A HEALING
INTIMACY

A HEALING INTIMACY

THE POWER OF
LOVING CONNECTIONS

Originally published as <u>Sexual Healing</u>

PAUL PEARSALL, PH.D.

CROWN TRADE PAPERBACKS
NEW YORK

Published by Crown Trade Paperbacks, 201 East 50th Street,
New York, New York 10022.
Member of the Crown Publishing Group.

Random House, Inc. New York, Toronto, London, Sydney,
Auckland

Originally published in hardcover under the title *Sexual Healing*
by Crown Publishers, Inc., 1994.

CROWN TRADE PAPERBACKS and colophon are trademarks
of Crown Publishers, Inc.

Manufactured in the U.S.A.

Design by June Bennett-Tantillo

Library of Congress Cataloging-in-Publication Data
is available upon request.

ISBN 0-517-88385-6

10 9 8 7 6 5 4 3 2 1

First Paperback Edition

E lei kau, e lei hoʻoilo i ke aloha.
(Love is worn like a wreath through
   the summers and the winters.)
Aloha wale ʻoe, e kuʻu ipo la Kalālani.
(I love you, my sweetheart, my wife Celest.)

CONTENTS

AUTHOR'S NOTE

Sexual health cannot be separated from physical health. The first step in any health or healing program is a visit to a trusted physician to work with you as a partner in developing a plan for total fitness. Many sexual problems are related to medical conditions that are most effectively treated at their earliest stages. Many medical conditions are related to sexual problems, and these too should be discussed with the physician. Never be afraid to discuss sexuality with your doctor.

1

THE HEALING POWER OF
SEXUAL CONNECTION

*It is not the threat of death, illness, hardship, or poverty that
crushes the human spirit; it is the fear of being alone and
unloved in the universe.*

Anthony Welsh

MY OWN SEXUAL HEALING

I had never known such helplessness and terror. I was blind and unable
to move. Even my eyelids would not open in response to my efforts to
cling to my tenuous connection with the world. I had just been taken to
intensive care following surgery for cancer that had spread through my
body and into my bones. I struggled to breathe and to move any part of
my body, and I felt totally isolated and alone. I heard the words of a
doctor pronouncing, "I think we've lost him." At that terrible moment,
I felt the miraculous effects of sexual healing.

Sexual healing is the process of enhancing the natural mending
capacity of the mind and body through pleasurable, meaningful, intimate, and sensual connection with a person you love. At my time of
helplessness and isolation, my wife, Celest, brought me back from
death's door and reconnected me with life. I felt the warmth of her
breath against my cheek, the wetness of her tears falling gently on my
eyelids, and the soothing and reassuring comfort of her fingers tracing
along my arms, chest, and the scars that lined my abdomen. "I love
you. I'm here. You'll make it, sweetheart. We'll make it together like

we always do," she cried softly in my ear. Like the electric paddles that shock a heart back to normal rhythm and bring a patient back to life, my wife's words seemed to be the catalyst for a flood of memories we had made together. As I lay near death, it was not *my* life that passed before my eyes—it was *our* life.

I remembered the times we had made love, laughed and cried together, raised our sons together, grieved together, huddled together in the gale of the catastrophes of daily living, and danced together through the chaos of a world that often seems so cruel. I strained again to open my eyes, and this time my eyelids responded. My wife's moist blue eyes were the first sign I saw of the magic of my sexual healing, of being connected again with Celest and with life. I was filled with an overwhelming sense of being one with my wife as she continued her sensuous and gentle massage. I panicked for a moment as she moved from my side to allow a nurse to take my temperature and blood pressure. My heart began to race until I felt her hands on me once again. In a few weeks, we would walk together from the hospital, and, as I write these words seven years later, I am completely cured of cancer.

"Remarkable," said the doctor in charge of the intensive care unit. "He's back. I guess we must have disconnected him too soon." Following my surgery, I had been removed from the life-sustaining respirator because it seemed that it was accomplishing little more than postponing the inevitable. From the biomedical point of view, my body had not sufficiently restarted when separated from its mechanical partner. But I had been disconnected from much more than a machine. My cancer, my chemotherapy, my whole-body radiation, my excruciating pain, and much of the medical treatment that had helped to repair my body and save my life had also isolated me from the essence of my existence. In my surrender of my body to modern medicine's mechanical miracles, I had forgotten why I was fighting to stay alive in the first place—to love and be loved, touch and be touched, hear and be heard, see and be seen, to share mutual memories, and to seek meaning in living with the person I love. My illness had caused me to become estranged from all that mattered, but our sexual healing had made me whole again. I knew at that moment that the reason we want to live and one of the most powerful ways to stay alive are one and the same—to connect intensely, sensuously, and intimately. I learned that—particularly when one is sick and afraid—the greatest gift anyone can receive is to be seen, heard, touched, and understood by another loving person. I knew that sexual healing is capable of making miracles, and this book describes the theory, process, and application of this most sacred human gift.

MY DISCOVERY OF PSYCHONEUROSEXUALITY

When we heal and are given a second chance at life and health, we sometimes make the mistake of going back to exactly the same lifestyle that contributed to our illness in the first place. What I learned from my own health and healing crisis helped me combine the areas of my professional training into a new approach to healing and a new field of medicine. I call this field *psychoneurosexuality* and define it as the study of the relationships among the brain in our skull, the mind as it exists throughout our body, the immune system that communicates with these systems, and the sexual system that expresses this entire health organization to another person.

Before my bout with cancer, I had worked for twenty years as a clinical psychoneuroimmunologist—a health psychology specialist who deals with the brain's interaction with the immune system. I had learned some remarkable things from my work in this new field of mind and body medicine that serve as a biological basis for psychoneurosexuality.

- I knew that the links between the brain, the body, and the immune system are strong and that our attitudes, thoughts, and feelings can make us vulnerable to illness and help us stay healthy and heal.

- I knew that healing is a built-in natural process that not only restores the body to health but also can result in lasting changes in our body and the way our mind works. Not only do we influence our healing capacity but the process of healing has a reciprocal influence on our mind, body, and lifestyle. Learning and loving help us heal, and the process of becoming healed or whole helps us learn and love.

- I knew that every cell in the body has tiny receptor sites resembling microcosmic antennae that are sensitive to the signals of chemicals from our brain. Every thought and feeling bleeds into our body, and our beliefs become our biology.

- I knew that every cell in our body is equipped with mechanisms for self-healing and that this innate healing process only works when each cell functions in harmony and connection with every other cell, and when we ourselves are in a harmonious relationship with our world.

- I knew that neurons, the cells of our brain and nervous system, communicate with one another by special conduction chemicals called neurotransmitters. I knew that some of these neurotransmitters, called endorphins, are capable of reducing pain and causing euphoria, that others are related to sleep and alertness, that some, like phenylethylamine, or PEA, influence how we experience love, and that some, called neuropeptides, can promote healing effects far downstream from the brain and all over our body.

- I knew that neurons from our brain communicate with the powerful endocrine system (our glands and hormones). The hormones that influence our moods and arousal communicate with these neurons, and every thought is a hormonal as well as a cortical event.

- I knew that cells from our brain also enter into and influence our bone marrow, where our blood and immune cells are made. Our thoughts and feelings do not stay in our head but actually are creating and re-creating our body every second. Every thought and emotion goes right down to the bone, where we are constantly being made.

- I knew that some immune system monocytes or immune cells pass into our blood and travel up to enter our brain, where they are transformed to glial cells, a special kind of connective brain cell.[1] I knew that our mind partially resides in our monocytes and our monocytes reside in our mind. I knew, then, that we don't have a mind and immune system but that we *are* both of these in one.

I had learned that this fascinating field of psychoneuroimmunology not only had remarkable potential to help people stay well, grow, and heal but, when misapplied and misunderstood, could also result in unfounded assertions of mind over matter, self-inflicted illness, and pressure to be a powerful disease fighter and self-healer. I had also learned, however, that how we give meaning to our lives profoundly affects how healthily we can live and how healing we can be.[2]

My professional background also included my establishment and directorship of a psychiatric clinic at Sinai Hospital in Detroit, Michigan. In this program, I combined my training and work at the Kinsey Institute for Research in Sex, Gender, and Reproduction at Indiana University and studies with William Masters and Virginia Johnson at their institute in St. Louis, Missouri, to design a treatment procedure for couples with sexual problems. I had seen firsthand how health relates to intimate relationships and how sexual happiness seems to enhance health. I had also observed that sexual distress is often accompanied by physical symptoms and illness. As director of behavioral medicine in Beaumont Hospital in Royal Oak, Michigan, I see daily the power of intimacy to heal and even reverse heart disease.

Combining my professional training and experiences with my personal health crisis and sexual healing taught me that all these factors—thoughts, feelings, caring, intimate touch, eroticism, and healing—can be united through sexual intimacy and meaningful sensuous connection with someone we love. The findings from psychoneuroimmunology can be combined with psychology and sexuality to help promote wellness. The chapters that follow will take you on a journey through this new field of psychoneurosexuality—PNS—and toward your own sexual healing.

SEX AND THE PENTAMEROUS MODEL OF SEXUAL HEALING

A primary assumption of PNS is that sexual healing is pentamerous—that is, it involves five key connections: self-esteem, a connection with self; intimacy, a connection with someone significant in your life; coherence, a connection with a sense of purpose, meaning, and manageability in life events and crises; mindfulness, a connection with the current moment; and sensuality, a connection with the physical body of someone you love as an intense physical expression and manifestation of all five levels of connection. This book will explore these factors, with a focus on the healing aspects of sensual connection, which are often ignored in the study of healing.

Sexual healing defines the term *sexuality* as the totality of one's maleness *and* femaleness, and it involves all that is masculine and feminine within each of us. It includes how we think, feel, behave, and believe on the most personal level. The World Health Organization defines sexual health as "the integration of the somatic, emotional, intellectual, and social aspects of sexual beings in ways that are enriching and that enhance personality, communication, and love."[3] It is this definition that is both the process and the goal of sexual healing.

At a time when, as pointed out by Jay Leno, sex is more dangerous than the cigarette afterward, sex is often viewed as a threat to health. Sexual healing offers a way to reclaim from hysteria and fear the most intimate and meaningful of human acts and to view sex as a way to connect and enhance our collective welfare. Let's look more closely at the five factors of pentamerous sexual healing that will be explored throughout this book:

1. Self-esteem: We connect with ourselves when our sexuality contributes to our awareness of who we are, what we are doing, and with whom. When we recognize how our sexuality affects our

5

health, the health of our partner, and the health of society in general. The sex of sexual healing does not involve escape or distraction from reality. It requires complete awareness of who we are and what our purpose for being sexually intimate is. Sexual healing always enhances the reputation we have with ourselves and our partners' feelings about themselves.

2. Intimacy: We make a healing connection through sex with another person only when we are honest, intimate, and responsible in our sexual expression and when we are sexually intimate *because* we love and not in order to find love. When we attempt to "have" sex, we are seeking a psychological or physiological high but not a meaningful connection. When we try to "do" sex "to" someone, we are using a person rather than loving and helping to heal him or her. When we attempt to have sex "for" a person, we are not remaining connected to ourselves and we make our partners users by making ourselves "usees." It is only when we have sex "with" someone that we are sexually healing by connecting intimately and meaningfully for the purpose of mutual growth and wellness. Author E. M. Forster wrote, "Only connect. Personal relationships are the important thing for ever and ever." His message reflects the intimacy of sexual healing.

3. Coherence: Sexual healing happens when we have sex with someone with whom we share our beliefs about the higher purpose of life and with whom we find even more meaning through the act of our loving. The sex of sexual healing is a connection of minds expressed through bodily intimacy. It requires a mutually expressed belief system that is accepted by both partners as their own "couple coherence."[4] Sexual healing is the shared physical expression of the discovery of the meaning of life—to connect. Psychologist Carl Jung wrote, "Meaningless is equivalent to illness."[5]

4. Mindfulness: Mindfulness means being aware of the present moment and its every sensation. Healing sex is sex *in* and not *for* the moment. The sex of sexual healing requires sexual intimacy that is unrushed; unimpaired by guilt, regrets, or self-recriminations from the past; and free from distractions and feelings of obligations waiting in the future. Sexual healing requires plenty of time, but author Duncan Calwell warns, "Americans have more time saving devices and less time than any other group of people in the world."[6] The sex of sexual healing is a slow, lingering, peaceful sex in which—at least for one moment—the eternity represented by the merging of the past and the future into the present moment is celebrated with someone we love. Mindful sex helps us join to overcome our regrets of yesterday and fears of tomorrow.

5. Sensuality: Sexual healing is connecting sensually with our own body and the body of our partner. It happens when we understand that sex involves much more than the genitals and the biomechanical stages of seduction, foreplay, sexual proficiency, multiple orgasms, and release of built-up neuromuscular tension and stress. Sexual healing involves a sensual connection on the molecular level, with every sense and cell merging in a melodic dance of molecules made healthier through our intimacy with our lover.

As you read about the five connections of sexual healing, you probably thought that sexual healing seems a difficult challenge. Miracles are never easy, and we are suffering from very complex and serious illnesses. The three major thieves of our quality of life are sarcopenia (premature loss of physical stamina and mental alertness), cancer, and heart disease. These killers cannot be vanquished by simple formulas. They may be so prevalent in part because of a lack of caring and connection in our modern world. They require strong medicine to help us get well again.

This book will ask you to make many difficult choices, to try many new and at first strange behaviors, and to think in a different way about health, healing, and sexuality. You will be asked to consider changing not only what you do in your most important and intimate relationship but, more important, why you do it. There is an old Zen saying, "Before enlightenment, chop wood and carry water. After enlightenment, chop wood and carry water." Throughout the pages that follow, you will read about research that shows that it is *why* we have sex more than *how* that leads to the healing power of sex. The path to being a sexual healer is difficult, but the rewards are great. Healing miracles are at stake.

Sexual healing transcends the popular mechanical, self-pleasure, and tension-release model offered by what I will describe later as the sex syndicate that has developed over the last fifty years. Much of what you have been taught about sex is wrong and without basis in scientific research. As author Artemus Ward warned, "It ain't so much the things we don't know that get us in trouble. It's the things we know that ain't so." The sex syndicate model of sexuality has become a popular folk myth, and it will be necessary to question the assumptions of that myth in order to learn the sex of sexual healing.

LONELINESS: THE NUMBER-ONE HEALTH RISK FACTOR

Psychologists Robert Ornstein and Charles Swencionis write, "We cannot communicate (connect) without affecting our bodies. There is no disease that kills people at the rate loneliness does."[7] As you will learn in this book, one health risk factor that underlies all the others is a sense of isolation, loneliness, a feeling of being disconnected. I remember writhing in the pain of the cancer eating at the marrow of my bones. I was overwhelmed by feelings of complete separation and isolation. It seemed that no one could know my pain or do anything to ease it. The only painkiller that worked was the loving contact of my wife soothing, holding, and embracing me. I am convinced that the neurochemicals and endorphins released when I was held and stroked by the person I love helped block my pain from my consciousness and that such connection is a powerful natural narcotic—the internal morphine of meaningful merging.

The joy and pleasure of being a part of life and loving may provide us with an intimacy inoculation that protects us from disease. The connections accomplished through sexual healing provide an intense way to avoid loneliness. I know of no other human behavior that can offer such intimate connection on so many levels at once.

PROOF OF THE POWER OF CONNECTION

In the book of Genesis, God said, "It is not good that man should be alone." Recent research is demonstrating that a sense of intimate connection has a real and measurable impact on our physical health.[8] Our connection with one another was vital in our evolution as we hunted, gathered, parented, and defended ourselves against predators. Our connection is still vital, and it has tangible influences that extend to every cell in our body. Every cell has to cooperate and connect with the others or we die.

Cardiologist Dean Ornish reports being able to reverse the clogging of the arteries around the heart in some patients not only by dietary and lifestyle changes but by helping patients through a process he calls "emotional open heart surgery." Sexual healing helps reverse sociosclerosis—hardening of the boundaries between two people. Emotional opening of the heart involves a reestablishment of intimacy, life purpose, and a sense of intimate connection. Dr. Ornish says, "A number of studies have shown that people who feel isolated have three to five times the mortality, not only from cardiovascular disease, but from all causes, when compared to people who don't feel isolated."[9] He adds that the lower mortality rate associated with feeling connected is independent of blood cholesterol level, blood pressure, or smoking.

That disconnection is the catalyst that increases the threat of established health-risk factors such as high blood pressure, high-fat diets, and smoking is illustrated by the fact that most people who have these risk factors don't get sick. Eight of ten people with three or more of the major health-risk factors will not have a heart attack in the next ten years. A vast majority of heart attack victims do not have any of the "biological" risk factors.[10] Investigative reporter Thomas Moore states that the risk factor strategy of predicting early death from being overweight, having high blood pressure, and having high blood cholesterol has proved a terrible disappointment.[11] We can account for less than 50 percent of deaths from heart attack by looking at risk factors.

There is clearly something else that accounts for sickness and health and that may be a key catalyst activating the negative effects of unhealthy behaviors. Sexual healing suggests that that something else is the disconnection factor.

In a study that tracked the health of people in Alameda County, California, for more than nine years, those who had strong and enduring connections with others had significantly lower mortality rates than those who reported fewer social ties and more feelings of isolation.[12] Another study showed that a community of Italian-Americans in Roseto, Pennsylvania, had an extremely low incidence of heart disease. Expecting to find a population eating a low-fat, high-fiber diet and jogging daily, researchers found instead a group of carnivorous, sedentary cigarette smokers. What seemed to neutralize the negative impact of these unwise behaviors was the fact that the community was extremely close-knit, with a great deal of connection, stability, and shared sense of life meaning. Surrounding communities with the same risky behaviors and less connection and closeness showed the expected high rate of heart disease.[13] Cardiologist James Lynch writes, "Growing numbers of physicians now recognize that the health of the human heart depends not only on such factors as genetics, diet, and exercise, but also to a large extent on the social and emotional health of the individual."[14]

It is not only the cardiovascular system that is protected by connection. When a sense of connection is increased or loneliness and a sense of isolation decreased, the immune system itself becomes stronger. One study of a group of thirty elderly people in retirement homes showed increased immune competence (more cells called natural killer cells or NK cells and other antibodies) when these people felt connected and cared for than when they felt lonely.[15] Other studies have shown that, even when people are under stress, a sense of connection can help increase the number of T cells (immune cells formed in the thymus gland).[16] These studies and many others document the facts that separation can lead to sickness and that intimacy heals.

THE HAMMARSKJÖLD PRINCIPLE OF SEXUAL HEALING

Because intimate connection is so important to sexual healing, it will be helpful if you can find a partner with whom to learn the principles and practices of psychoneurosexuality. I will be asking you to take the Pearsall Psychosocial Inventory in the Appendix of this book as a starting point for understanding all the dimensions of sexual healing. To learn the most from this test, you will need an intimate partner with whom to take it. While close friends, family, and colleagues are crucial to health and happiness, the full power of sexual healing requires one person with whom you connect on all five connection levels and with whom you choose to express that connection physically and sensually. One intimate and sensually demonstrative dyad is the core of sexual healing.

I call the concept of the healing importance of one two-person relationship the Hammarskjöld principle. Past Secretary-General of the United Nations Dag Hammarskjöld said, ''It is more noble to give yourself completely to one individual than to labor diligently for the salvation of the masses.''[17] Unfortunately, the great lovers of humanity in the abstract, such as Mahatma Gandhi and Albert Schweitzer, have not always been overly successful in their most intimate relationships. In modern psychology, there is the implicit assumption that exceptional psychological well-being is primarily a personal task. The pursuit of transcendent or transforming experiences, enlightenment, or personal power is often posited as antithetical to relationship and particularly to dependence on one enduring, intimate, sensual relationship.[18] Sexual healing is based on the opposite assumption—that the desire and ability to merge intensely with another person is crucial to health.

The Hammarskjöld principle of sexual healing asserts that one loving relationship between two people is the healthiest of all human acts because it allows pentamerous connection with self, another person, something more, the present moment, and sensual awareness of another body. Rather than viewing health as primarily achieved by introspection, withdrawal, and self-understanding, sexual healing is achieved through the daily challenge of maintaining a two-person relationship. Intimate bonding is biologically derived and a part of our genetic makeup, and, when we accomplish it, our health and healing systems achieve balance.

THE EVOLUTIONARY VALUE OF SEXUAL PLEASURE

Why does intimate sexual pleasure feel so good? Does any evolutionary value beyond procreation account for the great thrill that loving sex can bring us? I suggest that there is something in our genes that guides us toward intimate and loving connection. Sexual pleasure may be programmed into us as a signal to our brain that we are on the right track in preventing illness and staying well by making contact with another person. When we engage in intimate and meaningful sexual pleasure, we are rewarded twice. First, we feel very good physically and psychologically. Second, we gain long-term health and healing benefits by lowering what may be the leading health risk in America—disconnection on any or all of its five levels.

Although the current medical terrorism has caused us to doubt it, it is a fact that most things we do that feel good are usually good for us and for our world. There is species survival value in being strongly and intimately connected and gaining the health benefits of this connection. Charles Darwin proposed a theory called "inclusive fitness" or the value of prolonged connection between people to guarantee survival of one's own genetic material or DNA.[19] Perhaps "intimacy fitness," or close physical connection with a person we love, helps guarantee our health so we can live to pass on our own DNA. Survival of the most connected may be an evolutionary principle, so the strong drive for and pleasurable sensations of regular sexual intimacy help guarantee our efforts at maintaining connection with a partner.

Research supports the Hammarskjöld principle of dyad over group support as health enhancing. Studies at the University of New Mexico School of Medicine showed that, among 256 healthy elderly people, it was the ones who had close, confiding, one-on-one relationships who were healthier.[20] Several other studies point to the importance of one strong and intimate relationship in maintaining effective immunity, more endorphins or natural painkillers, and cardiovascular health.[21]

Almost fifty years ago, a classic study on the importance of one close, intimate, and physical bond was conducted by psychiatrist Rene Spitz.[22] He discovered that children raised in a foundling home and receiving good nutrition and medical care and regular periods of rocking and holding by several nurses still failed to thrive. Children raised in a penal institution and receiving poorer nutrition and less medical care but kept in close and regular physical contact with their own mothers (prisoners in the institution) did better. It was the one-on-one close physical bonding that seemed to make the difference.

So what if you don't have someone you consider a sexual healing partner or someone with whom you are intimately involved to learn about sexual healing and to take the psychosocial inventory? You can still learn to be a sexual healer. Find a close friend, colleague, family member, or neighbor who is willing to help you begin to understand sexual healing. You may find that, by understanding the areas of psychosocial connection that are not as dependent on a dyadal relationship, you can make more meaningful life connections in those areas first. These may serve as a starting point for finding that one special person. One of my single male patients said, "Looking at the issue of connection in all twenty-five areas of your test was like spinning the wheel of chance for other connections. I finally found someone after a few bad numbers, but I would not have found anyone if I wasn't out there looking to make more meaningful connections in my life. I think I became more connectionable."

THE PEARSALL PSYCHOSOCIAL INVENTORY

For more than twenty years, I have used my Psychosocial Inventory to help patients understand the complexities of sexual healing and the importance of connection in various aspects of their lives. Although it can be taken by an individual, this test is designed to be taken by couples. It measures twenty-five fitness factors related to connection. While I will be focusing on sexual connection, meaningful connection at work, at worship, and with friends and family members is also important, and the inventory addresses these factors.

Before reading any further, turn to the Appendix and take the Psychosocial Inventory with your partner. The time you spend taking the test and discussing the issues it raises will help you begin to understand the far-reaching effects of intimate life connection.

SEX AND THE TWENTY-FIVE PSYCHOSOCIAL FITNESS FACTORS

Here is an overview of all twenty-five psychosocial factors. Each has been shown to relate to how well we mobilize our connections with others in order to deal in a healthy manner with the stress and strain of daily living. Each factor is supported by current research showing that how we cope strongly depends on how well, how consistently, and how intimately we connect while we work, play, parent, and cluster together through the inevitable chaos and catastrophes that come with the privilege of being alive. Some of the factors are more directly relevant to sexual healing than others, but all relate to sexual health and have an impact on your sexual healing potential.

Twenty-five Psychosocial Connection Factors

1. Connected Codependence: This is the ability to be independent enough to be mutually dependent with another person and to take care of and be taken care of by another person at times of life crisis and illness. This is a sexual healing factor because consistent and adaptive mutual caring is essential to surviving the challenge of illness. While it is often viewed as a weakness, connected codependence can also be seen as an important interpersonal skill.

2. Caring Colleagues: This peer-group review factor is the ability to support and feel supported by colleagues at work or in other outside-the-home activities. It is an indicator of sexual healing potential because caring behaviors cannot be limited and practiced only when needed or desired. Our sexual character includes how we are in all our relationships; it is not a mechanical skill restricted to sexual intimacy. We bring all of who and how we are to our sexual healing relationship.

3. Positive Anticipation: This is the absence of the "Black Monday" syndrome. (It is a fact that more people die on Monday mornings than any other time of the week.) Positive anticipation is looking forward to the beginning of the work week and returning to work or routine life activities. It is a sexual healing factor because connection with one's partner is enhanced and maintained by general life energy and involvement rather than dread and cyclical ups and downs.

4. Creativity: This is feeling that you have generated something or done something of value to and appreciated by others. Creativity involves having pride in your work or life activities and feeling that you contribute significantly and uniquely to society. This is a sexual healing factor because self-dignity, self-esteem, and a sense of importance are essential for both partners in order for a strong sexual relationship to develop and evolve.

5. Hardiness: This is possessing the three C's—seeing problems as *challenges,* staying *committed* to your life purpose at times of stress, and feeling in *control* and knowing when you have no control and

it is best to "go with the flow." Hardiness is a sexual healing factor because "sticking it out together" and seeing illness and health problems as an opportunity to learn are central to healing.

6. Coherence: As described earlier, this is a feeling that life challenges are comprehensible, are manageable, and have meaning when internal or external events challenge our well-being. Coherence is a key sexual healing factor because it is the meaning of being intimate rather than the mechanics of sex that provides the healing power of sexual intimacy.

7. REST: This is the willingness and ability to find a time and place where you can be alone in peace and quiet. REST stands for Restricted Environmental Stimulation Time, and while social connection is vital to our health, just being by ourselves in serenity and tranquillity is also essential. This is a sexual healing factor because PTA, or Perceived Time Autonomy—the feeling of control over one's life and being able to find time to rest and reflect—helps us contemplate and remember the importance of finding the time to be intimate. REST-ing as a couple—being quiet, sitting together, and "being" instead of "doing"—are sexual healing acts. All our moments of quiet reflection do not have to be alone.

8. Caring Couple: This is living in an intimate and committed two-person relationship. Being part of a caring couple is another key sexual healing factor because, as pointed out earlier, one sexually intimate relationship is a more powerful health enhancer and protector than many less intimate and less committed relationships.

9. Sexuality: The ability to engage in regular, mutually pleasurable and fulfilling sexual intimacy is the physical, erotic, and genital aspect of sexual healing and the way our sexual systems express our sense of connection. Intimate sex and a new model of sexual response is a focus of this book because much of what we have learned from the sex syndicate about genital sexuality is misleading or wrong and therefore restricts our sexual healing potential.

10. Sensuality: The ability to enjoy touching and being touched beyond genital or sexual contact is another key aspect of sexual healing because gently connecting on a body-to-body and skin-to-skin level has a direct impact on the enhancement of our immunity and healing. Touch heals, and the sensual touch of a lover is the most powerful healing touch of all because the entire psychoneurosexual system is activated by it.

11. Connection: This factor is the ability to generalize a sense of con-

nection to people other than spouse, family, and close friends. Connection is an aspect of sexual healing because, although one intimate sexual relationship is the centerpiece of sexual healing, our ability to be kind, gentle, and caring with everyone is essential to community health, and community health is essential to all of our health.

12. The "Us" Factor: This is the ability to resist selfishness, self-involvement, and a valuing of the self only for accomplishment and control of others. The "us" factor is a sexual healing factor because the ability to think collectively and to see worth as a two-person rather than a one-person matter is essential to meaning and intimate connection.

13. Equanimity: This is the ability to resist anger and hostility. When we become angry, we are revenging on ourselves the mistakes of others. Equanimity is a sexual healing factor because anger only distances us from others or generalizes to our sexual interaction. One of my patients pointed out, "It's difficult to get in the mood when one of you is always in a bad mood."

14. Altruism: The ability to give, sacrifice, volunteer, and offer help and support to strangers is a sexual healing factor because it results in the "helper's high" that carries over to sexual relationships, enhancing these relationships and the immune systems of the people in them.

15. Optimism: Pessimists tend to take problems personally. They see problems as pervasive and characteristic of the "black cloud" that seems to linger over their heads. Pessimists view negatives as permanent, beyond control, and inevitable manifestations of their own inadequacy or constant bad luck rather than natural and necessary aspects of daily living. Optimists see things from a nonpersonal, nonpervasive, and nonpermanent perspective and resist ruminating about negatives. Optimism is a sexual healing factor because sexual interactions are not personal but mutual; one negative sexual experience does not have to generalize to another; and sexual interactions change and, like life and love, grow and mature.

16. Serenity: The ability to underreact to stress and to show quiet dignity under duress is a sexual healing factor because sexual joy requires acceptance of one's own and one's partner's shortcomings to the same extent that we celebrate one another's strengths. The soul attracts what it secretly harbors, so personal agitation and hostility—however denied—tend to draw these reactions from others. The key to resolving conflicts is the phrase "always without bitterness."

17. **Pride:** This is freedom from shame. Pride is a key aspect of sexual healing because shame restricts our ability to feel accepted, desirable, and deserving of caring commitment in the eyes of our sexual healing partner.

18. **Mirth:** The ability to laugh regularly and hard is a sexual healing factor because shared humor is a way of dissipating stress and can serve as an aphrodisiac. Laughter usually results when a mutual insight draws two people together in a sudden sharing of a sense of the absurd even when things seem hopeless and senseless. When we laugh, things don't cease to be serious and even sad, any more than when we cry things cease to be funny and ludicrous.

19. **Weeping:** The ability to cry regularly and openly is a sexual healing factor because crying is another way we dissipate stress and purge our bodies of the waste products of the stress hormones. Like laughing together, crying together can result in an intense feeling of empathy, sympathy, connection, and sharing.

20. **Smiling:** Not only do we show our feelings by our expressions but we also come to feel in accordance *with* our expressions. By smiling even when we don't feel like smiling, we program and strengthen our healing system. It is almost impossible not to smile back at someone who smiles at you because smiling is a powerful connection device. This is a sexual healing factor because conveying and modeling a sense of joy and acceptance sets the stage for sexual advances. Dozens of types of smiles are found cross-culturally, including a "sex smile" or copulatory gaze—widening the eyes for about three seconds, dilating the pupils, showing the upper teeth, tilting the head to the side, and then looking down toward one's genitals.[23] Try the "sex smile" with your partner; you'll see an immediate response and a return smile.

21. **Response-Ability:** A *reaction* is a reflex over which we have no control. A *response* is a considered and thoughtful action. Unlike other animals, humans can choose between reaction and response. The response-ability factor refers to our willingness to take responsibility for our behaviors and feelings rather than helplessly attributing them to external forces or the behaviors of others. When we say "You make me upset," we give up our power, but when we say "I'm getting myself upset," we become powerful. Response-ability is a sexual healing factor because sexual pleasure and intimacy

require that we work to *be* the right partner and not to *find* the right partner. In sexual relationships, we usually get who and how we are, and we tend to attract what we reward.

22. Esteem: The ability to see one's self-worth independently of accomplishments, attainments, and achievements is a sexual healing factor because self-esteem involves a balance between courage and self-assertiveness and a strong consideration for another person, both of which lead to more fulfilling sexual intimacy than self-pleasure or self-sacrifice alone.

23. Vulnerability: This is the ability to give the gift of self by sharing sincere feelings openly and spontaneously. It is the absence of alexathymia or the inability to give words to our feelings. Vulnerability is a sexual healing factor because when we model open self-expression, our partners usually follow suit.

24. Faith: This is the ability to show trust and recognize that we not only believe what we see but can see what we believe. Faith is believing in something more than just the day-to-day physical realities of living and in the existence of a higher power and purpose in life. This is a sexual healing factor because sharing faith and a belief system with our partners strengthens our loving bond by making it more adaptable.

25. Ceremony: The ability to engage in rituals that give continuity and a sense of consistent meaning to our life is a sexual healing factor because there is a natural, melodic rhythm of loving and sensuality that can develop between sexual partners. Following simple rituals such as dinner together at the same time in the same seats and holiday celebrations helps maintain ties with our past and confidence in our future. This sense of predictability allows the comfort, steadiness, and freedom to love in the now. Sexual healing is based not on the excitement of variety but on the safety, security, and validation of sameness.

THE STRUCTURE OF THIS BOOK

There are three parts to this book. In Part I, you will read about the basic theory of psychoneurosexuality and sexual healing. You will see how sickness is as necessary to life as health and how too much health might actually shorten your life by weakening your adaptability and healing skills and robbing life of its meaning. I will describe how the immune system works and how it interacts with the sexual system, the psychochemistry of coupling, how myths of healing have often restricted healing capacity, how shame can interfere with healing, and how a healthy guilt can help you heal. I will discuss two syndromes of vulnerability to illness that are related to lack or imbalance of sexual health and show the new way of thinking about "us" rather than "self" healing that underlies sexual healing.

In Part II you will read about a new way to understand sexual intimacy and human sexual response as they relate to sickness, health, and healing. I will describe the development and influence of a still powerful sex syndicate that provides misleading and often health-damaging advice regarding sex. You will learn a new model of human sexual response based on tone, melody, and rhythm rather than tension, muscles, and secretions. Finally, you will explore a new psychology and sociology of sexuality that challenges many popular concepts, such as the danger of codependence and the importance of self-fulfillment.

In Part III you will discover how to become a sexual healer by applying the ideas you learned about psychoneurosexuality and sensual intimacy explored in Parts I and II. You will read about the health risks of too much sex and not enough intimacy, how to identify your sexual healing style and the sexual style of your relationship, and how to design your own sexual healing program. Finally, you will learn about the impact of aging on sexual health, how to turn the changes that come with getting older to your sexual healing benefit, and how cancer and heart disease can be healed sexually.

I invite you to take a new view of the purpose of health, the process of healing, the role of sickness in your life, and the possibility that sexual intimacy is one of the most powerful healing forces.

PART ONE

THE
NEW FIELD
OF
PSYCHONEUROSEXUALITY

---

*In the deeper reality beyond space and time,
we may all be members of one body.*

Sir James Jeanes

2

ILLNESS IS THE TEACHER, INTIMACY IS THE LESSON
The Purpose of Sickness and Health

Our life without love is like the coconut in which the milk is dried up.

Henry David Thoreau

THE MOST POWERFUL HEALING FORCE IN THE WORLD

"Why me?" cried the woman sobbing in her husband's arms. "Why do I have to have this cancer? What did I do to deserve this? What a terrible, terrible waste. Why? Why would God do this to me?"

Her husband held her closer and answered with his own question. "Why us, sweetheart? Why did this happen to us? The cancer is in your body, but it's happening to us. I never knew how much you meant to me and how much a part of you I've become. I'll never let you go. I'll always be with you." The husband began to cry, and the couple tightened their embrace.

Suddenly, the wife pulled away, held her husband at arms' length, and stared directly into his eyes. "My God, look at us," she said. "In thirty years of marriage, we've never held each other and cried together like this. You've never talked to me like this." She hugged him close, and they cried again. "I've never felt closer to you than right now. I've never felt more complete. I love you."

As a hospital staff psychologist, I had been asked to talk with this woman about her depression in the face of her diagnosis of breast cancer.

While I was speaking with her in her hospital room, her husband had arrived. I offered to leave, but they both asked me to stay.

I knew that depression and fear are realistic, natural, and in some ways necessary reactions to cancer or any life-threatening illness, particularly if we have others with whom we can share our reactions. I knew that personal support and comfort are important in coping with serious illness. I had read that women with metastatic breast cancer live significantly longer than medical predictions if they meet regularly in support groups with other women with cancer and that something about this support seems to help mobilize natural healing forces in their bodies.[1] As a psychoneuroimmunologist, I knew that there is some mechanism in our bodies, awakened by our connection with others, that does not emerge when we try to fight or flee from illness alone. But as I watched this couple, I began to understand that there may be an even more powerful force than general social support. The love and intimacy between these two people revealed that—in addition to friends, family, and fellow patients—connection with one person in an intense, intimate, loving relationship may ignite the most powerful healing energy of all.

The wife's cancer had spread throughout her body, and her prognosis was poor. Most of the doctors thought she would not live out the year, but the couple lived on to love together for more than ten years. When she was asked a few years ago if she was cured, she responded, "I guess you're only cured when you live long enough to die of something else. I can tell you this. Cancer can cure neurosis and shrink distances between people. My husband and I are more in love than ever before."

Last year, the husband fell and broke his hip. Surgery and hip replacement were necessary, but he resisted. "I have to be there for my wife," he said. "She's not doing well now. She's in a wheelchair and very weak. I have to be there for her." The surgeon reassured the husband that the surgery was needed and that, although all surgery is risky, this procedure was comparatively common and safe. "But I must be there for her," said the man. When the wife's condition worsened, the doctor explained that the husband would be more mobile, strong, and able to be of more help to his wife if he had his hip surgery. On the day the wife entered the hospital to begin treatment for the recurrence of her cancer, her husband reluctantly agreed to his operation, stating yet again, "Please remember, I must be there for her."

As the oxygen mask was placed over his face, the husband whispered one final time, "I have to be there for her." As the surgeon was scrubbing in preparation for the surgery, she heard urgent talking and the buzz of the alarm of the heart-monitoring machine echoing from the operating room. She could see through the small window in the scrub room door that the anesthesiologist was pounding on the patient's chest as stimulating drugs were being injected directly into the man's heart. Even before the anesthesia had been administered and despite the medical staff's best efforts, the husband's heart had stopped beating. The surgeon rushed in to help the other doctors, but it was too late. Tears rolled down the surgical masks of everyone in the room as one of the scrub nurses whimpered, "He never knew it, but his wife died an hour ago."

While the wife's death was not unexpected, no one to this day can give a medical reason for the husband's death. "I think I have an answer," said the surgeon, who herself had been a cancer patient. "He kept telling us, didn't he? We just didn't understand what he meant. He said from the very beginning that he had to be there for her, and he was. He was there to meet her."

The infinite healing love of this couple illustrates the life-prolonging influence a loving bond exerts on our natural healing powers. The wife had lived far beyond medical expectations, and the couple's love had grown. The power of intimacy to heal goes beyond anything we now understand in modern medicine, but I suggest that sexual healing can work miracles. Sexual healing represents a source of connection and wholeness that transcends mere physical survival. Because it offers connection on all of the five levels of human bonding mentioned in Chapter 1—with self, another, something more, the present moment, and sensual unity—it has the power to make us whole forever and beyond the constraints of our physical existence.

We all must eventually release our lives, but we never have to give up our loving. There will come a time when we all will be beyond a cure, but none of us has to be beyond healing or becoming whole. Wholeness is the objective of intimate connection, and it transcends our years of life. Individuals are mortal, but loving and intimate relationships are forever.

The research you will read about in this book is beginning to show some of the physical mechanisms that may relate to the power of sexual healing. Much more must be learned about the connection between the mind, body, and healing, but 2 million years of evolution has taught our bodies to respond in a healing fashion to intimacy and caring. Beyond simple healing platitudes and self-help approaches are strong scientific findings showing links between the mind, intimacy, the body, and healing. By understanding and applying these links to our own lives, we can forge a chain strong enough to hold us together at times of health crises, at the very least add years to our lives, and defy medical statistics that are too often self-fulfilling prophecies.

THE NECESSITY OF SICKNESS

I learned much about sexual healing from the couple just described and from my own sexual healing. I also learned from them and other couples with similar stories that sickness can serve very important and healthy purposes. If health is wholeness, illness is a reminder—a call for intimate reconnection with the purpose of our loving, and that purpose is to love and be loved.

When I watched the couple in that hospital room, I remembered that they had seldom touched before. The husband was a doctor on the staff at my hospital, and I had known him and his wife for years. They traveled together, raised children together, and solved the problems of daily living together, but I had never heard them talk so gently or seen them touch so tenderly. The illness seemed to have taught them to value their opportunity to connect during their living years and to do so on an intensely emotional and physical level. Our medical approach often sees health as the absence of measurable symptoms, ignoring a key reason for health—the sensuous and meaningful relationships that it allows us to engage in.

This couple was learning the lessons of intimate connection. The wife was discovering how to reach out for the intimacy she craved more strongly than ever before. The husband was learning that all the success, money, and material things he brought to the relationship were meaningless in comparison with the greatest gift of all—his own demonstration of his love and sharing of his feelings. Husband and wife were learning through the challenge of sickness to reach out physically before physical connection was no longer possible.

Illness is to some degree always caused by disconnection and lack of wholeness—a separation between organ systems within the body itself or within our life relationships—and the healing of illness requires a repair in our relationship rupture. Sexual healing is a powerful way to achieve that reconnection with ourselves, our lover, our life purpose, the present moment, and the intimate physical sensations of our lovers' touch.

HEALING, HEALTH, AND THE CONNECTION FACTOR

When we are sick, there is a biological breakdown in one or more body systems, which results in a biochemical imbalance. There is a disconnection between body systems and an interference with the body's natural collective and cooperative coping and growing processes. Illness is a natural part of our body's development; science has shown that all growth is chaotic rather than orderly and predictable. We get ill because we are always changing, and change is necessary for development and maturity. Sickness is necessary for health because it is a part of how we evolve through the life cycle. All illness eventually will be characterized by physical discomfort and pain, but our suffering can be a signal of the need for reconnection that arises from the necessary and natural rhythm of the chaos of our growth.

When we get sick, most of us reflect to some degree about how and why we are living. Individuals become ill, but social context and relationships are where illness is expressed. We may have bodies, but we are also part of a social body. We are connected to those around us, so illness is always a social event as well as an individual experience. We recover our health through healing, and healing means becoming whole and reconnecting with our world. Health is not an end. It is a means. The purpose of life is not to be healthy, but one purpose of health is to find higher purpose and more meaningful connections in our life.

We cannot always be cured, but we can always be healed. To *cure* means to fix and repair. Some diseases are too devastating to be cured. We die because we are mortal, not because we failed to believe and love enough. But we can always be healed, because *healing* means reconnecting. Healing is the process of learning from and through illness and seeing our sickness as a catalyst for life change in the direction of more meaningful connection. By curing, we can sometimes temporarily reestablish body system balance, but imbalance will always recur. By the process of healing, we become whole again through our stronger connection. Self-healing is a myth because we can never be completely healthy or heal completely all alone. Health is connection, and healing is working to maintain and enhance our connections even when we are the most afraid and vulnerable.

THE DANGER OF BEING TOO HEALTHY TOO LONG

Learning to be a sexual healer requires assuming that it is necessary to be ill sometimes and that it can be healthy to be sick. Too much health can result in physical stability but emotional stagnation from lack of personal growth. I suggested in Chapter 1 that the pleasure of intimacy is strong because it is adaptive and evolutionarily constructive to connect intimately. The social need growing out of illness—the suffering of sickness as inspiration for healing—is also evolutionarily necessary because it drives us toward reconnection and the maintenance of our connections. In some ways, there is an evolutionary principle of "survival of the sickest" if by *sickness* we mean a dominant and insistent need to connect on more and more intense and meaningful levels. Connection guarantees the continuation of our genetic identity and the survival of humanity and the world.

Modern medicine often teaches that disease is a sign of weakness or failure, but in reality, sickness is as necessary to our life as health. Health isn't strength, it's balance. Sickness isn't failure, it's a challenge. A sick child's first response to illness is to seek the physical comfort of his or her parents. The loving parent's first response to a sick child is to hold and gently stroke the child and urgently reaffirm caring connection and a loving, intimate bond while healing progresses. We are never too old to need connection to help us heal. The elderly seem sometimes to regress to childish behaviors because something within them—an intimacy imprint—is reaching out for the closeness they had at the beginning of their lives and need so urgently at the end.

CONNECTION COMPLACENCY

Becoming healthier and staying that way is challenging, but being in a state of health can sometimes lull us into connection complacency. We don't feel we need others as intensely when we are well and thriving. Health is a quiet between the storms of change and a brief recess from life, soul, and love development school. We don't seem to learn much from health because it does not get our attention as strongly as does illness. Those who claim to be perfectly healthy all the time may be self-absorbed people who focus on and protect their individual physical condition but neglect their relationships. Physical health helps us be effective individuals but not necessarily caring and loving people. *Total health* is a humble state of being well—a health shared with those around us and experienced in full awareness of our mortality and vulnerability. It is accomplished in loving interaction with others and credited not just to our own health fitness practices but to loving intimacy with those around us.

Health is convenient, and it allows us to go about our daily lives without paying too much attention to why or where we are going and with whom. It allows us to focus on doing, but it distracts us from the importance of being. We need our times of health to get things done, but we learn most when we suffer and are ill because these are the times when something within us remembers that we cannot survive alone. We must never allow feeling good to distract us from the importance of feeling love and loving. We can celebrate and share our healthy times with those we love, but we must never become arrogant about our health or take sole credit for it. We are never finally whole and complete, so we can never truly be healthy once and for all.

To test the hypothesis that too much physical health might not be healthy in the long run for whole person development, talk to people who have never been ill or loved someone who has been terribly sick. Talk about love and caring and the meaning of living in the present moment. Then talk to people who have known illness, pain, and suffering in their own lives or the lives of people they have loved. You will notice immediately that those who have known illness seem, as psychologist William James suggested, born into a universe two stories deep. They seem reborn into a universe of love and depth of meaning more profoundly human and connected than the chronically and egocentrically healthy. They have sipped too deeply from the cup of sickness and pain to ever forget its taste. As a result of their healing through sickness, they seem more complete and whole than those who have never been sick or helped heal and love someone who has been seriously ill.

THE DISEASE DECISIONS

This book will describe my research and the work of others that documents that, when you are ill, you need to do more than decide what you will *do* to get better, what magic medicines or technical procedures you should use, or who you should find to "cure" you. You will also have to decide how you are going to *be* sick and with whom.

Illness can cause us to face two major disease decisions. The first decision is "Who will heal with me?" The next is "How will we find more intimate connection?" Illness reminds us that we have been behaving too separately; that we have been too selfish, detached, self-consumed, or disregarding of our place with and for others; or that even more intimacy than we currently experience is needed. No one has proved that a specific disease is caused solely by selfishness and separation, but we can use our sick times as reminders of what really matters in sickness or in health—loving and connecting. Our suffering can set us back or draw us together; the choice is ours. A major lesson of illness is that none of us is really self-sufficient.

This is a book about going beyond being strong, fighting illness, and overpowering disease to the greater challenge—creating and maintaining intimate life balance. We live in a society that teaches that competition is more important than connection, fighting more important than flowing, and self-assertiveness and power more important than dependence and interdependence. Sexual healing challenges each of these assumptions. It requires more balance than strength, more cooperation with another person than competition against an illness, more selflessness than selfishness, and more intimately relating than mechanically repairing.

We often seem to divide ourselves into two categories—healthy or sick. I suggest that we are all always a little healthy and a little sick because we are always undergoing the chaotic process of life. We are all works in progress. Health is a matter of finding creative and shared meaning in the natural chaos of life, and sexual healing involves searching for that meaning with another person. Whom we travel with and how we travel with him or her toward our inevitable physical end is the key aspect of sexual healing—an intimate journey through our short time here on earth. We don't have to be two individuals sharing separate spiritual experiences. We can be a joined spirit sharing and eventually transcending a brief but wonderful human experience of togetherness.

HEALING MYTHS EXPLODED

The self-healing model of fighting illness and struggling to stay healthy contains many assumptions about health and healing that are not supported by research. Sexual healing challenges each of these myths.

Ten Healing Myths

1. **The Self-healing Myth:** I have emphasized that self-healing is impossible because all healing involves a rebalancing of a system. Your body, your relationships, and society are all involved. Body parts, people, and the social body are all systems that must get along if healing is to take place. Health is not an individual event. Healthy people cannot remain healthy for long when they live in places characterized by stress, violence, and environmental pollution, all of which are forms of disconnecting from the natural, peaceful, caring, clean, and safe world we all crave. Despite modern medicine's focus on the individual patient, when it comes to health and healing, all boundaries are delusions. When cells in the body disconnect and behave selfishly, they proliferate, grow out of control, and kill the system in which they exist. If one body system fails to cooperate with another, illness is always the result. If we act without regard for our world and the social body as well as our own bodies, the planet itself will get sick and die.

2. **The Illness as Enemy Myth:** Both sickness and health are natural

states of the human condition, not opposite ends of a wellness continuum. If we see illness as an adversary, getting better as a war in which we fight disease, we are in constant fear and alertness rather than a shared celebration of living. In my own experience with serious illness and from my patients' reports, I have learned that we fear illness because we fear separation. The ultimate human anxiety is dread of the disconnection that can accompany life-threatening illness. All fear is experienced in part as a sense of separation—from others, from health, or from the pleasure of a healthy body. By focusing on our connections, we can lessen our fears by reducing the sense of separation.

3. The Grief and Guilt Are Bad Myth: If you never feel guilt, you are not taking risks to establish strong and loving relationships. In our struggle to connect, we sometimes make mistakes, go too far, try too hard or not hard enough. Like illness, guilt is not necessarily a punishment but a teacher instructing us toward new and more constructive ways to love and relate. If you never feel guilty, you have not reflected clearly and intensely about your responsibilities in your interactions with others. If you have never grieved, you have never loved, because grief is the natural reaction to the loss of a love. If your heart never aches, perhaps it is underused.

Grief and guilt can be good for your healing because they provide impetus toward connection. Blaming oneself for becoming sick is always destructive, but paying attention to feelings of guilt for not trying hard enough to love and connect can lead to more intimacy. Self-pride and loving connection bring us joy and health, but reflection on our failings and despair at our losses are equally important in strengthening our physical and emotional health. The current popular psychology emphasis on avoiding guilt and moving rapidly in brief stages beyond our grief leads only to repeating the mistakes that may have restricted full intimate connection in the first place. *Bad guilt* is self-blame resulting in withdrawal, but *good guilt* is a longing for more connection that can lead to stronger human bonding.

4. The Feelings of Love Heal Myth: The self-healing model suggests that feelings of love can heal you. There is no doubt that loving feelings are health inducing, but these feelings do not come without loving behaviors. As you will read later, feelings of infatuation can make you sick by resulting in a shower of stressful chemicals that can impair the immune system. Healing love derives from caring acts and not spontaneous and romantic emotional reflexes. Healing,

loving feelings are not overwhelming impulses, they are the result of the mutual decision to demonstrate consistent caring and connection. Romantic impulses may initiate a try for intimacy, but they will never sustain it. Healing love is not only emotional, it is volitional. While attraction, infatuation, and strong attachment are powerful and stressful physiological events built into our reproductive imperative, each of these responses, when prolonged, can weaken immunity and interfere with healing. It is the lasting intimate bond achieved by loving acts over time that can help save your and your lover's lives. Understanding that the healing fruits of love are derived from the behavioral roots of reflective, considered, meaningful loving acts is central to sexual healing.

5. The No Pain, No Gain Myth: Pleasure heals. Although the new medical terrorism often teaches that anything that feels too good can't be too good for our health, sexual healing is based on the opposite lesson. Sexual healing suggests that if something you do *with* someone else enhances the relationship, feels good, and fits well and constructively with the world, it is probably very good for your health. You can eat enough fiber to turn into a rope, but if your relationship is tied in knots, you will not remain healthy for long or enjoy the physical health you have. Anything that hurts you or your relationship is not good for your or your lover's health. If there's heartache and pain, there's probably no gain.

6. The Positive Thinking Myth: Just as sickness is the opposite side of feeling well and both are necessary for healing, negative thinking is as important to health as positive thinking. The effort to think only positively negates the power of negative thinking and the inevitable emotional rebound that occurs from negative to positive. A challenge of sexual healing is to learn to think realistically together and face illness with a sense of mutual challenge, commitment, and control.

The advantage of sexual healing is that we can emotionally boost one another if we learn to accept the good with the bad. There is no evidence that negative thinking or attitudes cause illness or that positive thinking cures disease. Sexual healing research suggests, however, that mutual acceptance and sharing of a range of emotions promotes healing.

7. The Codependence Myth: A common belief of what is often called the "recovery" or self-help movement is that to err is dysfunctional and to forgive is to be codependent. The term *codependence* was originally used to describe the tendency of anyone (although it is

usually women) to stick it out with someone who is "addicted" to some substance or self-defeating behavior. Sexual healing teaches that mutual dependence or codependence, self-sacrifice, forgiveness, tolerance, and caring for someone else through a long and persistent crisis can be one of the most health-enhancing acts in the world. Sexual healing also teaches that, while human acceptance should be unconditional, loving empathy should *not* be unconditional. It should be earned within an endearing, enduring, responsible, and intimate exchange between two caring and mutually nurturing partners. This is the connected codependence factor in the Psychosocial Inventory you took while reading Chapter 1.

8. The Movement Myth: Motivational speakers shout at their audiences about ways to change their attitudes and get motivated by their systems. There always seems to be another "movement" in popular psychology—behaviorism, psychoanalysis, humanism, transpersonal psychology, Gestalt psychology, and dozens of others, and popular books and seminars preaching the merits of each new movement abound. Recent research indicates, however, that it is the individual's faith and not the movement or program itself which has the most impact on behavior change and health.[2] The result of belief is called the placebo effect, and it works best when the belief is shared and confirmed by another person. We need fewer movements and more moving toward and with one another if true healing is to occur.

   Sexual healing is not a motive, an attitude, or a new therapy movement, it is a set of intimate and caring behaviors intentionally exchanged with another person. Sexual healing asserts that motivation does not come before a behavior; it follows behaviors. As I discussed in self-healing myth 4, we feel love when we behave lovingly. Self-healing myth 8 extends this idea to the general motivation-feeling-behavior relationship in all life activities. Sexual healing challenges the assumption that changing feelings will change your life. It asserts that changing your life can change your feelings. The best way to feel like having a sexually healing life is to *be* more intimate more often. Don't wait to feel it. Do it. Don't marry someone you can't seem to live without. Marry someone you are ready to learn to live with. The only proven aphrodisiac is sexual activity. Doing it makes you want to do it more than wanting to do it leads to doing it. No new movement or therapy ever healed anyone. People connecting is the true act of healing.

9. The Pursuit of Longevity Myth: Self-healing is designed to achieve

the long survival of the self. Sexual healing is a way of finding meaningful intimacy every moment of our lives. There are dozens of books about how to add years to your life, but sexual healing's focus is to delay the "disconnection zone" that is caused when sickness results in separation rather than merging. It is more concerned with your love span than your life span. Sexual healing views the purpose of health to be the opportunity to live a life of intimacy and not just to live long enough to end up alone. When we fear death, we tend to live *for* the moment. When we cherish connection with all the dimensions of living, we live *in* the moment. It's not the years of your loving but the loving in your years that makes life and health worth having.

10. The Macho Myth: Modern medicine, until recently, has been dominated by men and the male view of the body and health maintenance. Healing was seen as a matter of the *yang* or traditionally masculine characteristics of individual will, strength, power, and hard work. The more *yin* or traditionally female characteristics of empathy, vulnerability, acceptance, and gentleness have been neglected. The self-healing movement has also suffered from a machismo complex, which teaches that we must face our disease head-on, take full self-responsibility for getting better, win the war against cancer, fight heart disease, defeat illness, keep up our defenses, and wipe out viruses. Some patients feel that they are weak or failures if they cannot "win" their struggle against their illnesses. Sexual healing suggests that we re-yin-ify, or balance the yang and yin of healing by combining the wonders of the mechanical aggressive approach to illness with a sharing, tender, connecting, collective approach to mutual healing.

Sexual healing is an androgynous process that combines the strengths and counterbalances the vulnerabilities of both gender role perspectives. The next chapter explores the way our immune system functions and how a new view of immunity that is based on balance, caring, acceptance, connection, and cooperation rather than a guerrilla warfare orientation against illness can set the stage for sexual healing.

3

INTIMACY AND IMMUNITY
The Biological Power
of Shared Meaning

Most of our most highly valued cultural heritage has been applied at the cost of our sexuality.

Sigmund Freud

MEANING AND MEDICINE

The man's body was bloated with cancerous tumors larger than oranges. The doctor had already drained almost two quarts of milky fluid from his chest, and the man could barely breathe. His immune system had completely shut down, leaving him without the one tool we all need to be safely connected with our world. Lymphoma, the same cancer that had nearly killed me, had spread through this patient's lymph nodes. The hospital staff were doing all they could to make the man comfortable until what they were sure would be his inevitable death.

But this patient was not ready to be separated from his world. He had heard of an experimental cancer drug called Krebiozen and wanted to try it. The doctors at this hospital were scheduled to begin testing the drug but knew that it was far from ready for patient use. Most thought that this patient was much too sick to be helped by any medication, but one doctor went beyond the mechanical approach and stayed connected with his patient. He thought that, if his patient was not ready to be disconnected, he would not disconnect from him. Against the protests of his colleagues, the doctor followed his patient's wishes and injected the Krebiozen. The treatment was given on Friday night, and most of the staff returned home almost certain they would never see their patient alive again.

On Monday morning, instead of finding a gasping and dying man in his bed, they found their patient walking the corridors and talking pleasantly to the startled nurses and other patients. Within ten days, he was completely free from his disease. In contradiction of all medical logic, the patient's hope and refusal to disconnect from life combined with a doctor's willingness to stay connected with his patient's hope had worked a miracle.

After two months of health, the patient read newspaper reports that research had shown that Krebiozen could not be an effective cancer drug. Within days, he relapsed and reentered the hospital. His body swelled, and the tumors returned. His doctor was convinced that something more was at work than mere biochemistry and that the rebound of the man's immune system had been related to his beliefs, feelings, and attitudes. The Krebiozen was a placebo, and, as I mentioned in Chapter 2, this false pill was made strong by the faith of the patient, shared and confirmed by his doctor and others who chose to believe with him. What makes a placebo effective is a shared belief in its power. The placebo effect is not a mere research or clinical nuisance. It is every bit as real as the effect of any medicine. The pill may be made of sugar, but its power is real.

Although Krebiozen was not showing positive results in most patients, the doctor again listened to this patient's pleas not to give up. "It must have been a bad form of the drug," said the patient. The doctor went along. He knew that all his patient had was hope, and he decided to use that hope. He decided to tell his patient that a "new, improved, and stronger Krebiozen" was now available and that he would try the stronger drug. He then administered the placebo. Within days, the tumors were gone again, and the patient returned home healthy and happy.

Months later while the man was traveling, a newspaper story reported that the American Medical Association had finally declared Krebiozen a "worthless drug in the treatment of cancer." Far from his doctor, alone and frightened out of his hope, the man died.[1] This verified case and hundreds of other documented examples of "fatal" diseases disappearing require more than a mechanical explanation for the nature of illness and healing.[2] Such cases are often attributed to the power of the patient's own hopes and beliefs, but I suggest that there is an additional factor at work. In every case of a miracle cure attributed to hope and individual positive attitude, there is someone else who helps to make the miracle and create the healing. Doctor, nurse, wife, husband, or other close person is always a coconspirator in mobilization of the natural healing powers of the human body. There is always someone else who believes and cares with the suffering person, helps to validate his or her faith, and will to stay connected. Hope, faith, and love are essential to healing, but sexual healing suggests that you can't have the first two without the third.

The hundreds of shared miracles documented in scientific reports and case studies indicate that our immune system—the system that protects us from illness and heals us when we are sick—is not separate from who we are, how we think, how we believe, the meaning we give the illness and healing, and particularly the value of having someone to heal with. No one can maintain faith, hope, and belief in total isolation. Faith is a collective effort.

Immunity is highly subjective, reactive, subtle, and responsive. It is not an objective, reflexive, biochemical system that works independently of how we feel about life and with whom we live and love. Sexual healing is possible because our immune system is not "in" us but *is* us. It is selectively responsive, and it is a way of giving a meaning of connection and caring to our lives.

One of the most important aspects of sexual healing is that our immunity is responsive to intimacy. Author Norman Cousins was a pioneer and leading spokesman for the mind-body medicine revolution in the early 1980s. He beat the odds and recovered from serious illness and a heart attack. Many people read that a positive attitude, humor, and hope had been responsible for his survival.[3] While all these factors were important and emphasized by Cousins in his own writings, a careful reading of his books and my discussions with him indicate that his loving relationship with his wife and the shared faith of his doctors were central to his eventual recovery. If, as in the Krebiozen case, meaning can have such a significant biological effect, then mutually found intimate meaning for life is what makes sexual healing so effective.

THE IMMUNE SYSTEM: A PRIMER

The system that is so profoundly responsive to meaning and connection and that rests at the core of our sexual healing system is one of the most wonderful phenomena in nature. Even researchers who work every day in the study of the immune system find it endlessly complex and almost overwhelming in its intricacies. One of the founders of psychoneuroimmunology, Dr. Robert Ader, when asked how he felt about studying immunity and its relationship to feelings, thoughts, and behaviors, said in awe, "I'm scared to death."[4]

The immune system is often seen as a defensive and warlike part of the body, but you will read later that such a view may program our immune system to behave combatively rather than help us connect safely with our world. Immunity does not just function as a lonely sentry ready to kill an invader. It also functions as a partner with our brain and body to help us connect with what and who is healthy for us, and it helps make us whole. Unless we tell it otherwise by the way we live, think, and love, it is more a gentle giant than an angry warrior. To help you understand this important part of the sexual healing system, here is a brief description of the body's primary means of being well connected.

The immune system contains cells which alert it to a substance that is attempting to connect with us. These cells work with the mind to determine if a healthy relationship is possible. If not, they help rid our system of this antigen or "foreign body." Key cells of the immune system are called lymphocytes, including T cells, which come from the bone marrow and are developed further in the thymus gland. We have helper T cells that get rid of elements that do not connect in a healthy way with us; suppressor T cells, which help keep our immune system from overreacting and attacking us; and killer T cells, which remove cancer cells and virus-infected cells. Fast-reacting B cells move within our humoral or fluid immune system to produce antibodies (sometimes called immunoglobulins). These antibodies dispose of illness-producing agents. Cells called phagocytes clean up the waste left after the process is complete. Large cleansing cells called macrophages are particularly efficient cleaners, capable of removing toxins such as the debris of smoking cigarettes that can clog our lungs. All these cells communicate with cells and fluids from our brain and glands.

There are many other cells and processes in our immune system, and this description is grossly simplified. Our miraculous immune system, however, represents only one of the three *I* factors in the sexual healing equation. Intimacy and isolation are also important elements in our healing status.

THE THREE *I* FACTORS OF SEXUAL HEALING

- Intimacy: This is the skill of being physically, emotionally, spiritually, and mentally connected with someone else and the world around us and of maintaining that connection. As you have read, a sense of intimacy doesn't just happen. It is the result of choosing to behave in caring, loving ways with another person. It is not a mysterious cosmic occurrence but the result of active and tangible caring with someone else. Sexual healing is something we do to feel rather than something we feel like doing.[5]

While this book focuses on the physical, sensual, and sexual behaviors that go into intimate connection, our thoughts, beliefs, and feelings are also crucial to the nature of our relationships. Many excellent books deal with the emotions of intimacy as they relate to healing, but far fewer deal with the sexual component of healing love that is the focus of this book.[6]

● Independence: I spoke in Chapter 1 about the REST psychosocial factor and the importance of finding quiet time alone to reflect and contemplate about life's meaning. Independence is the skill of being constructively alone and balancing closeness, connection, and dependence on another person with the ability to maintain intimacy even when physically separated. To be healthily isolated, we need to feel connected beyond physical presence.

Psychologist Steven Covey points out that only independent people can make the choice and commitment to engage in an interdependent relationship.[7] Independence, however, does not mean being self-involved, suffering from the self-sufficiency delusion, or not needing and being needed by anyone else. Sexual healing begins with the assumption of self-deficiency and the belief that no one can be healthy alone. It means assuming the responsibility to work toward wholeness rather than being led through life adjusting to one event after the other without unifying meaning. Independence from the point of view of sexual healing implies being willing and able to be connected to and responsible for ourselves and our lives while we work hard to become fully connected with someone else. The true test of independence is not how self-sufficient we are but whether we can be sufficiently selfless to connect totally with another person.

● Immunity: The third of the three I's of sexual healing—the immune system just described—is not only a body system but also a learned interactional process. Researchers have discovered that the immune system can be conditioned or taught. Experiments have shown that when rats ingest salt water and then swallow a substance that lowers immunity (cyclophosmamate), their immune systems are eventually weakened when they drink the salt water alone. The rats' immune systems learn that salt water is associated with something that weakens them.[8] Our own immune systems can also learn and make associations, and our relationships can become immunotoxic.

While we tend to assign central importance to our brain, research is not clear as to whether the brain or the immune system is dominant in our interaction with the world. Some researchers suggest that our immune system is so sophisticated and subtle that it is a body-brain that thinks and may even be our "sixth sense."[9] Our immune system senses in ways we cannot yet measure or even imagine. Not only does it respond to our brain but our brain responds to our immune system. When our immune system senses something is happening that needs attention, it tells us how to think as much as we tell it how to function through our thoughts. European neurophysiologist Hugo Besedovsky suggests that our immune system is an extension of the brain and a "peripheral receptor organ."[10] Like any receptor organ, the immune system signals the brain. Psychiatrist Joel Elkes describes the immune system as a "liquefied nervous system."[11] Sexual healing is based on the view that our immune system, our brain, and our mind are all one interactive organ system.

As you will read in Chapter 4, sexual healing also views the immune system as a sexual and sensual organ. It courts and rejects, senses, reacts, is aroused or turned off, becomes excited or depressed, learns what turns it on or off, marries or joins us to life and can—as happened to the man with lymphoma at the beginning of this chapter—divorce itself and therefore us from the world. Biochemist J. Edwin Blalock has shown that some of our immune cells produce chemicals called peptides that are nearly identical to those in the brain and nervous system.[12] He concludes that one of the functions of our immune system is "to serve as a sensory organ."[13] Scientist Ted Melenchuk of the Institute for the Advancement of Health states, "The immune system is a sensory system for molecular touch."[14] We may be merging with others and our world on levels even our brain and mind don't know about!

Just as the rats' immune system learned that salt water had the same effect as the cyclophosmamate immune depressor, we teach or condition our immune system every day through our thoughts and feelings. We instruct ourselves and therefore our immune system in what and who to resist and to accept, how much to react or underreact, and how to keep in balance. When we talk to ourselves, our immune cells are listening. These cells are very literal, and what we tell them about the nature of our life becomes the disposition of our immune system and how it will learn to talk to us. Our immune system *is* us, and we have the power to incorporate it into sexual healing to help us heal and stay well.

When it was first discovered that the mind and body were not separate, that the mind could help heal the body, and that we could help promote that process, a "me over my mind and my mind over my body" sequence evolved that still dominates much of the popular health literature. The remainder of this chapter discusses a different orientation to healing based on new research.

OUR SHARED IMMUNITY

I suggest that our immune system works most efficiently if we view it as connected to and interacting with the immune system of our lover. We now know that women's menstrual cycles are affected by the presence of other women and that they can fall into a common pattern.[15] We also know that the presence of a man biochemically influences menstrual cycles and fertility.[16] As in the case of the man at the beginning of this chapter, sexual healing asserts that it is not only our own beliefs which become our biology. Our shared beliefs, feelings, and attitudes combine with those of the people closest to us to influence our own immunocompetence.

The erroneous belief persists that a person can perform a "self-healing" by using the proper mind power methods. Sexual healing depends much more on meaning than method and on the meaning of illness and health found through connection with another person. One of my patients, a car dealer in the sexual healing program with his wife, said, "I think I've discovered what autoeroticism is, and it's making us sick. We have a fixation on our cars. We're driving alone in them and hardly ever touch anyone else unless we have an accident and have to get out of our car. Our sex and our whole life is like that too. It's like we're alone in our skin-mobiles, driving along alone through life. Sometimes we have an accident and make a connection with someone else, but we get hurt because we don't know how to connect safely." This man is referring to our tendency to see our body, our immunity, and our health as our own rather than as intimately connected with the lives of everyone around us. We are often more worried about what we might catch *from* someone else than encouraged by how we might be healed *with* another person. We know how to speed, pass, and surpass others, but we are less skilled in merging and flowing together safely.

Scientist Arthur Eddington wrote, "We often think that when we have completed our study of 'one' we know all about 'two,' because 'two' is 'one and one.' We forget that we still have to make a study of 'and.' "[17] This book is about the *and* factor in healing and sensual and sexual ways in which intimate connection can help us merge and mobilize our immune and healing system.

THE MIND IN OUR BODY

For sexual healing, we need new definitions of *brain* and *mind*. The *brain* is the mass of neurons in our skull. There are more connections between the neurons or brain cells than there are stars in our solar system. The brain is an organ—a massive thinking gland that secretes powerful substances that flow everywhere within us. It is a health maintenance system without compare, and its primary job is to keep us alive whether or not we are connected in regardless of someone else staying alive.

The *mind* is us. The mind is our consciousness and awareness. The mind uses the brain to think with, but it is much more than the brain. As you read in Chapter 1, the cells of our brain and the cells of our immune system communicate, interact, and interchange. To understand sexual healing and immunity, we must also understand that our brain works with our immune system and does not control it. We react with our brain, and we respond to loving with our mind.

"It's like our brain is having sex with our body in the missionary position," said a nurse. "I think it's a form of brain-ism or brain-bias. Everyone talks about the mind over matter or mind over the body. Why does the mind always have to be on top?" While it is true that the mind is much more than the brain, neither the brain nor the mind presides "over" the body. The mind and the brain with which it thinks are not masters doing things "to" the body but are always with and within the entire body. Research now teaches two new lessons about the mind:

1. *The Brain Has Left the Head:* We know that the cells and neurochemicals of our nervous system go far beyond the brain tissue in our skull. The endorphins or pleasure chemicals we once thought were only in the brain have now been discovered throughout the body. Former Chief of Brain Chemistry at the National Institute of Mental Health Dr. Candice B. Pert writes, "I can no longer make a strong distinction between the brain and the body."[18] It looks more and more like our consciousness can, as Dr. Pert suggests, "be projected into various parts of the body."[19] The next time someone says that the brain is the most important organ in the body, remember that this is only the bragging of our selfish brain, which is unaware of the mind directing it. The spirit of our mind and the stuff of our brain permeate the entire body system.

2. *The Mind Has Gone out of Its Body:* It is not only our brain and our mind that heal us but the mind we share with those we love. New evidence from physics indicates not only that our brain has left our head but that our mind or consciousness has lost its body by con-

necting with all other minds. Evidence now exists that the mind transcends the body to interact with and influence those around us.[20]

Physicist Erwin Schrödinger stated, "Mind is by its very nature a singular tantum [concept]. I should say: the over-all number of minds is just one."[21] New age medicine typically assumes that when the mind plays a role in recovery, it is the patient's own mind doing the healing. Sexual healing asserts that other minds heal us too! In a now famous study, a cardiologist at the University of California Medical School studied almost 400 heart patients. The entire group received the same medical treatment, but one half were prayed for and the other half were not. Neither the patient groups nor the doctors and staff were aware of which group was prayed for. The prayed-for group had far fewer complications, required fewer antibiotics, never needed endotracheal intubation or a "breathing tube," experienced less pneumonia, had less need for cardiopulmonary resuscitation, and had fewer deaths than the control group.[22] This "healing at a distance" reflects what physician Larry Dossey describes as "coming home . . . returning to our original, undivided, larger Self, the part of us that connects."[23]

One of my patients put the issue clearly when she said about her healing from cancer, "I'm not sure why I'm healing, but I'm sure of one thing. It's beyond me and between my husband and me." Her comment summarizes the nature of sexual healing and exposes the myth of one lonely mind over one separated body.

SOUL AND STUFF

Sexual healing does not differentiate the matter of the body from the matter of the mind. Everything in the universe is made of the same stuff. The elements that make up the stars are also the elements that make up our bones. The mind is not composed of a mystical spiritual something generating some form of paranormal energy through the body. Our minds, the minds of those with whom we connect, and our bodies are—like everything in the world—both matter *and* energy. It's the meaning we give to our lives and our loving that causes the transformations we experience as stuff and spirit.

Long ago in order to allow dissection of the human body, a divine deal was struck between physicians, eager to learn about the mechanics of the body, and the church, eager to protect the soul housed somewhere in the body and mind. For years, Leonardo da Vinci performed dissection and made remarkably accurate medical drawings, but he did so in secrecy for fear he would be hung for blasphemy. Negotiations between the cutters and the church finally resulted in placing the soul up in the brain and under the exclusive purview of the church. The cutters were given the body to work on so long as they remembered that the body they were cutting was entirely separate from the brain, where the soul lived. The soul was safely sequestered in the cognitive control tower. The effects of this deal are still felt today as the brain is seen as over and separate from the body rather than within it. The body is still often seen as a chemically driven muscle, organ, and bone bag directed by its brain.

Dr. Candice Pert describes the brain, mind, immune system, and body connection as a "psychosomatic communication network."[24] The mind-over-body approach to healing grossly oversimplifies the mind and immune system connection. Mind and matter are not separate; they represent an infinitely complex system that, like quantum physics, some feel will never be completely understood.

The guiding principle of sexual healing is Oneness and connection, not control, power, and self-direction of a single, separate body system.[25] "Self"-consciousness is mere illusion. The divine deal was a sellout of our soul and our healing power of our mind because it separated these two infinitely connected systems. Sexual healing puts us back together again.

TWO BODIES, ONE MIND

"I have to think of sharks eating my cancer cells," said the young mother receiving her weekly chemotherapy. "My daughter has a psychology class in college, and her teacher says that visual imagery can cure you." This woman was intimidated in her attempt to heal by the myth that mind control works by aggressive mental imagery. Since the later 1970s, several books and seminars have taught visual imagery for healing heart disease, cancer, and other serious illness.[26] There is good evidence that certain types of visualization may help promote healing.[27] Unfortunately, most of the work in this area has again focused on individual visualization rather than the development of shared healing images.

Much of the work in visualization borrows heavily from Eastern religious approaches. Yoga, meditation, and other techniques are often suggested to patients without mentioning the key message of the spiritual philosophy from which they sprang. That lesson is one of connection. The word *yoga* derives from the Sanskrit word meaning "to connect," and the original intent of practicing yoga was to connect profoundly with "the way" or the world and universe and all that exists. Now, however, patients too often find themselves listening alone to audiotapes of someone else's idea of healing rather than sharing the creation of healing imagery.

Recent research on meditation reveals that the most successful practitioners of this 4,000-year-old technique experience associations and thoughts concerned with sexuality, relationships, and dependency on someone else. Meditation does not mean separation. Psychologist Roger Walsh reports that experienced meditators shown Rorschach cards designed to measure our unconscious psychological impulses spoke of conflicts concerning dependency, marital satisfaction, and sexuality that had grown from their meditation.[28] Even when we are completely focused and mindful, it appears that our need to connect is ever present.

Sexual healing as I will describe it differentiates between individual visualization and connective imagery. *Visualization* is done by an individual in the attempt to instruct the body directly in healing via specifically chosen images, such as clogged arteries being forced open by mechanical blasters or cancer cells being eaten by killer bees.[29] *Connective imagery* refers to mutually created thoughts that elicit sensory qualities, such as feelings of warmth and arousal.[30] Sexual healing utilizes the intimate shared imagery technique in which two minds combine into one Mind to paint sensuous, healing pictures of health. Here is one example.

One of my patients was a twenty-seven-year-old man with testicular cancer. He was a police officer, and he prided himself on his rugged individualism and independence. He felt that this particular form of cancer was demeaning to his masculinity. He was ashamed of his illness more than frightened by it. His wife had read about the use of visualization in cancer treatment. She suggested that her husband try to visualize little bombs blowing up his cancer cells, but he resisted her suggestion and was becoming more depressed.

As I do in all cases of sexual healing, I saw the couple together rather than examining the patient alone. As we talked, it became clear that no one had spoken to this couple about the mutual effect of the illness. No one had asked them about their loving, their sex life, and what had happened to their relationship. As often happens in cases of cancer in the genital area, all touching, intimacy, and sexual interaction had stopped on the day of the diagnosis. The idea of bombs blowing up cancer cells that were growing in this man's testicles was even more demasculinizing for him. I worked to help the couple talk openly about reestablishing intimate connection, touching, holding, and making love. I clarified that the cancer could not be transmitted by lovemaking and designed with them a connective imagery approach in which they formed a healing unit rather than a caretaker-caretakee relationship. Rather than trying to explode the cancer, they worked together to squeeze the cancer cells back into connection with the rest of the body cells so that they would produce cooperative, caring cells rather than competitive cells killing through their selfish disregard for connection.

Rather than the husband sitting alone trying to visualize attacks on his cancer, the connective imagery designed for this couple involved sitting together in the nude and looking into each other's eyes. They thought about their love for each other, the times they had made love, and the sensual feelings they had experienced. They stroked each other and embraced. The wife reported, "Sometimes we end by making love, but usually we hold one another and cry. I feel so much a part of it all now instead of responsible for just helping him." The husband reported, "I don't want to destroy and murder my cancer cells. They were made inside me, so they are a part of me. I just want them to stop reproducing, quiet down, and become normal again to fit in with the rest of my body. When my wife and I hold one another, it settles everything down and I think it's bringing those overgrowing cells back into the team with my other cells."

This mutual imagery approach has been effective for many of my patients. This man received the news that he would require surgery to remove his testicles. Following the surgery, the couple continued their imagery, and four years later, there is no sign of cancer in the man.

In the search for the metaphor of our illness, we fail to seek the meaning of sickness in the context of our relationships to those we love.[31] We try to tune in to our own body and its sensations rather than our relationship with our partner and the sensations that interaction can create. We often try to discover what we failed to do for ourselves that would have been more positive and healing rather than what we can do with someone else intimately to heal together.

An approach to illness that emphasizes personal visualization rather than connective imagery contains two dangers. First, it can distract us from connection by involving us in private reflection, turning inward instead of reaching out. Second, it can make our partner a concerned bystander rather than an integral participant with us in our healing.

RESPONSIBILITY FOR OUR ILLNESS OR OUR HEALING?

One of the most invidious mistakes occurring among patients suffering from serious illness is assuming full responsibility for the fact that they have become ill or are not being cured. Sexual healing assumes that we can share our responsibility for healing and that no one yet knows all the factors that cause disease. One of the most caring and concerned physicians I have ever met, cancer surgeon Dr. Bernie Siegel at Yale University, formed the Exceptional Cancer Patients Program.[32] He met with groups of cancer patients who worked hard to be strong, think positively, not be depressed, show no regrets or guilt, and were exceptional in their willingness to fight their disease. Although Dr. Siegel didn't mean to imply anything other than hope and caring for his patients, I'm afraid that I would never have qualified for his group. I am distressed by the implication that there are cancer patients who are less strong or skilled than those exceptional healers who love right, feel right, and believe powerfully enough. I believe I would have fallen into the WIMP cancer patients category—the Worried, Immature, Mad, and Pessimistic group.

Dr. Siegel speaks and writes about the healing power of maturely facing our problems, dispelling all anger and learning to love unconditionally, and being optimistic and hopeful. I was often childish, angry, in a state of denial, and completely depressed or pessimistic. My wife and sexual healing partner was there to help with these emotions, but they seemed as much a part of my healing as the more positive feelings discussed by Dr. Siegel. Unfortunately, some of Dr. Siegel's thinking has been interpreted to mean that death and disease are failures rather than natural parts of life and that any negative feeling is potentially lethal.

Dr. Siegel writes, "I have learned to not bitterly regret anything. Life is too short and too precious to spend time regretting."[33] While this sounds good, it is seldom a realistic orientation for most of us. We are only human, and we do regret, ask why, and become bitter. The advantage of sexual healing is that we have an intimate partner to counterbalance our regrets with hope, our fear of optimism, our irrationality with reason, and our surrender with courage. The rebound from negative feelings to positive depends on connection with another person accepting us in our down times while pointing the way to hope.

Dr. Siegel's emphasis on hope and a positive attitude is only part of the healing equation. He comes closer to the point of true sexual healing when he quotes psychiatrist Karl Menninger as writing, "Love cures two people. The one who gives it and the one who receives it."[34] Although Dr. Siegel and others in the self-healing orientation often mention love and healing in the same sentence, they seldom speak of the hows, whys, wheres, and whens of the sexual and interpersonal aspects of this two-person loving. Self-confidence and belief in the power of the self are the focus rather than the learning of intimate and sensual connection. Such connection may not save our lives, but it safeguards our souls through our living.

Physician David Spiegel writes, "We die because we are mortal, not because we have the wrong attitude."[35] He and Dr. Siegel have debated—often heatedly—in medical journals regarding the role of psychosocial factors in healing.[36] Dr. Spiegel has conducted research into the role of psychological and social support in illness and healing. He concludes that social support may improve the quality of life and even add years to survival but that miracle cures from love, hope, humor, and compassion are unlikely.[37]

Dr. Spiegel's emphasis on the importance of social support—including support group and family counseling sessions—transcends Dr. Siegel's focus on self-healing, but it does not discuss sexual healing and the role of two-person sexual relationships or the Hammarskjöld principle described in Chapter 1. He speaks of support groups to help us through serious health problems and points out that we can learn much from our illnesses through such social support. There is no doubt that group support is useful, but the impact of a sexually intimate partner helping us through the rough times or working together to maximize the natural healing processes is crucial. Sexual healing values the combination of sympathy and empathy that can most often be found in intimate two-person relationships.

EMPATHY OR SYMPATHY?

Empathy, the centerpiece of many support groups, does not imply agreement or shared acceptance of meaning. It implies only full and deep understanding of what a person says and feels. Sympathy, on the other hand, is a judgment that a feeling is legitimate. It is an agreement with another person that his or her thoughts and feelings are correct. Empathy involves the effort to understand a person's feelings, but sympathy involves the effort to join with a person in the endorsement of feelings. Empathy involves acknowledgment of another person's feelings, but sympathy validates and accepts them as authentic fact.

Healing is enhanced by the empathy that can be found in support groups, but sexual healing goes further. It combines the comfort of empathy with the validation of sympathy between two loving people. The empathy of social support is helpful, but the unqualified sympathy of a two-person shared support system is the key to sexual healing.

SICKNESS SHAME SYNDROME

Noting a link between our thoughts and emotions does *not* mean that we *cause* our own illness. If there is a need to blame when what we do to heal seems to fail, we should blame the procedure and not ourselves. Doctors know some of the things that contribute to the etiology of disease, but no one knows *the* cause of most diseases. Smoking, drinking, exposure to hazardous substances, genetic factors, diet, stress, and many other variables no doubt place our health in jeopardy, but the majority of people who are exposed to these risk factors do not succumb prematurely to the disease that would be predicted by them.[38] There is something more at work, but the issue is far too complex to assert that anyone "caused" their disease.

I have seen a dangerous side effect from the self-healing approach. There is a frightening increase in sickness shame or feelings of failure for becoming sick. The Sickness Shame syndrome is brought on by a set of unfounded assumptions about health. These include three common guilt inducers:

1. The Responsibility Error: Because the mind and body are so strongly interactive, we are totally responsible for our own recovery. We are partly responsible for our own well-being, but there are too many unknown etiological disease factors and influences over which we have no control to assume that we alone are responsible for illness.

2. The Reality Error: Mind creates matter, so we create our own reality. As you have seen, the mind *over* body approach is inaccurate and even dangerous to health and healing. Mind and body are so interconnected that to see one as causing the other is impossible. The brain does constantly create the body, but the body and immune system interact with the brain, constantly feeding back to and recreating the brain. Sexual healing is one way to remake the mind, to mold it with love shown through intimate body connection.

3. The Grief Error: Depression and grief impair immunity, so negative emotions make us sick. All emotions contain lessons for the key health factor of the sexual healing approach—connection and intimacy. Being sad, angry, hurt, depressed, bereaved, and lonely does affect our health, but these emotions can also urge us to connect with others more profoundly and intimately. In effect, depression and grief can be motivators for sexual healing.

Negative feelings should not be purged and avoided at all costs. They are *essential* for healing because they can result in a biological afterglow that follows all anguish. Psychologist Richard Solomon at the University of Pennsylvania has done extensive research on the biology of emotions in both animals and humans.[39] He has discovered the "opponent-process principle," which asserts that every human emotion triggers its opposite. The pain and fear of serious illness eventually result in a rebound of relief and even a sense of euphoria as we become stronger for our pain. There is a psychobiological price for our pleasure and an immunoenhancement reward for our suffering—an aftershock for the up times in our life and an afterglow for the down times. There are eventual health dividends for our suffering and liabilities or debts for the delights of our pleasure. The new age assertion that we must always be positive not only results in undeserved guilt when we can't be cheerful but prevents us from experiencing our natural melancholia and the health-enhancing biological rebound that inevitably follows. Plato wrote, "How strange would appear to be this thing that men call pleasure! And how curiously it is related to what is thought to be its opposite, pain. Wherever the one is found, the other follows up behind."

PREPARING FOR SEXUAL HEALING: FORGIVENESS

At the beginning of their program in sexual healing, I ask my patients one question: Have you forgiven yourself? Patients often assume I am asking if they can forgive what they did to "cause" their illness. I make it clear that I am asking something much broader: Have they forgiven themselves for any guilt and shame for what they think is their lacking a positive attitude or being unable to avoid negative feelings, not succeeding in controlling their bodies with their minds, feeling too depressed or grieving too long, or not having the "right" self-healing orientation. I explain that no one causes illness all alone and no one gets better all alone. I teach them that depression, grieving, and negative feelings are as essential to healing as more "positive" or "up" emotions. Self-blame is as irrelevant to healing as self-credit.

To help my patients begin the process of sexual healing, I ask them to take the Sickness Shame Syndrome Survey. I ask someone who knows the patient very well to score him or her at the same time, and then the patient and partner discuss the results.

Sickness Shame Syndrome Survey

0 = NEVER	**3** = VERY OFTEN
1 = SOMETIMES	**4** = ALMOST ALL THE TIME
2 = OFTEN	

1. _____ Do you feel guilty for becoming sick?

2. _____ Do you feel self-blame for allowing a disease to develop or for not trying hard enough to avoid illness?

3. _____ Are you embarrassed by your illness because you feel it shows that you have a less-than-healthy upbeat attitude about life?

4. _____ Do you feel anger and hostility toward others for helping your disease happen to you?

5. _____ Do you have a complete self-sickness psychological theory for why, how, and when you became ill?

6. _____ Do you quote new age, codependency, and recovery movement concepts in support of what you did to bring on your problem?

7. _____ Do you try multiple and futile attempts at "new age" or "holistic" approaches (astrology, channeling, crystals, iridology, chakra realignment, simplified quantum physics–based metaphors, etc.) in order to "cure" your illness?

8. _____ Do you ruminate about one major life or love error that "caused" the illness—the "illness imprint"?

9. _____ Have you tried extreme nutritional changes (enemas, megavitamin use, macrobiotics, etc.) and given up almost everything you enjoy in the process?

10. _____ Are you overcompensating for perceived disease-causing psychological errors (for example, trying always to be extremely positive and loving because you were not positively loving enough)?

11. _____ Do you try to teach others how to avoid causing their own illness by using your failed self as an example—assuming a health guru role?

12. _____ Are you angry with health-care professionals and those attempting more traditional treatments because they "have not seen the way" and are getting in your way by not accepting the "new" healing ideas?

13. _____ Have you turned to a "new religion" or recovery support group to heal your inner child or make up for the alleged love deficiencies that caused your illness by seeking support from strangers?

14. _____ Do you have feelings of fear that you are reluctant to express because you will seem weak or show the wrong attitude?

15. _____ Are you working hard to cover deep feelings of sadness?

16. _____ Do you feel a lack of knowledge about your disease while having many ideas about why you have it?

17. _____ Has there been a breakdown in your communication and rapport with your doctor?

18. _____ Is your family pulling away from you because they think you have changed and become strange or difficult?

19. _____ Do you feel fatigued because of the energy required to "keep up the act" of being a positive healer and efforts to avoid natural grieving for the loss of your health?

20. _____ Do you try to deny real symptoms that may signal that the disease is worsening because getting sicker is interpreted as personal failure or evidence that your explanatory model of your illness was wrong?

21. _____ Do you try to suppress resentment of those who are not sick and secretly wish that they would "know how it is"?

22. _____ Do you attempt to elicit admiration or pity by stoicism and courageous acts and speech? Do you attempt to be the perfect patient?

23. _____ Do you talk a lot about intimacy and connection while turning away or not having time for sexuality, caring, or closeness with significant people in your life?

24. _____ Are you on the lookout for any new book or talk-show expert that might have the answer to the "why me" question?

25. _____ Do you use a lot of simple psychology or new age phrases ("in recovery" or "in denial" or "dysfunctional") rather than talk directly and specifically about your unique experience of your symptoms and feelings?

We all feel a little shame and guilt when we are ill. We live in a society that views sickness as a failure or weakness rather than a natural and necessary aspect of the privilege of our soul spending some brief body time here on earth. We all have to pay our "disease dues," but we still feel a little like failures when we don't feel well, particularly when we suffer from major illness. Here is the scoring system for the Sickness Shame Syndrome Survey.

Sickness Shame Syndrome Survey Score Interpretation

70–100	SERIOUS SHAME (interferes with sexual healing)
50–69	SELF-BLAME (slows sexual healing)
20–49	BORDERLINE BLAME AND SHAME
0–19	TYPICAL SELF-DOUBT

The higher your score, the more you may be impairing your healing process, the more likely it is that you have wrongly identified a single or limited cause for being sick, and the more probable it is that your explanation of your illness is based on fear, misunderstanding, and disconnection from those who would provide a more complete and measured way of understanding illness and healing in an intimate connection context.

DIVIDENDS OF SUFFERING AND LIABILITIES OF JOY

Unless our purpose in life is only to survive individually, we can take some comfort even when we suffer from serious illness. When we are challenged by disease, we may take solace in the fact that there is always some dividend—in our learning, self-growth, or increased closeness and mutual meaning. We are wise to remember that, even at our most joyful moments, our humanness and vulnerability mean there are liabilities. The natural chaos and crises of living will always exact their toll, payment for the journey of the developing human spirit.

If it seems unlikely to you that catastrophic disease or injury can sometimes have relatively rapid positive emotional results, consider the findings of a study of auto accident victims left permanently paralyzed from the neck down. Within three weeks of receiving the news from their doctors and after days of sorrow, tears, and ''down'' emotions, happiness was the prevailing emotion of this group, and their level of happiness was higher than that of a control group who had not experienced injury.[40] In my own research with men and women told that they had a form of cancer or life-threatening heart disease, those who allowed themselves to be down and negative for a while benefited from the afterglow of these negative emotions the most.[41] The rebound may not be as rapid as in the case of the men who broke their necks, but it can occur if we stay connected.

There are two warnings about the emotional rebound factor. First, people who complain and agonize over minor illnesses and setbacks do not seem protected by this phenomenon. It is catastrophe and not inconvenience that results in a bounce back to an enjoyment of living. Second, the invisible or less visible injuries and handicaps—such as some forms of cancer, learning disabilities, and autoimmune diseases—may not lead to the rallying of social support that sudden and dramatic injury seems to elicit. A part of the rebound phenomenon results from the resumption of social connections, and isolation may cancel out much of its effect.

THE BONDING BUFFER

When we have someone to support us through our crises and help us find meaning within them, and when we have someone to help us temper our exhilaration with the perspective of a full and rich life that has both pain and pleasure, we derive a buffer against both endless despair and delusional delight. When we have someone with whom we can be physically intimate and with whom to confirm our connection during our struggles, we may manage stress and depression better. By doing so, we relieve our body of the added burden of coping with stress and free it to do its best in dealing with our illness. Stress signals that you are not able to maintain meaningful connection with others, and stress reduction requires reconnection.

Stress reduction workshops are popular, and millions of dollars a year are spent by companies to offer stress management for the individual. My own programs in coping with stress emphasize participation by partners to work toward more connection on the five levels of sexual healing. Just as no one heals alone, no one can effectively cope with stress alone. Research recently published in *Annals of Internal Medicine* shows that meditation, biofeedback, relaxation, cognitive therapy for thinking about stress differently, and other methods have little long-range effect.[42] It is the major change to a more connected life that helps us cope and thrive.

While there is no evidence that any single approach cures any major life-threatening illness, there is evidence that our lives can be prolonged by loving support. A healing balance in thinking and feeling is promoted by the presence of a concerned sexual healing partner for whom the patient is also concerned. The terms *caretaker* or *caregiver* are often used, but I suggest that a sexual healer is a "care-sharer," who benefits as much from the healing process as the person who is the identified patient.

4

THE DISCOVERY OF A NEW SEX ORGAN
Loving for the Health of It

Love resides in the brain. It is the organ of love.
Paul Chauchard

The best cure for hypochondria is to get your mind off your own body and on someone else's.

Anonymous

A NEUROCHEMICAL WEDDING

At the restaurant, the man sat across the table from the woman he had been trying to date for months. When she passed him at work, he could feel his pulse quicken. She had been interested in getting to know him from the first time she saw him. When she met him at the watercooler, she sometimes felt her face flush. They had never said it, but their bodies spoke the language of romantic attraction.

As they talked, her hand touched his. "I've wanted to get to know you since we first met. You're a very attractive man," she said softly. He felt his hands begin to sweat, and his penis began to get erect. He placed his hand on top of hers and answered, "I've felt just the same. You're beautiful." The woman felt her pelvis warm and vagina moisten. Almost instantly, a social romantic connection became physical, was translated up through all the levels of the brain, back down through the glands of the body, and was experienced and expressed all over their bodies and in their sexual organs. Because of an intimate and sensual moment of connection, the immune systems of these two people were altered by their connection and the neurohormones that surged through their bodies. Receptors like tiny locks on immune cells called lymphocytes responded to the chemical keys of their hormones. Two entire body systems were responding in unison, and, however temporarily, a neurochemical wedding had taken place.

BRAIN, SEX, AND IMMUNITY

We required physical examinations of all the patients in our sexual treatment program. As I worked with our patients, I wondered if it was more than the stress of sexual problems and relationship conflicts that seemed to impair their immunity. I saw the impact and pattern of their sexual experiences and relationships translated into an internal body language and changes in their immune status. As the sexual problems were reversed by the reestablishment of intimate sexual communication and the partners felt connected on all the levels of sexual healing, the health of the patients improved. Certainly the stress of their problems had lifted, and their general health behaviors likely improved in the absence of such stress, but these factors were insufficient to explain the speed and extent of their recovery and the improvement in their resistance to illness. There is no doubt that their newfound sexual intimacy played a direct role in their healing. It was through my recognition of the relationship between sexual health and general wellness that I discovered the psychoneurosexuality dimension of healing and the fact that our immune system is a sensual organ.

Current research is supporting my preliminary findings and showing that joyful, mutually fulfilling sexual intimacy has a salutary effect on our hearts and immune systems and may even be a powerful analgesic, or painkiller. A recent study showed that 65 of 100 women who were treated for heart attacks reported feeling sexual dissatisfaction before hospitalization. A study of 131 men found that two thirds said they were having significant sexual problems before their heart attacks. Psychiatrist Alexander Lowen states, "A lack of sexual satisfaction should be considered for further study as a possible risk factor for heart disease."[1] Dr. Dudley Chapman, a professor of obstetrics and gynecology at Ohio University College of Osteopathic Medicine, studied women with breast cancer. He reported that those who felt content with the sexual intimacy in their lives had better levels of T cells—the white blood cells that help rid our bodies of unhealthy elements. In my own clinic, men and women reported less severe migraine headaches, women reported fewer and less severe symptoms of premenstrual syndrome, and both genders reported reduction in symptoms related to chronic arthritis.

The psychoneurosexual connection of thought-feeling-brain-body–immune system–genitals is strong. The cortex or thinking center of our brain influences every part of our body, and our body in turn influences our cortex. The sex centers of our brain are directed by both body and brain signals. These centers include the limbic system, which sits like a cap on top of our spine and is a center of our most basic emotions; the amygdala, which is sensitive to pleasure and novelty; the hippocampus, which responds to intensity and change; and the septal region, which responds to strong emotional stimulation.

Another important sex center is called the brain's brain. It is the hypothalamus, which controls the 4 F's of fighting, fleeing, feeding, and, to put it more politely, sex. When messages interpreted as pleasurable reach the hypothalamus, a series of reactions occurs which causes strong body reactions associated with passion and other aroused states, including flushed skin, sweating, increased heart rate, and heavy breathing.

Some theorists suggest that sex causes love because it provides the biological and neurochemical arousal that motivates us to pair up to multiply. Others say that love causes sex by providing the emotional impetus to become physiologically aroused with another person. Still other theorists suggest that love and sex exist in a spurious relationship because they are both caused by a third factor—the need to be aroused.[2] Sexual healing suggests that love, sex, and the arousal they bring are all paths to fulfilling the need we all have within us to be more complete human beings by connecting intimately with another person. Among the many drives within us is the most powerful—the instinctual drive for intimacy.

Each of the regions of the brain important to sexual arousal is also important to the regulation of our immune system, and each sends messages to our hormones and immune cells that help control their amounts and effectiveness. When we feel turned on, our immune systems respond with us.

While it always functions as an interactive whole, our nervous system can be understood as divided into two parts: The *voluntary nervous system* deals with our movements and physical activities. The *autonomic nervous system* deals with bodily functions that are less under our conscious control, such as breathing, sweating, and heart rate. The autonomic nervous system in turn is divided into two parts: The *sympathetic system* turns us on, and the *parasympathetic* calms us down. The *sympathetic* and *parasympathetic* systems communicate directly with the *pituitary* gland, the key endocrine gland, which regulates the hormones of our body. The ACTH (adrenocorticotropic hormone) the pituitary secretes signals the adrenal glands to release corticosterones and epinephrine (or adrenaline). These secretions influence our immune system. When the sympathetic system (the activating and alerting part) goes into gear, the middles or medullas of our adrenal glands respond to ACTH and secrete epinephrine (adrenaline). Epinephrine is an excitatory hormone that prepares the body for action. This SAM system of Sympatho-adreno-medullary secretions, when chronically activated, can disrupt the immune system by overstimulating and in effect exhausting it to the point of lowered effectiveness.

When the parasympathetic or counterbalancing calming and controlling part of our autonomic nervous system responds, the outside coverings or cortexes of our adrenal glands react to ACTH and secrete a corticosterone called cortisol. This is a slower-acting psychochemical, and in its presence our immune system may be slowed in its development of immune cells, their numbers may fall, and the immune system may become less vigilant for unhealthy cells and antigens. The PAC or Parasympathetic-adrenal-cortical pattern of response is a less agitating mechanism than the SAM system, and connective balance between these systems is key to health, healing, and balanced immunity.

If we experience too much fear, anger, or anxiety in our relationships, our SAM system overreacts and disrupts our immune system. Because the excess SAM epinephrine can send our immunity into imbalance, our immune cells may overreact to our own body (causing autoimmune diseases) or to outside elements (resulting in allergic reactions). Too much depression, disgust, or despondency in our relationships may slow our internal chemistry because our PAC system overreacts. Its excess cortisol makes our immunity sluggish. It may underreact to outside elements (infection) or to our own body cells that are mismade or overgrowing (cancers). Every act of love and intimacy becomes an act of immunity, and if we find healthy connection in our relationships, we protect and heal our body by helping the SAM and PAC systems work together in harmony.[3] Psychoneurosexuality suggests that we view our intimate relationships as choices not only regarding who and how we will love but also in terms of how these relationships may affect our health and the health of our partners.

TESTING YOUR PSYCHONEUROSEXUALITY SYSTEM

You have seen how all our thoughts and feelings translate powerfully to an internal neurochemical environment. Some of our most intense emotions are related to our intimate sexual relationships. How we are responding sexually is one indicator of how our psychoneurosexual (PNS) systems are functioning. Who we are, how we feel about ourselves, and what life means to us are all involved to some degree when sexual intimacy is considered. Our sexual thoughts and feelings result in some of the most rapid and powerful changes in our psychoneurosexual systems. You can discover just how strong and responsive your PNS system is by trying the following experiment.

After you read these instructions, sit down alone in a quiet place. Think about the most erotic, sexual experience you can imagine. Picture the person you would like to make love with. Think of her or his body, how it feels when you touch and stroke each other, what you would like to do with this lover. If you are not distracted by other thoughts, you will notice that your body begins immediately to respond to your sex thoughts. You may note a slight warmth in your pelvic area. Your pulse may quicken, your breathing rate increase, and your muscles will probably tense slightly. Your genitals may even show some response. You might also notice that, if you pay too much attention to your body or feel self-conscious or embarrassed, the natural reaction will quickly reverse.

In this test, you probably experienced arousal of your psychoneurosexual system. If you became nervous, embarrassed, or anxious or had thoughts of prior sexual failures or fears, your SAM system overreacted and the balance necessary for sexual arousal was disrupted. If you thought that sex would not be possible, that you were not worthy of your fantasy image of a partner, or if you felt depressed or even disgusted at the thought of sex, your PAC system blocked the PNS system from even beginning its pattern of secretions. The PNS is a two-way system. If you caress your erotic zones, you may discover that you will begin to think about your lover and experience images of him or her. An intimacy imprint is in the brain, and it is activated by erotic zone signals just as the body responds to the mental images of your lover.

There is no clearer evidence of the mind-body connection than the direct and immediate response of our bodies and genitals to our sexual fantasies and our brains to our erotic body signals. The warmth and physical arousal you may have felt are caused by neurochemicals and hormones pouring through your body, and your immune cells are an integral reactive part of this sensual shower. Intimate, mutually caring and warm sexual intimacy and imagery are caused by and help to promote a SAM-PAC balance, and the psychoneurosexual effect is better health and healing.

THE MEANING OF THE MASSAGE

When our genitals are stroked and touched, signals are sent to the lower part of our spine, called the sacral region. If we simply react without thought and attribution of meaning to the stimulation, erection of the penis and lubrication of the vagina may result within seconds. If we think positively and with love and caring about the stimulation, the reaction intensifies. If we think negatively and with fear or disgust, the reaction is interrupted. We decide if sex signals from the sacral region will be brought up to our brain for processing, and we give the meaning to the massage. We decide by volition and not just emotion if a sexual encounter is a quickie for fun, an obligatory payback, or an expression of deep affection. We give the meaning to our relationships, reacting with guilt, disgust, fear, anxiety, hope, trust, or caring. Each of these reactions writes a psychoneurosexual prescription for health and healing or injects a dose of health-threatening psychochemicals.

Sexual healing is possible when we give a meaning of intimate connection on all five pentamerous levels. Sex that involves these five connections of sexual healing—self-esteem, intimacy, coherence, mindfulness, and sensuality—results in a balance between the SAM and PAC systems, and our immune system balances as well. Feelings of self-degradation, alienation, meaninglessness, distraction, physical awkwardness or discomfort, and the anxiety and depression that can be associated with these states challenge rather than balance our immunity.

SEXUAL PROBLEMS AND IMMUNITY

There are several ways of classifying sexual problems, but the most common complaints are problems getting sexually aroused (difficulty achieving penis erection and lubrication of the vagina), problems having orgasm (ejaculatory incompetence and anorgasmia), and problems having orgasm too soon (premature ejaculation or vaginal contractions). In Part III, I will discuss the two additional problems of compulsive sexual behavior and hypoactive sexual desire. All these conditions have direct effects on and are affected by the psychoneurosexual system.

In order to become sexually aroused, the parasympathetic or the relaxing part of our nervous system must be primarily in control. We can't get turned on when we are afraid, threatened, stressed, or worried because that is when the sympathetic nervous system starts to take over, and the fight or flight response rather than the touch and hold reaction dominates.

Too much SAM too early in the sexual interaction and the psychochemistry becomes countersexual. The body gets too excited, and sensual intimacy is blocked.

If we have difficulty becoming aroused, achieving erection, or lubrication of the vagina, we are experiencing too early interference and too much sympathetic stimulation of our nervous system. I have never seen a patient with difficulties with erection or lack of vaginal lubrication who did not report some degree of health problems such as allergies, nagging and chronic illnesses such as colds or flu, and often more serious diseases such as heart disease. No doubt many other factors are related to such illnesses, but the PNS system's hyper-SAM reaction is a part of the vulnerability to these diseases.

If we experience difficulty having sexual orgasm, it is likely that we are not getting the timely dose of sympathetic nervous system neurochemicals. We need a spurt of excitement of the SAM system at just the right time in order to experience orgasm. However, an overdose of SAM because of the stressful meaning we may be giving to a sexual encounter (fighting) or a blocking of the SAM by the PAC system because of disgust or fearful insecurity (fleeing) destroys the flow of our intimate exchange. As figure 1 indicates, just the right balance between feelings of safety and security are scintillation and physical sensations results in the most intimate and therefore the most healing sex.

It is not just the individual's SAM and PAC systems that must be in balance. The nature of the relationship itself and whether it is running too hot or too cold also determine whether the sexual encounter will be healing or stressful. You will read later about the PNS hot reaction to the thrill of attraction and the addictive high of infatuation. When safety and security are lacking, things heat up, but the fire can cause illness. You will read how the PNS system reacts coldly to the helpless lovesickness of attraction and numbness of the love-blindness of detachment. Too little scintillation and sensation, and the sexual system can freeze up to contribute to illness.

When we are intimate within a sexually healing bond, the SAM and PAC systems are in perfect balance because our relationship is in balance. The loving meaning we are giving to what we are doing and with whom we are doing it results in a PNS prescription that soothes rather than burns or freezes our body systems. We are not thrilled to distraction, infatuated to desperation, attached in surrender, or detached in resignation. These four states are mere reactions to our body chemistry. When we are sexual in a healing bond, we are turned on just enough. Our SAM and PAC systems are in harmony. We are alert enough to tune in completely to our

FIGURE 1

Sexual Healing and Balancing the SAM and PAC Systems

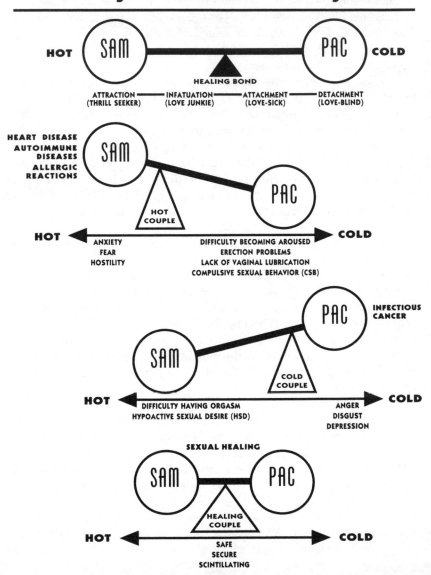

partner but trustful and secure enough to be vulnerable to him or her. The result is arousal, excitement, strong bodily response, euphoria, pelvic contractions, flushing of the skin, and eventually complete muscular and body relaxation. When the hormones are in such erotic harmony, there is no more immune-balancing and -enhancing act than loving, meaningful, connected sexual intimacy. When they are not in such balance, I have noticed that many patients—both men and women—with problems having orgasm are prone to arthritis, immune diseases such as lupus, chronic infections, and even cancer.

THE IMMUNE SYSTEM WE CAN TOUCH

If you could collect all your immune cells and put them in a bag, they would weigh about two pounds. The immune system is composed of about a trillion lymphocytes and 100 million trillion antibodies, and it is entwined throughout our body and brain. The biggest part of our immune system is our skin—the largest of all our body organs. We don't usually think of our skin as an organ of immunity, but it is one big, living, breathing body bag full of immune cells.

The most obvious way our immune systems come in contact with one another is when we touch and rub skin. Punch us and we bruise as immune cells rush to the scene to effect a repair. Cut us and we bleed as millions of immune cells begin to weave a web of repair, clean out bacteria, and rebuild the skin itself. If we become nervous and frightened, our skin may develop bumps and rashes. Gently caress us, hold us, and sensually stimulate us, and our largest immune system organ is soothed by the signal that there is loving life in the universe beyond our own body making contact with us. Whisper gently in our ear, and the hair on our skin might stand up in excitement. Say something sexually suggestive, and our skin will blush. Just before orgasm, a slight reddish rash appears on our chest and cheeks.

We can see all these changes in our wraparound immune organ, and these changes are more clearly evident than the changes going on in our lymphocytes. They represent and demonstrate, however, the degree to which our entire immune system reacts to our thoughts, feelings, and sexual intimacy. Every act of sex is an act of immune stimulation. Our erogenous zones are centers for collection of immuno-enhancing signals, and our genitals specialize in receiving and sending potentially immune-balancing messages. When we make physical contact, much more than a symbolic healing touch occurs. Our immune systems embrace.

THE MAGIC TOUCH OF THE NIGHT NURSE

She came to me late at night. I could sense her presence by my bedside, and I could feel her looking down at me. During the late hours on the bone marrow transplant unit, I would long for the touch of my wife. On most nights, I could hear only the crying, retching, and groaning of the patients around me. Strangely, the sounds of our pain seemed reassuring signals that the battle was still joined and that we were all still fighting for our lives. Around three in the morning, things would quiet down as pain medications and sleeping pills began to numb the unit. I felt afraid and alone in the darkness of my room. Every drop of the medicine going into my veins seemed to sting a little more because of my separation from my wife, and I seemed to feel the cancer cells eating away at my hips. It was about that hour that she would come to me to perform her healing touch. I would pretend I was asleep, but I know I didn't fool her. I would feel her hand on mine as she whispered comforting little songs. Her touch soothed me and made me feel safe. She gently stroked, patted, and rubbed my hands, arms, legs, and face, and I felt strengthened. After several minutes, she would gently kiss my forehead and walk quietly from my room, but I knew she would return the next evening. I knew she would bring her healing energy to me.

I never knew her name, although I have many guesses. She was one of the night shift nurses or aides, and she would comfort me in my wife's absence and keep me connected through her tender touch. She was a connection surrogate standing in for my wife, and while only my wife could truly help me maximize my healing, the mysterious night nurse helped save my life with her tenderness.

THE SEXUAL HEALING PROFESSION

Many doctors, researchers, and sex experts may have largely ignored the power of sexual healing, but there is one profession that has led the way in trying to understand and offer healing through intimacy and physical contact and connection. Like my secret night healer, many nurses have long been practicing the "healing touch" and have been less reluctant to speak openly about it.[4] Perhaps because nurses spend so much time with patients and are able to observe and participate in the healing process more directly than most physicians, they have seen intimacy and gentle touch heal. Few nurses would be willing to call their healing touch sexual healing, but physical connection with a caring person is one of the five connections that compose sexual healing. The surrogate touch cannot bring all five of the connections of sexual healing to bear, but it can help maintain the tenuous ties to tenderness that can be severed by distance from our sexual healing partner. Surrogate touch cannot fully heal us, but it can help sustain us until our sexual healing partner arrives.

Listen carefully in hospitals, and you will hear doctors speaking of mechanical analogies such as hammertoes, mallet finger, funnel chest, clubbing of the fingers, lockjaw, sandpaper rashes, cannon shot sounds in arteries and sawing-wood heart murmurs.[5] Nurses speak this mechanical language too when they have to, but they are medically bilingual. Many of them can also speak the language of tenderness, caring, touch, support, gentleness, hope, and the human spirit. It is most often nurses who bring and unwrap the flowers, cry with and for patients, and offer "relief from your discomfort" with a gentle massage rather than "knocking out the pain" with a needle injection.

Traditionally, it has been nurses who come in closest contact with our most intimate body parts and functions. Whether it's professional training, the femaleness or yin that both male and female nurses bring to their work, their own willingness, or the plain responsibility for the day-to-day survival of their patients, nurses deal daily with sexual healing. Through their comforting touch, they help keep patients connected when so much is happening to wrench them from a sense of safety and security. One of my male nurses never left my room without hugging me, rubbing my chest, and holding my hand for a few additional moments. He seemed to know the power of the healing touch, even joking one evening that "we've got to get your T cell count up. Let me sit here awhile and hold your hand. I'll help boost your immunity."

Nurse and academician Dolores Kreiger, at New York University, is a pioneer in the study of therapeutic touch through which the hands are passed near but do not actually contact the body.[6] The effect of touch similar to that studied by Kreiger was researched by Dr. Daniel Wirth. He found that full-skin-thickness surgical wounds were healed in days by what he calls "non-contact therapeutic touch," even when the patients did not know that such touch was being administered.[7]

"TOUCH TEMPLATES" AND ORGAN MEMORIES

Research on animals has shown that gentle touch and stroking leaves a powerful imprint on their health. Animals that are petted and cuddled when they are young tend to age less rapidly, fewer of their brain cells die as they age, and their memory seems better far into their later years.[8] As physical organs develop, they seem to be capable of remembering gentleness and love and tend to respond to these gestures in a healthy fashion at a later time. Animal immune systems are strengthened by early handling, and the more the touching the more active the immune system in later life.[9] Close handling and nuzzling seem to produce long-term positive health and sexual effects. If a mother rat was sprayed with lemon scent and then suckled her offspring, the offspring would respond more intensely in sexual encounters as adults when lemon scent was placed on their sexual partners. The imprint of the pleasure of intimate connection resonated from their past.[10]

BYPASSING OR OPENING THE HEART

There is emerging evidence of the validity of physical touch as a healing factor.[11] This research shows that measurable physiological changes take place when we are touched gently by someone who cares about us and for whom we care. Reduction of blood pressure, slowing of breathing, lowering of the amounts of stress hormones epinephrine and lactic acid in the blood, and relaxing of muscles have been recorded in response to tender touch.[12] The healing nature of touch derives from its role as the confirmation or reconfirmation of an intimate connection—the physical verification that "we are here together" and that we mean something and find meaning in life together.

One of the most common forms of surgery in the United States is heart bypass surgery. A heart bypass is done when the heart becomes separated from the rest of the body by the clogging of the arteries which nurture it. The heart surgeon constructs arterial detours around these blockages or, in some cases, forces the arteries clear by a procedure called angioplasty. Both heart bypass and angioplasty are ways of mechanically going around the heart or forcing it to stay connected to the body, but there may also be sexual healing paths to reestablishing our heart connection.

Remarkable work by Dr. Dean Ornish, a cardiologist at the University of California School of Medicine in San Francisco, has shown that clogged arteries can be cleaned out solely by behavior and lifestyle changes. Dr. Ornish has documented overall regression of coronary artery disease in patients who made four major lifestyle changes: a low-fat vegetarian diet, a program of moderate aerobic exercise, stress-management training, and connection through group support.[13] The effects of these changes were dose specific. The more assiduously a patient adhered to the program, the more marked the clearing out of the arteries.[14]

The patients who were most successful in sticking with the program were those who also confronted the factor of intimacy and connection in their daily lives and developed better and more intimate connections.

Dr. Ornish states, "I think that the sense of isolation is often at the root of or leads to chronic stress, which, in turn, may lead to heart disease."[15] He speaks of emotionally "opening the heart" through social support and helping patients reestablish a sense of connection with themselves, others, and a higher purpose and meaning in life. He has shown on angiography—X rays of the heart—that the arteries around the heart are cleaned out by significant changes in behavior maintained in part because patients are able to feel connected again.

Dr. Ornish says, "We all have a memory, sometimes a dim memory, of how good it feels to feel connected and intimate with other people."[16] I believe that every organ in the body contains such a memory and that sexual healing works because these fond remembrances are acknowledged and fulfilled not just interpersonally but also on a physical level. In psychoneurosexuality terms, intimate physical connection promotes autonomic equilibrium, which is conducive to immune system balance and efficiency.

Unfortunately, the way we sometimes go about trying to recapture our memories of gentle caring and a sense of connection and closeness makes us feel even more isolated. We begin to believe that wholeness and meaning are gained by achievement and acquisitions. We assume that superior sexual skills or selecting and seducing a prized sexual partner will bring us the sense of connection we so desire. Strive as we might, we seem to fall short. To feel more involved in life, we become more self-involved. We harden our attitudes, and we solidify our arteries in the process.[17] Psychosclerosis leads to arteriosclerosis, but sexual healing is one path to opening the attitudes and the arteries, reversing both psychosclerosis and atherosclerosis, and helping us to realize and fulfill our organ memories of connection. As T. S. Eliot wrote, "There is only the struggle to recover what has been lost."

SENSUOUS HEALTH AND BONDING BOOSTS

The word *sensuous* means "perceived by or affecting the senses" and "readily affected through the senses."[18] Our immune system matches all these characterizations and should be viewed as a sensuous organ system. Conditions that influence our loving and connection have profound effects on our psychoneuroimmunological status. As PNI researchers have gathered more data on just how sensitive or sensuous the immune system is, they have begun to focus on emotional reactions in addition to the depression, shame, grief, and guilt I have discussed.

Psychologist Janice Kiecolt-Glaser and her colleagues at Ohio State University College of Medicine studied the reactions of the immune systems of medical students to the stress of examinations. Dr. Kiecolt-Glaser administered psychological tests and took blood samples to assess immunodeficiency—number of lymphocytes and their effectiveness—in the students. She found not only that the stress of exams impaired the immune status of the students but that those students who said they felt lonely had even more depressed immune systems than those who felt stress but had someone to be stressed with.[19] Intimacy may be an effective "bonding buffer" against the negative effects of chronic stress.

Stress has been shown to lower our body's resistance to upper respiratory infections and herpes.[20] Studies of astronauts returning from three Skylab missions showed that their immune systems were significantly impaired by the stress of reentry and splashdown.[21] The stress of attending college can lower immunity.[22] Stress has been shown to make the symptoms of a common cold worse because of its effect on our immunity.[23] The National Academy of Sciences concluded that the grief and depression that follow the death of a spouse decrease our immune defenses and also increase the risk of having a heart attack or stroke.[24] This evidence and other research add support to the ideas that the immune system is sophisticated and extremely sensitive and that it reacts to all the events of our lives. By establishing an intimate physical relationship with another person, we can bring into balance our immune system. The one behavior that our immune system responds to best even when it is under pressure is intimate connection.

Our immune system feels and behaves as lonely and helplessly or as lovingly and connectedly as we do, and it may be even more sensuous—more sensitive and reactive—than any other body system. It does not depend on our eyes, yet it is capable of sensing acutely what and with whom we want to connect. It does not depend on our ears, yet it responds to sounds to which our ears are deaf. It employs our skin to "feel," yet it feels and senses in a much more complex and discerning way than we can imagine. When it feels alone and isolated, it pines and becomes powerless. When it feels challenged and fearful, it can love us to death with its passionate burning. When it feels loved and loving, it is capable of loving us to health. When our intimate connection is actualized by erotic physical contact, the immune system is massaged, soothed, and comforted into an erotic equilibrium that helps us cope with almost any threat to our wellness.

IMMUNOIMPOTENCE

When we feel disconnected and isolated, our immune system's capacity to protect us diminishes. When we shrink away from others, our immune system recoils, cringes, and constricts. When we fear that we are sexually and sensually inadequate or unable to connect, we experience learned helplessness and our immune system begins to be helpless too.

Martin Seligman has studied the effects of "learned helplessness," or learning through experience that our actions are ineffective in reducing stress. He discovered that helplessness depresses both the number and effectiveness of our immune cells.[25] Studies on rodents given inescapable shocks showed that they were more likely to develop cancer and that—as if their immune systems had learned to be helpless too—their cancer would go unchecked by an inadequate immune system response.[26] All this evidence indicates that our immune system is not within us, it *is* us, and it is one of the most sensuous, responsive, intimate, sensitive—and therefore sexual—systems in the world.

If we think of sexuality as only the physical or genital aspects of connection, we neglect the fact that our whole psychoneurosexual system is involved in every one of our intimate encounters. When we begin to think of our intimate relationships as ways of stimulating, programming, balancing, and strengthening our immune system, we are beginning the process of sexual healing. We accomplish immunopotentiation or produce immunoimpotence by how we sexually relate. Sexual healing involves not only what we do to whom but also, more important, physical expression of how we think, feel, and believe about our healing partner. The sexual aspects of a healing physical connection will be explored in Part II.

5

THE DEVELOPMENT OF A SEXUALLY HEALING RELATIONSHIP
Courting Health or Disease

Those who know how close the connection is between the state of mind . . . and the state of immunity . . . will understand that the sudden loss of hope and courage can have a deadly effect.

Victor Frankl

POTENTIAL LOVERS AS ANTIGENS OR EROTOGENS

"I have never felt more totally alive, more fully complete, or more happy in my life," said the woman about her lovemaking with her husband. "Just looking at him turns me on and makes me feel great."

"Just looking at my husband makes me feel weak or turned off," said another wife. "Our lovemaking has become a hassle. Every time he wants to make love, I want to find an excuse. I feel bad for hours and sometimes days after we make love. Even when he calls on the phone, I get down."

These two opposite accounts of sexual experiences illustrate the range of feelings we can have when we attempt to relate intimately with someone. You read in Chapter 4 that our every thought and feeling translates to our internal biology and immune status. Because of the connection between our brain, body, and immune system, our attempts to relate are particularly significant for our health and healing.

Antigens are elements which challenge our immune system when they attempt to connect with us. Our immune system keeps us safe by recognizing that these antigens are not a good match with us and ridding our body of them. A person in our life may function as a human antigen, to whom we react with stress and emotional turmoil. Excess stress chemicals are released, our immunity weakens, and we become healing impaired. Another person may be a potential *erotogen,* or welcome and healthy addition to our living. We feel safe, soothed, happy, fulfilled with this person, and our immune system easily helps us maintain and nurture our connection with him or her. The antigenic people in our lives threaten our health, but the erotogenic people are good for our health.

SEXUAL ATTRACTION AND THRILL SEEKERS

When we meet someone we consider a potential sexual and loving partner, we engage in the first step in every sexual encounter as well as every immune event—perception. In response to as yet unmeasurable signals from our immune system as well as our brain, we decide based on past experiences, preferences, fears, and fantasies whether we want to or should be intimate with this person. We determine if we feel threatened or comforted, attracted or repulsed. "Wow, he or she turns me on. I've got to do something to get this person together with me" might be the perceptual response. Or, we might think, "Oh no, what a jerk. I have to figure out a way to reject this fool." Like our immune system, our sexual system determines friend or foe.

Accompanying our perceptions concerning the status of our connection with someone else, our hypothalamus and other sex centers of the brain, which you read about in Chapter 4, send immediate signals throughout our body. When we feel strong attraction, our sympathetic or activating part of our nervous system goes into gear. The hypothalamus (with adrenocorticotropin) tells the pituitary gland (with its adrenocorticotropic hormone) to stimulate the adrenal glands, epinephrine is released, and we get turned on. Some people are almost addicted to the turn-on of constant attraction and the epinephrine that accompanies it.

People who are epinephrine addicts are thrill seekers. They can't seem to get enough of being high and find themselves seeking more and more feelings of attraction by finding a variety of partners. They look for excitement to come from a projected image of a person rather than from within a relationship. For them, new and different are good, and the adventure and risk of the courtship chase are even better. Thrill seekers enjoy the hunt but quickly tire or become bored when commitment, maintenance, and sameness enter the picture. Their immune system is as agitated as they are, and their excess epinephrine stirs up the immune system, tires it out, and severely overextends its adaptive capacity over time.

A major healing and immune risk for thrill seekers may be their tendency to misattribute their aroused state to a person when they may be turned on by factors other than personal attraction. Psychologists Ellen Bersheid and Ellen Walster have researched the tendency to misidentify what is causing us to be aroused and the possibility that we can be attracted to our own state of arousal rather than by the intensity of interpersonal relationship.[1] By causing physical stress in volunteers and then showing them pictures of men and women, persons under chemically induced stress reported being more turned on to the people in the pictures than a control group who had not been stressed. In another study, by psychologist George White, men were asked to run in place until their heart rate and respiration increased (signs that epinephrine is being released). Another group sat quietly. When asked about their response to a woman researcher in the room, the men who had been running reported being very turned on while the men at rest did not.[2]

Psychologist Alan Lee suggests six styles of loving.[3] The first two types, *eros* love (from the Greek word meaning "sensuous and romantic")—intense, exciting, and thrilling love—and *ludus* love (from the Greek root word meaning "insincere and ridiculous")—a playing at the game of love with many lovers—characterize the thrill seeker. The attraction addict is after the thrill of it all and continually tries to get higher by finding more and more exciting love and lovers rather than a more and more meaningful relationship.

Our ability to establish strong and healing relationships is enhanced by going beyond the chronic hormonal high of attraction and the danger of mislabeling arousal for caring and love. The two-component theory of emotion suggests not only that our emotions lead to arousal but that we may assign an emotion such as love or sexual attraction to the state of arousal itself, which may have been induced by something entirely different.[4] A sexually healing relationship requires clear identification of why we are aroused and certainty that we are responding to the relationship and not an image representing a psychochemical high.

INFATUATION AND LOVE JUNKIES

After perception, the second phase of our sexual healing system's courtship is our assessment of whether we have the emotional, cognitive, and sexual coping capacity to be intimate with a person in a healthy and satisfying way. We react by determining what constitutes a sexual stimulus, then we respond by assessing our potential to be safely sexual with this stimulus.

After we have been attracted to someone, we move into a phase of infatuation. This phase is always short-lived, but it is characterized by the presence of another neurotransmitter—phenylethylamine, or PEA. Phenylethylamine is the romance chemical, and we feel euphoria and excitement when it is present. When we are infatuated with someone, we experience a PEA rush that diminishes in about a year and half if we see the person relatively regularly or in about four years if we see him or her less often. Presence seems to make the heart grow less infatuated.

When we react rather than contemplatively respond to our lover, we can become fixated or stuck in the courtship sequence. If we allow our biochemistry rather than our mind to direct us, we are unable to progress beyond romantic reflex to meaningful intimacy. It is natural for us to become thrilled or infatuated with someone, but we will never discover sexual healing if we keep recycling through preliminary courtship phases designed to draw but not keep us together.

Like the thrill seekers reacting to epinephrine, infatuated people crave PEA. They become love junkies who are in love with love and who regularly fall in and out of what they think is love but is more likely to be lust. Like any junkie, the love junkie develops a tolerance for PEA—a little is no longer enough. And, like any excitant neurohormone over time, PEA can have negative effects on our health and immunity.

In terms of the Lee types, the love junkie's love would be called *mania* love from the Greek word meaning "agitation." This type of love is distracting, characterized by intense conflicts and arguments. The mania love junkie's love life is one of many breakups and makeups. The thrill seeker is placed at health risk by his or her chronic high. He or she abandons relationships when the thrill is gone and the romantic "fix" seems less satisfying. The love junkie's health risk stems from his or her proneness to a roller-coaster ride of the brief highs of passion and the prolonged lows of separation.

Sexual healing requires that we move beyond the brain and body chemistry of attraction and infatuation to a more meaningful, stable, enduring relationship. It requires that we not seek a series of new partners so we can enjoy the thrill of it all but that we learn to love the person rather than the PEA high.

ATTACHMENT AND LOVE-SICKNESS

A key time in the development of a sexual healing relationship takes place when we have transcended attraction and infatuation. A sexual healing decision must now be made. Will I attach, detach, or bond? Some people develop *attachment,* a needful, dependent, insecure, and uncertain relationship with another. Attachment is accompanied by another set of neurotransmitters, the endorphins. These lower the level of PEA, quieting the system and calming things down. Unfortunately, attachment is so comfortable, so easy, so soothing, and so seductive that we can become addicted to attachment and not grow within our relationship and help our relationship grow. Attachment is an easier option than detachment or bonding. It is so comfortable that we may elect to suffer in comfort or stay in an unfulfilling relationship rather than make the effort to bond or to detach from a relationship that is not mutually gratifying.

People who are addicted to the neurochemistry of attachment are the lovesick. They are numbed by the comfort of their endorphin-induced comfort and fear leaving the safety of this comfort to seek what may be a more demanding but more meaningful and less dependent relationship. In terms of the Lee classifications, the attachment junkie or love-sick person engages in *agape* love (from the Greek word meaning "to be overwhelmed to the point of personal sacrifice"), suffering for the good of the partner at the expense of his or her own health and engaging in a child-parent type relationship.

DETACHMENT AND THE LOVE-BLIND

Another loving style is detachment, in which a person passes through the attraction and infatuation phases but can't seem to accept the challenge of forming and maintaining a sexual healing bond. It may be that hypopituitarism is partly responsible for a type of love-blindness. Adrenocorticotropin from the pituitary gland is not maintained at adequate levels, and the biochemical impetus to attach or bond is lost. More often, however, the love-blind chooses not to look with love or to make the effort necessary to see love. Like a child with a learning disability, the love-blind does not "read" the signs of loving. Unlike the learning disabled child, however, the love-blind can learn to be love-literate through the necessary effort to connect on all five levels of sexual healing.

The love-blind person just "does not seem to get it" when it comes to bonding. Intimacy doesn't seem to be a turn-on, so there may be a regression to search for a higher high of more intense attraction and/or infatuation with a new partner. The love-blind enters relationships reactively but drops out to seek more intensity elsewhere, ends relationships passively or by neglect, or surrenders to what he or she feels to be a dull but practical interaction. In Lee's classification system, the love-blind may show a *pragma* (from the Greek word meaning "serviceable and functional") style of relating. He or she stays in the relationship as a way to get the tasks of daily life done in an efficient manner, but the relationship is not a source of joy and meaning. Once the initial attraction and infatuation wear off, the love-blind does not attach or bond. He or she falls into complacency. This is a love that is quick to fall into but even faster to fall out of. The love-blind tends not to choose attachment over detachment, because attachment requires too much self-sacrifice and not enough thrill. Usually, the love-blind tires quickly of the titillation of attraction and the excitement of infatuation and prefers to remain in a nonintimate but comfortable relationship that does not grow.

Even when the love-blind stays in a relationship, he or she puts little effort into its growth. Work, hobbies, and other friends take precedence over the relationship, and the love-blind person may resent encroachment by perceived demands from the partner for a more bonded interaction.

HEALING BONDS

If we successfully negotiate the courtship path through the psychochemical pull of attraction and infatuation, the temptation to the comfort of attachment, and the escape from mutual relationship responsibility offered by detachment, and we do not become thrill seekers, love junkies, or love-sick or love-blind, we can discover the true sexual healing relationship of human bonding. *Bonding* is a process of two mature adults choosing to care forever for each other, give to and take from each other in balance, and meet crises together with a sense of challenge, commitment, coherence, and mutual control.

One neurohormone present when we bond is oxytocin. Unlike the epinephrine of attraction, the phenylethylamine of infatuation, the endorphins of attachment, or the deficiency in ACTH of detachment, oxytocin is a psychochemical which induces a sense of deep caring, protection, and tender empathy. Unlike the agitation of epinephrine, excitement of PEA, lulling calm of the endorphins, and numbness of insufficient ACTH, oxytocin contributes to intense closeness, trust, and sensual feelings shown by cuddling, holding, and sensual intimacy. Oxytocin helps to balance our immune system; it is the same hormone that is secreted when a mother nurses her baby and when we have intense orgasmic experiences. It is a neurochemical of intimate connection.

In Lee's classification, the bonded relationship's love is a *storge* love (from the Greek word meaning ''companion or friend''). Storge love grows from a deep and enduring friendship that shares many common beliefs. It does not come from an unexplained attraction, a mysterious high, a romantic thrill, or childish dependence, and it transcends compla-

FIGURE 2

Courting Sexual Healing

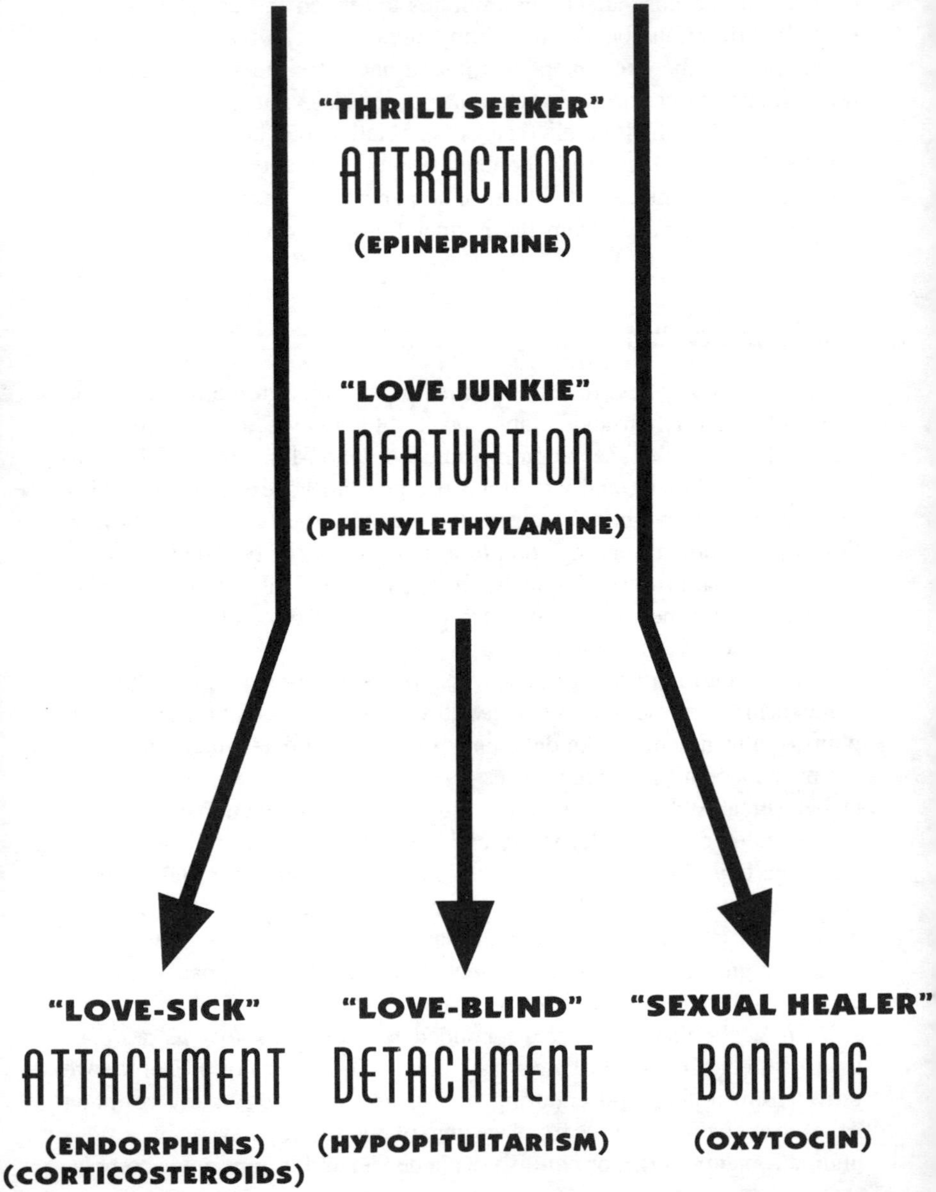

"THRILL SEEKER"
ATTRACTION
(EPINEPHRINE)

"LOVE JUNKIE"
INFATUATION
(PHENYLETHYLAMINE)

"LOVE-SICK"
ATTACHMENT
(ENDORPHINS)
(CORTICOSTEROIDS)

"LOVE-BLIND"
DETACHMENT
(HYPOPITUITARISM)

"SEXUAL HEALER"
BONDING
(OXYTOCIN)

cency in constant effort to grow and to nurture the loving. Bonding is based on connective codependence and interdependence, and while the other relationships described here may result in some degree of healing through human companionship, they offer little more than support groups of strangers meeting to confront a common problem. It is the bonded relationship that is capable of the most powerful sexual healing process.

RESPONDING OR REACTING TO THE STRESS OF LOVE

Stress is defined as the perception of physical or psychological threat *and* the perception that our coping mechanisms are inadequate to meet the perceived challenge.[5] Since stress is a perception and we are the perceiver, stress is us! Stress is how we are and how we cope, not something or someone that happens to us. Stress happens when our gut tells us we need to connect but our behaviors and choices are tentative and selfish.

When we accept the central assumption of sexual healing—that every act of connecting and disconnecting and every act of sexual intimacy is an act of health or threat to health—we recognize that mindfulness about the meaning of the connection is a crucial step in dealing with stress and in sexual healing. Too often, we are sexual reactors rather than sensual responders, and learning response-ability is another important phase of sexual healing.

A key step in understanding sexual healing is to learn to differentiate between a sexual response and a sexual reaction.[6] A *sexual reaction* is primarily a physical reflex. It involves our bodies telling us what to do and deals only with the first part of the perception cycle—sexual stimulus detection. A sexual response is a considered and thoughtful action that we choose to make based on our prior experiences and hopes for the future. Thrill seekers, love junkies, the love-sick, and the love-blind are reactors. People in bonded sexual healing relationships are responders and not simply glands with feet. They pay attention to the meaning of their loving more than the power of their hormonal pressures.

A CASE OF CAICS

A syndrome is a combination of symptoms, feelings, and behaviors all or most of which consistently indicate the presence of a disease or an abnormal condition. My research and clinical work indicate that there is a predictive set of signs associated with people addicted to attraction and infatuation. The thrill seekers and love junkies I have interviewed over twenty years, because of how they think, how their thinking influences their psychochemistry and immunity, and how the neurochemicals in their bodies affect them, tend to be prone to a syndrome I call CAICS, Chronically Agitated and Irritated Cardiovascular Syndrome. Here is a list of the symptoms of CAICS:

Symptoms of CAICS

1. Hint of a headache: Recurrent feeling of almost having a headache or that a headache is coming on.

2. Talking stomach: Gurgling sounds from the stomach and intestines, often elicited in response to other people's stomach sounds. Frequent heartburn, perhaps because the heart is overheating as a result of chronic irritation.

3. Irritability: Tendency to overrespond to noises and to be startled by others and proneness to become quickly angered by small things.

4. Turtle Tunnel: Shoulders raised toward ears, tunneling the neck between the tensed shoulder muscles.

5. Internal Blushing: Feeling a "rush" or as if the blood is surging through the veins and arteries. This reaction is the result of constantly feeling that personal worth is exclusively a matter of doing rather than being. We feel in a rush to get our share and translate our rush to our cardiovascular system.

6. Pleonasm: Because of trying to say too much too fast, using many words to say very little and stumbling over words, reversing the first letters in words, and so on.

7. WISC-ing: Wheezing, itching, snorting, and coughing. This is "love stuttering" or the brain's choking on words of love longing to come out but blocked or hurried by our consumption with doing, getting, and achieving self-fulfillment.

8. Colon Calls: The frequent feeling of having to have a bowel movement and passing of gas.

9. Nagging Backache: Feeling chronically tense in the lower back, groaning and holding the lower back.

10. Reactive Cholesterol Levels: Cholesterol count varying greatly in response to stressful times.

11. Day's-end Droop and Droppings: Feeling exhausted and totally spent at the end of the workday or as the end of the day approaches.

Upon returning home, dropping shoes, coat, and clothes on the way into the house. (One wife described her husband's return home as "like a snake shedding his skin or like little lizard droppings leaving a path to the bedroom.")

12. Libido Spasms: A tendency to go through periods of intense need for "sexual release," which is really stress relief, followed by longer periods of no interest in sex. A tendency to feel agitated after sex.

The more of these symptoms a person has, the more likely he or she is either to be in a relationship based solely on attraction or infatuation or to feel unable to stay in a relationship and make it grow and mature. The irritability, fatigue, erotic withdrawal, and hyperintensity alternations, and the illnesses and diseases that come with chronic autonomic agitation by epinephrine and PEA interfere with the relaxed, sensuous, and meaningful sexuality that is necessary for sexual healing.

Sex for the thrill seeker or love junkie is a way to turn on, get off, or maintain arousal. Sex is a release without a deeper loving reason, and a form of claiming entitlement rather than expressing erotic interest in response to the true identity and essence of another person. These hot loving styles are distractions from tension rather than a celebration of connection.

A CASE OF CFIDS

The initialism *CFIDS* stands for Chronic Fatigue Immune Dysfunction Syndrome. This syndrome results from the constant aggravation of the autonomic nervous system. People who detach from their relationships and people who are addicted to attachment and stressed by concerns for the survival rather than the thriving of their relationships tend to suffer from this syndrome. These people, who are prone to love-sickness and the numbing and narcotic effect of the endorphins associated with it, have presented the following symptoms in my interviews.

Symptoms of CFIDS

1. Too Tired Too Often: Feeling exhausted much of the time and talking often about how tired they feel.

2. Weakness: Feeling physically and muscularly weak and noticing that it takes effort to "get their energy up."

3. Melancholia: Feeling of vague sadness and despair without specific cause.

4. Subjective Fever: Feeling warm even to the touch, but with no measurable body temperature or a slightly depressed body temperature.

5. Mild Sore Throat: With no signs of infection or redness, the throat feels sore. Sometimes accompanied by repeated attempts to clear the throat and taking of throat medications or lozenges.

6. Painful Lymph Nodes: Nodes in the neck, armpits, or groin feel tender or sore but are not enlarged.

7. Memory Lapses: Difficulty remembering names, numbers, and directions.

8. Confusion: Easily distracted and disoriented (missing exit on freeway, losing keys, looking for eyeglasses that are on one's head, and so on).

9. Thought Flashes: Spontaneous and distracting thoughts that occur at unlikely times in unlikely places (while in an important business meeting, worrying about whether the dog was fed or where the car is parked).

10. "Gone Gazing": Tendency to drift into the self or totally tune out while gazing into nothingness.

11. Lack of Lab Findings: Doctor unable to find any significant irregularities on blood tests and physical exam.

12. Libido Loss: Lack of interest in sex or sensuality. Tendency to feel tired and drained after sex.

The more of these symptoms a person has, the more likely he or she is to think about the relationship in a dependent, insecure, apprehensive manner. The person is often too tired for real tenderness because of the mental and physical effort of protecting what she or he sees as a relationship susceptible to the slightest problem or dissatisfaction, which could bring its end.

THE LOVING BRAIN

The levels of the brain may be described in archaeological terms. The 500-million-year-old part of our brain is our reptilian brain. It contains the reticular activating system (RAS), which is the turn-on and turn-off mechanism for our body. The reptilian brain deals with basic life processes and keeping us alive. A newer part, called the paleomammalian brain, is about 200 million years old, and it is where our limbic system is. This is a brain area that processes our most basic emotions, and it is from here that the thrill and infatuation of relationships are relayed throughout our body. The newest part of our brain is only 50 million years old; this neomammalian brain is where we think and find meaning and connection. The rational left hemisphere and more emotional right hemisphere of the cortex or outside layer of our brain are joined by the newest part of our brain—the corpus callosum. The one-million-year-old corpus callosum is a set of fibers that allow the logical left and romantic right hemispheres to communicate and work together.

The most evolved part of our brain, the neomammalian or new brain, is the part with which we can choose to think clearly and make rational choices. It is where we give the meaning to our lives, our lovers, and our loving. Unlike other animals, governed by the older levels of the mammalian brain, humans can consciously select what level of the brain they will allow to direct their lives. We can use our higher brain to work toward sexual healing by reflecting, contemplating, considering, and intentionally connecting and disconnecting on more than a physiological, emotional, or addictive basis. Our new brain is where true loving and sensual response rather than mere physiological and neurohormonal sexual reaction are possible.

The new or loving brain is the director of sexual healing. It can go beyond the "turn me on" and "what's in this for me" orientations. Our new brain can think about the meaning of sexual encounters and relationships rather than just the physiological pleasure or variety and multiplicity of partners. Sexual healing is first and foremost meaningful and thoughtful personal connection. The loving level of our brain can override the impulses and chemical preferences of the lower parts of our brain, but we must be ever vigilant for the primitive imperatives within us. They still start the processes that precede bonding, but they do not have to control them.

Our immune system is instructed by us when we select the level of our brain that will be in charge. It runs hot or cold or rationally connected depending on our neurological choice. You have read that our thoughts do not begin or end in our brain and nervous system. Our every thought translates to neurochemical changes throughout the body, and neurochemical changes can influence our thoughts. There is no real barrier between the brain and the body.[7] Many of our daily life reactions—including our sexual reactions—take place primarily on the lower two levels of our brain, but sexual healing requires that we keep our minds on the meaning of our loving. Falling in love is actually falling out of the more evolved and more human level of our brain. Being and working to stay in love is a choice made on the highest level of our humanity.

When we perceive a sexual stimulus, we make two key decisions: Will I have sex or be sexual? and Will I make love or connect lovingly? When we pay attention to these decisions, we are selecting the level of the brain we will love with. If we simply react, we use our reptilian brain and "do" sex to someone or for self-release and relief. Such an approach worked well when sex had to be fast because a predator might be approaching. Quickie sex had evolutionary value because it kept our ancestors alive to have sex another day. But in our modern world, quick and reactive sex can lead to illness when we ourselves and how we think about our intimacy have replaced predators as the real threat to our survival.

Healing sex makes our impulses subservient to our principles. If we have sex to "come" or have an orgasm and to get turned on, we follow our impulses. If we have sex to seek variety, challenge, and conquest, it is our biology rather than our spirit and consciousness which is directing us. We can decide to share our sexuality with someone as a physical expression of our choice to connect forever.

The neocortex or new brain can exercise control over the hypothalamus, pituitary gland, septal region, amygdala, and hippocampus housed in the older and more reactive parts of our brain. When we make the conscious effort to respond instead of react sexually, we activate our higher brain to give meaning to what we are doing, why we are doing it, and with whom. The "sex and immunity cycle" begins with either a reaction or a response—it is our choice. Reactions such as attraction, infatuation, and attachment can stress us or burn us out, but considered, rational, loving responses can lead to meaningful healing bonds. A person using his or her cortex for caring and intimacy shows the following characteristics:

Characteristics of a Caring Cortex

1. Energetic: Seldom feels tired, falls asleep almost immediately when going to bed, and awakens refreshed. Feels as energetic at the end of the day as at the beginning.

2. Symptom-free: Doesn't have nagging headaches, heartburn, stomach or bowel problems.

3. Serene: Tends to be calm and patient. Seldom overreacts, even at times of crisis, and appears at ease.

4. Superimmune: When colleagues and family members get sick, tends not to catch their colds or flu or to have milder symptoms when sick and to rebound faster.

5. Attentive and Alert: Has good long-term and short-term memory and can be counted on to remember small details.

6. Organized: Follows daily rituals, knows where things are, has an effective filing system, and is almost always on time for appointments.

7. Focused: Responds to questions directly, hears what is said, and seems to be "present in the present" instead of distracted or somewhere else.

8. Happy: Tends to look and feel happy, smiling, laughing, and joking.

9. Expressive: Easily expresses feelings without overexcitement or defensiveness. Uses a few words to say a lot rather than a lot of words to say little.

10. Optimistic: Realistically optimistic and able to bring out the optimism in others. Optimism is rational and in balance with reality and responsible behaviors, not self-delusional.

11. Sensuous: Enjoys the beauty of music, art, nature, and people and speaks of this enjoyment often. Enjoys touching and being touched and hugging and being hugged.

12. Libido Balance: Enjoys having sex regularly and often and feels energized and content after sexual experiences.

The more of these characteristics a person shows, the more likely it is that he or she is responding with the loving brain rather than reacting with the lower and older parts of our reactive ancestry. The more of these characteristics you and your relationship show, the more healing power is present because each is a factor that helps the immune system stay in an adaptive and not an overreactive state.

THE MYTH OF SEXUAL TURN-ONS

Nobody "turns us on." We turn ourselves on and off by how we perceive, react, or respond to people and events in our lives. We can choose how to think about people and things, and by doing so, we choose how we will love. When we simply react rather than reflectively respond, our bodies react in a SAM or "hot" fashion and our cells behave in the same anxious, fearful, hostile, cynical manner as our brain thinks.[8] When we think in a cold or PAC style and are worried, reluctant, and distrusting, our bodies' healing properties can freeze up and react in a more cool or even "cold" or defeated, depressed, lonely way, and the cells of our bodies respond in kind.

In effect, every time we have sex or connect with someone else, we select the brain sex organ we will use to start the process. While all of our reacting and responding are going on, the thymus gland, where our immune cells are being produced, is making love too. The fluids of sexuality are not just vaginal secretions and ejaculation but the cortisol emitted from the cortexes or outer shells of the adrenal glands and catecholamine (adrenaline and noradrenaline) produced by the inner core or medulla of the adrenal glands. These immunosexual fluids affect our immune status by influencing the thymus gland, where the T cells are being produced.[9]

We never just get "sexually excited," we get psychoneurosexually excited, and our autonomic and immunologic systems respond as much as and even more than our breasts and genitals do. We all experience a sexual flush of neurotransmitters, endorphins, and immune cells every time we have sex. We literally put our hearts and our health into every sex act, and the level of the brain we use to make love determines whether that flush is healing or hurting us.

We now know that our immune system is directly involved in all our responses, particularly our response to events that "stress" or challenge our system. Sexual reactive arousal can be one type of "stressor" because it alerts and may over- or hyperarouse our entire body and mind. We know that sex which causes excessive stress (hot reaction) or feelings of alienation and despair or fear and guilt (cold reaction) can result in shrinking or impotence of the thymus gland.[10] Seeing every one of our sexual encounters as potential disease causers or as intimacy inoculation helps promote sexual healing by allowing us to reflect on and not just react to our need for sexual connection.

THE DULCINEA EFFECT

We create our own turn-ons and turn-offs. We can create our lover by how we choose to see our lover rather than simply react to an image. I call our ability to turn on to a lover rather than be turned on by a lover the Dulcinea effect.

In the novel *Don Quixote,* the hero meets a street prostitute. This poet-knight chooses to see this woman not as a whore but as someone with great beauty, kindness, and virtue. He gives her a new name—Dulcinea. Because of his loving point of view, he creates a woman of love and attractiveness. When the knight is dying, he calls his lover to his bed to remind her that she will always be his Dulcinea. The knight had created what turned him on, responding to his lover's inner beauty and not reacting to material and worldly signals. Our lovers come to be as we are and not just as they are, and the stress or strain of passion or pain is mainly in our brain.

PROTOTYPES OF PASSION

Years ago, a research team at Beth Israel Hospital and Harvard Medical School injected people with a small dose of epinephrine. The lymphocytes of those injected noticeably increased in number at first, but after thirty minutes the number dropped to lower than normal levels. The amount of epinephrine was less than you would release in your body if someone just said *"Boo!"* or if you had a brief encounter with someone who might be a sexual threat instead of a treat, yet the immune system seemed startled, hyperaroused, and then reactively depressed.[11] It was almost as if the immune system had an unfulfilling quickie and then left to call a cab.

It appears that T 8 suppressor cells are released in higher than normal number when we engage in behavior which startles and arouses us but for which we find little meaning, connection, or coherence. Such stress reaction is similar to a sexual reaction in which a person becomes stimulated, is reactively aroused, and then feels depressed and alone when reflecting in postromantic remorse about the meaninglessness of his or her behavior. Even when we are startled, if we are able to find meaning and feel that we can cope immediately and well with what startled us and if we are able to make a safe connection, our immune system quiets down and returns to balance.

Just as our immune system must determine whether a cell in our body belongs in our system, we make sexual decisions about who we will be intimate with. Each decision and its impact becomes a guide and lesson for our immune system, and the meaning we give to our connections with others becomes a passion prototype for our immune system. Hot reactive sex followed by cool feelings of regret or loneliness can eventually teach our immune system to be as nonselectively promiscuous and disconnected as we have been in our intimate decisions. Every time we connect with someone else, we are teaching our immune system how to function: Our passions become prototypes for our immunity and healing.

Unfortunately for our health and healing, when we become addicted to psychochemicals and a reactive love style, our immune system weakens much as any junkie's immune system eventually becomes ineffective. It does not learn to recognize the danger of who and how we love, and eventually becomes poisoned by its own addiction. As a result, we become defenseless against the loving style that so endangers our health.

THE POSITIVE SIDE EFFECTS OF A BONDED RELATIONSHIP

I have pointed out how dangerous to our health love addictions can be. Fortunately, loving relationships are the most powerful of all healing forces. Our immune system remembers love and healthy lovers, seeks such love again, and works to maintain it when it is established. It feels just as we feel, is soothed by caring and sensuality, and is wounded by cruelty and aggression. Consider some recent research concerning a tender, caring connection.

Researchers have shown that the touch of the hand of someone we care about can help prevent atherosclerosis.[12] Even animals respond to the touch of someone who cares. In a study at Ohio State University, rabbits were fed an extraordinarily high-fat diet designed to induce blockage of their arteries. When it was discovered that only half the rabbits on this diet showed atherosclerosis, the researchers were puzzled. Upon further study, they noted that only the rabbits in the higher cages in the laboratory showed the expected blockage. It was finally discovered that the woman feeding the rabbits was short; she had to reach up to feed the rabbits in the high cages but took out the rabbits in the lower cages, stroked them, and comforted them while feeding them. The study was repeated three times, always with the same result. The rabbits that were talked to softly and stroked gently and caringly did not develop atherosclerosis.

Another study showed that surgical patients who had their hands held by someone who was emotionally close to them while blood pressure and temperature were taken had lower blood pressures and less elevated temperatures. Another study showed that patients with close social support were able to leave the hospital earlier, had fewer complications following their surgery, and recovered faster at home than those who were not so sensuously treated.[13] Intimacy and connection have been shown to strengthen the immune system by "turning it on."[14] Some researchers are going so far as to conclude that "love is more important than healthy living."[15]

Minister Bernard Larson writes that the quality of our relationships may have more to do with how often we get sick and how soon we get well than our genes, chemistry, diet, or environment.[16] In this chapter, I have emphasized the fact that sensual, caring, bonded relationships are the interactions that protect our health and help make us well. In the last chapter in this part, I discuss the sexual thoughts that can help program our psychoneurochemistry for healing.

6

LEARNING TO THINK
IN A SEXUALLY HEALING WAY
Healing Hearts with Mending Minds

It has been said that love cures people, both those who give it and those who receive it.
Physician Robert Mack*

We have no indication where precisely psyche leaves off, and only reflex and neurophysiological events remain.
Ludwig Von Bertalanffy

TRAIN RIDE TO GRIEF

The roar of the crash could be heard for miles, and in a matter of seconds, the lives and health of dozens of families were changed forever. A speeding train carrying commuters home from work jumped the track, roared along the ground digging up grass and knocking down trees, and finally stopped in a pile of twisted steel. Bodies, briefcases, and train seats were strewn down the hill near the siding, and a deathly quiet fell over the carnage. The only sound was the hissing of steam and the flapping of evening newspapers that were moments ago in the hands of the tired fathers eager to relax at dinner with their families.

Just a few miles away, some of the waiting wives looked up from their cooking, puzzled by a faint rumble. The dishes and glasses set in anticipation of their husbands' return began to tremble, then suddenly stopped. Much more than dishes was to be shaken on this terrible day.

* Robert Mack was a surgeon who completely restructured his life after surgery for lung cancer. He died in his sleep six years after his diagnosis while listening to restful, sensuous music. See R. Mack, ''Occasional Notes: Lessons from Living with Cancer,'' *New England Journal of Medicine,* vol. 311, no. 25 (1984), pp. 1642–43.

Twenty-six of these women would wait for hours wondering where their husbands were, fearing more for their safety as every hour passed. Finally, a knock on the door would tell them even before they answered it that they would never see their husbands alive again.

The announcement on the television was brief. "Today, a train heading for Melbourne, Australia, derailed. Twenty-six men were killed. The accident is under investigation." Not only did this 1978 disaster change forever the lives of these poor families but it would drastically change the way illness and the process of healing are understood.

THE DISCOVERY OF PSYCHONEUROIMMUNOLOGY

Psychiatrist Roger Barthrop offered counsel and support to the grieving widows of the train wreck victims. He also monitored their health, including taking blood samples to assess the status of their immune systems.[1] What he discovered contributed to the birth of the field of psychoneuroimmunology (PNI), the study of the relationship between thinking, feeling, and the body's brain and immune system that underlies psychoneurosexuality.

Dr. Barthrop discovered that the lymphocytes—cells in our immune system that protect us from viruses and other abnormal or unhealthy cells—became less numerous and less active in the widows. Three weeks after the loss of their husbands, the widows' immune systems were in a state of depressed surrender, reflecting their grief and despair. The terrible tragedy of the train crash had shaken these women to the very marrow of their bones, where our immune cells are formed.

For the first time, it was documented in humans that the immune system could become as depressed as the person within whom that system functioned. It was shown that the immune system reacts as we react and, as I pointed out in Chapters 4 and 5, that it functions as a sensory organ.[2] Not only does our brain affect our immune system but how we think, feel, and believe about intimate relationships such as the marriages destroyed by the train wreck was shown to have powerful immune and healing influences.[3] The evidence presented in these first six chapters supports the fact that our thoughts and feelings affect our immune status, and learning to think interdependently rather than independently is a key to healing and health. The field of psychoneuroimmunology has crashed into medicine's awareness, and psychoneurosexuality extends this area of study to the reciprocity between our connections with others and our health and healing.[4]

What we call our mind uses our brain to think with, but you have seen that the mind is not housed only in the cerebral cortex. It is to be found in some form in every cell of the body. When we say we have a "gut feeling," we are being biologically accurate. Neurotransmitters help the cells in our brain communicate with one another. One recently discovered type of neurotransmitter is a neuropeptide. This substance is made up of amino acids, and it is found in the chemicals in our brains (neuro) and stomachs (peptide). Having feelings in the pit of our stomach and feeling torn apart are more than metaphors, they are descriptions of the interweaving of our immune and nervous systems to make a mind of our entire body. We literally "embody" our thinking and feeling, so we either embody thoughts of connection, relationship, and integration or thoughts of separateness, isolation, and autonomy. Our thinking style becomes a curriculum for the living style of every cell in our body.

The body is the outward manifestation of our mind—the brain's public presentation of itself. We constantly create ourselves and our world by how we think because our thoughts help create the psychochemical environment in which every cell in our body is made. Lord Byron wrote, "With our thoughts, we make the world." Detective Sherlock Holmes observed, "I am a brain, Watson. The rest of me is a mere appendix."[5]

Not only do our thoughts and feelings affect our immune system but our immune system also "thinks." When we perceive threat or challenge, you have read that our brain influences our hormone system, which in turn influences our immune system. At the same time, the white cells of our immune system react independently, secreting their own form of stress chemicals.[6] The immune system doesn't have to wait for the brain to tell it to react; it reacts at the same time the rest of us does.

THOUGHTFUL CELLS AND THE NEED FOR MORE RESEARCH

When the widows experienced the depression and loneliness of their loss, their feelings and thoughts were translated directly into the tissues and fluids in their bodies. More recent studies offer even stronger evidence of how grieving and bereavement—two major feelings of disconnection—are reflected directly in our immune systems' response and how feelings become biology.[7] One study demonstrated that—for two months after the deaths of their wives from breast cancer—bereaved husbands' lymphocyte responses became less effective.[8] Like the grieving widows, the widowers developed sad immune systems with sluggish cells.

We still need to learn much more about how the brain, immune system, and endocrine system talk with one another. Research in this area is complex, and there are many unanswered questions about the depression and immunoimpairment link. For example:

- The immune alterations in depressed and lonely people are relatively small compared with the immune changes experienced in reaction to major physical illness. For example, they are nowhere near the magnitude of the immune impairment in AIDS patients. No one yet knows if a small immune impairment is enough to contribute to serious illness, but it is likely that any change has some impact on our health and healing.

- While it has been clearly demonstrated that immunodysregulation or imbalance and deficiency occur in disconnected, lonely, depressed, and grieving people and that these people tend to develop more illness and die sooner than those showing less depression and grief,[9] it may also be that people who are widowed, divorced, or otherwise disconnected from a meaningful intimate relationship are more likely to react by drinking to excess, using drugs, failing to exercise, or eating and sleeping poorly because no one is around to help monitor their health behaviors. All these behaviors affect the immune system. This qualification of the findings, however, does not negate the fact that life events translate eventually to immune system changes. Whether it is the feeling or the behavior accompanying the feeling that causes immune impairment is still to be determined, but how we relate is beyond question an immune system event.

- It may also be that the mechanics of illness—even in its earliest stages—result in depression because the immune system cells and other body systems sense the presence of as yet unmeasurable signs of illness and react by creating a psychochemistry of depression within the body. Illness makes us sad as much as sadness can make us ill. Researchers have shown that one of the best predictors of future health—even better than complex laboratory testing—is high self-health-esteem or a general feeling that one is healthy.[10] We may have an inner sickness sense that, if we pay attention, lets us know how healthy we are because our immune system "thinks" and talks to us as much as our brain talks to it.

- Perhaps people who feel isolated and depressed become more sensitive to their health and report their illness more quickly and often, thus artificially raising the reported frequency of illnesses related to depression and isolation. Is it not also possible that our stressed immune system is sending out neurochemicals that communicate with the higher brain to let us know that something isn't right within us?

Despite these qualifications, there is sufficient evidence to assert that isolation and loneliness are health and immunity risks. Exactly how and to what degree will require much more research. All the possibilities in the preceding list are also the results of disconnection and isolation, and it is not *only* the immune system which is affected by a sense of separation. As physicist Max Planck pointed out, we can never understand any system in the universe, from the stars to the quantum world, unless we regard the entire system as a whole.

There is no debate that our immune system is sensitive to varying degrees to our sense of disconnection and the despair of feeling isolated and unable to maintain meaningful relationships. The more recent studies which attempt to take into account the qualifications I have just outlined show that single, separated, divorced, or widowed people are two or three times more likely to die prematurely than are those in long-term relationships.[11] Psychiatric drugs which help relieve symptoms of depression such as loneliness and a sense of detachment and hopelessness also improve immunity.[12] Beyond the burden of proof lies the burden of prudence, and new research clearly indicates that it is prudent to pay attention to the issue of intimate connection as a health-protecting and healing factor.

Cardiologist Carolina Thomas at Johns Hopkins University writes, "Thirty years of intensive research . . . have so far failed to discover the single 'cause' of cancer, heart attack, or mental illness. The time has now come to consider another concept of disease etiology."[13] I suggest that this concept should include the issue of connection and sexual healing in addition to preventive medicine and self-healing approaches.[14]

ESCAPE FROM MEDICAL TERRORISM

"There he goes again," said the wife, looking wistfully through the window. Her eyes followed every bounce of his step as her husband jogged by their house. He was singing loudly to the music only he could hear through his earphones, and he never looked to see his wife waving. "That man could win the American Heart Association man of the year award. When he dies, they're going to have to beat his heart to death with a stick just to bury him." She was sitting on the arm of the couch as she had often done, relegated to the role of passive observer of her husband's flight from the fear of illness.

Her hair was carefully combed into a new style, and she was wearing a new blouse, slacks, and shoes. She had tried to get his attention this way before, but it seldom worked unless his health program had been completed and he could put in what he called "a little quality time with the love of my life." "I thought we just might make love tonight after dinner," she continued. "But as usual, he got up from the table, left me and the dog sitting there, and went out jogging. At least this time he didn't take the dog. He was a little upset with me that the grams of fat in the dinner I made were a little over the amount in his program. He writes it all down, and even though it was within his doctor's guidelines, he seemed annoyed that it wasn't perfect by his own standards. He always says he wants his cholesterol to be half of his IQ. Sometimes I think that means we should shoot for about forty."

Like this woman's husband, many of us have become health hostages. As I discussed in Chapter 1, our worries about our health often make us try to avoid illness and pain rather than embrace wellness and pleasure. We speak of preventive rather than enhancement health, about avoiding heart attack instead of nourishing a healthy heart, about the right pulse rate rather than enjoyable exercise, and about avoiding dangerous foods rather than enjoying sharing a healthy meal with someone we love. We seem ever on the lookout for new ways to outrun the grim reaper.

RUNNING RISKS AND THE RISKS OF RUNNING

"I hurt in places I didn't know I had places," panted the young attorney. "I run miles a week, and my doctor said I'm in great shape. My knees are so sore I can hardly walk, but my cholesterol levels and HDL-LDL ratios have been outstanding. They may have to carry me into court, but at least I won't collapse of a heart attack."

I was interviewing this woman for my book as she and several other women completed their three-times-weekly workout at their gym. I watched as more than fifty doctors, teachers, and housewives stretched and strained to the beat of the song "She Works Hard for the Money." Each of these men and women was here alone. I assume that their lovers were somewhere else working as hard on their own health. Knee braces and elbow bandages were everywhere, and occasionally one of the exercisers would fall to the floor in sweaty surrender. "Push yourself. Only you can do it" came the call from the leader. "No pain, no gain!" Had she, have we, forgotten that pleasure heals? Have we lost sight of the fact that most things we try to accomplish alone seem not to bring us the happiness we hoped for?

The treadmills all had only one tread, no double path for two to use together. Some machines had video games attached to keep the exerciser involved, but even these games were warlike competitions against oneself or a robot. The pursuit of health seemed to have become a personal challenge. The cardiovascularly fit but romantically unfit husband previously described was on this same lonely journey, and, as a result, his physical health seemed stronger than his marital health. The jogging junkies and spa addicts seem to fear for their own lives more than for the lives and well-being of their relationships. As we run from the risks to our health, we run the risk of running out of time to love and be loved.

RISK OR FEAR FACTORS

Like many of us, the jogging husband had been frightened by the "heart disease risk factor" myth. It is clearly documented that the leading risk factors for heart disease include smoking, high blood pressure, and high blood cholesterol. Certainly, these factors should be avoided or treated when possible. The presence of just one of them doubles your statistical chances of having a heart attack. If you have two of these factors, your risk increases by four times, and with all three you are six times more likely to develop heart problems. All this is ammunition for the health terrorists and healthism fanatics, yet most people who have a heart attack (nearly 80 percent!) have none of the major risk factors.

Even if the goals of exercise and eating programs are valid, compliance with sound health practices is greatly enhanced when we have someone to share with us in the healing adventure.[15] In our "Change of Heart" program for atherosclerosis reversal by lifestyle changes including working toward more intimate connection and decreasing psychosclerosis and sociosclerosis (hardening of the boundaries between people), all our treatment is done with couples rather than individual patients. The Pearsall Psychosocial Inventory you read about in Chapter 1 is designed for couples, and the entire program is focused on interactional rather than self-health. Although some of our patients come with close friends or family members as their healing heart partners, most come with their spouses. Compliance with dietary and exercise recommendations is much higher throughout our program and after than it is in programs designed for a one-patient approach.

Cardiologist Dean Ornish, whose research I discussed in Chapter 4, emphasizes the impact on our health of how we think about our relationships to life and other people. He writes, "Providing people with health information is important, but it is not usually sufficient to motivate lasting changes in behavior. If . . . we address . . . issues of inner peace, contentment, meaning, value, and intimacy, then that individual is more likely to make choices that are life-enhancing."[16] The more assiduously we adhere to good health practices, the better our health, and adherence requires connection with others to provide the coherence or meaning and motivation to continue and a stronger shared purpose to be healthy.[17]

THE WHY BEHIND THE WAY TO HEALTH

A key aspect of sexual healing is the assumption that why we do something is as important as the doing.[18] As I explore the issue of sexual healing, it is important to remember that sexual behavior can heal or slay us depending on the motivation behind it. Sex can be abusive and isolating or one of the most transforming, healing, and transcendent of all human experiences.[19] We should exercise, eat wisely, and avoid health-risking behaviors, but we only continue in these endeavors if we have a reason to do so. Sexual healing suggests that the purpose of staying healthy is to stay intimately connected.

Although she was masking her pain by trying to joke, the jogger's wife could not hide her sadness and loneliness. Her words reflect what I consider the single major problem in the quest for health in America: the way to wellness has become essentially a lonely journey. We are firmly entrenched in a self-help, self-knowledge, and self-health orientation. We exercise, walk, jog, eat, and often even have sex alone. We have become more able to count calories and grams than to count the family members sitting quietly around us as we slowly and joyfully share our meal. Even though cholesterol count has been valued as a health indicator way beyond its ability to predict heart disease, we are better at knowing our cholesterol count than at counting the meaningful moments we spend in loving connection.[20] We act as if our health depends on us alone and social or family obligations are either requisites that are often in the way of our individual health plans or quality time commitments necessary to receive the proper dose of social support as indicated in the latest health bulletin. In our rush to become healthy, we have forgotten to ask why we want to be healthy. As a result, much of our exercise and many of our other health maintenance behaviors are much less effective than they might be if we employed sexual healing for their underlying purpose.

Just as good sex requires more than in-bed competence, sexual healing means more than physical intimacy with a loving and loved partner. It is also a way of thinking about life, love, and our lover and making the effort to extend the intensity of the caring in our basic loving unit to all areas of our lives. It means eating together, exercising together, contemplating or praying together, and connecting for health instead of disconnecting to save our health from what we view as the endless obligations of a rushed and hassled life. Our homes often become our hassles, and sexual healing requires a more hassle-free, purposeful way of thinking about our lives by thinking more about relating and intimacy and less about self.

Comedian George Burns jokes that at his age he is still able to get turned on, he just has more trouble getting plugged in. While Mr. Burns is punning in reference to sex, his comment reflects the lesson of sexual healing. Our fixation on outrunning and undereating disease may offer some short-term protection to the body's machinery and allow us to grow old, but until we learn how to stay plugged in or intimately tuned in to one another, we will not have the energy to live happily, hardily, and lovingly no matter what our cholesterol count may be.

SEXUAL HEALING AS AN END AND A MEANS

The nice part about adding sexual healing to your health-care regimen is that it is both a delightful means and a joyful end. If one purpose of health is to love, then what could be better than working toward that goal by loving now? After he and his wife completed the sexual healing program, the jogging husband joked, "I've given up half of my jogging time and added more loving time with my wife. I'd sooner have her on my lap than do a lap. It not only feels great to be with her, but my knees aren't sore anymore. And my wife isn't sore at me anymore either. Hell, I almost ran right past her and out of my marriage. What would my health have been for then?"

One of my doctor friends relates the following story illustrating how we may have missed the point about healthy living: An old man came to his doctor complaining that he could no longer seem to have an erection. The doctor said, "You need more exercise to clean out those arteries. Run five miles a day, and call me in a week." After the week had passed, the call came as scheduled. "How are your erections now?" asked the doctor. "Much better, thank you," said the patient, "but we haven't had sex in a week." "Why not?" asked the doctor. "You said run five miles a day. I did, and I'm having erections, but I'm thirty-five miles from home."

We can have what we desire most—meaningful intimate connection—by making the pursuit of erotic intimacy or "erobics" as important as doing aerobic exercise to protect our hearts or eating less fat to prevent cancer. We can have the end and the means at the same time, without dangerous side effects and without cost. If there was a medicine capable of accomplishing such results, it would be seen as a miracle drug.

COGNITIVE CONNECTION AND SEXUAL HEALING THOUGHTS

Sexual healing is not only making love together it is also making meaning together. Beyond the urging to "think for ourselves," sexual healing requires learning to think cooperatively with another person. Here are six sexual healing thought patterns to begin your journey to healing by connection.

Sexual Healing Thought Patterns

1. Think About Us: If you don't think about and with someone else, you won't think much of yourself. It has been assumed that you have to think for and of yourself because that is the path to self-esteem, but sexual healing asserts that collective thinking is the way to happiness and health. Despite changing sexual roles and mores, the increase in divorce rate and spouse abuse, and across the variety of occupation, social class, sexual orientation, and religious or political beliefs, most people crave a close, loving relationship with another person over all else in life.[21] Although we have been encouraged over the last decades to be assertive, be self-fulfilled, and find our "space," we seem only to have ended up more distant from one another.[22]

2. Love Someone to Love Yourself: The first love is two-person love. The mother-child bond beginning in the uterus is a collective and dyadal love, not self-love. The idea that we have to love ourselves before we can love someone else is popular, but sexual healing is based on the opposite assumption. We can only love ourselves *after* we learn to give and share love with another person. There is evidence that close personal intimacy produces transcendent personal experiences, even at times when everything seems to be falling apart in one's individual life. Personal fulfillment does not automatically lead to intimacy, and fixation on it can interfere with loving. However, interpersonal intimacy almost always leads to personal fulfillment.[23] If you want to be personally fulfilled and healthy, you must focus as much or more on your relationships as you do on your own health status.

3. Think About Finding More Connection and Less Individual Space: Interdependence leads to independence. We often hear about the need to "get away from it all," and I have already suggested that

elective times of being alone can help promote intimacy. However, too much individual space can create a vacuum of loneliness and a decrease in the ability to be intimate. Intimacy and shared space promote psychological health in both partners, while meditation and self-fulfillment efforts tend to produce private lessons of meaning relevant only to the meditator and therefore of value only to his or her health.[24] As you read earlier, sexual healing is accomplished by a merging of minds and not by withdrawal into the individual mind.

4. **Think About Strength as an Interdependent Trait:** Learning to share mutual dependence with someone else leads to more interdependence, and interdependence rather than independence makes us strong. Cooperation rather than competition strengthens us. Strong-willed and hard-driving individualists did not create the greatest accomplishments in our world. It was cooperation and personal connection that resulted in social progress. It is sometimes assumed that dependent people are weak and prone to becoming more dependent. But evidence shows that close, mutually dependent intimate relationships result in more—not less—personal growth.[25] As you will read later, so-called codependence is a cure and not a disease and functional, not dysfunctional. All studies of extremely hardy and healthy people indicate that interdependence, mutual sympathy, and strong affectional and sexual feelings for another person are key indicators of health and hardiness.[26]

5. **Think About Compliance and Docility Rather Than Self-representation and Assertiveness:** It's what you give and not what you try to get that makes you healthy and heals you. It's what you are willing to learn more than what you think you have to teach that makes you grow and develop. Compliance and docility are not signs of weakness. *Compliance* means to go along instead of against, and *docility* means to be teachable. Both are indications that a person will learn, be open, and merge with another to experience all that life has to offer. The scarcity hypothesis suggests that there is only so much of the Essential in this world and that one must struggle to get his or her piece of the pie. Sexual healing suggests that we can make a whole new pie together through giving, helping, and caring. People who are willing to work to give and learn within a relationship instead of trying to take from it for self-growth have been shown to be psychologically and physically healthier than their more self-focused counterparts.[27] Researchers at Harvard Medical School have shown that just watching someone being giving, sharing, and altruistic produces positive changes in the immune system. Medical stu-

dents watching a film of Mother Teresa ministering to the sick were tested for their immune status. All of them experienced a measurable strengthening of immunity—a form of helper's high.[28] Being the right partner in an intimate relationship is more important than finding the right partner, and altruism is much more healthy than assertiveness.

6. Think of Your Health as Inseparable from the Health of Another Person: Health is a collective care system. It is often assumed that health is your own concern and responsibility, but health is impossible without connection. You have read that there is now well-substantiated research supporting the conclusion that isolation and lack of intimacy are a major risk to health.[29] It is not possible to take care of one's own health because our health is intertwined and inseparable from the health and illness of those around us. The word *health* itself comes from the word *whole,* and sexual healing is the process of maintaining and enhancing healthy systems—not selves.

As a sexual healing learning experience, I ask my patients to combine the results of their medical tests. I ask them to add up their blood pressure scores, body temperatures, and lists of physical complaints and healing strengths. While doctors must focus on the individual meaning of these scores to intervene when we are ill, I think we can achieve an insight into sexual healing by also seeing these scores as related to and affected by each other. This simple exercise has led to productive discussions by my patients about the overall health of their system rather than just their selfs.

Sexual healing implies a new view of healthy living based on these six points about thinking together instead of just for ourselves. Sexual healing employs a new definition of health that includes intimate relationships at its core. We need to see our relationships not as places where we can aggrandize our egos but as places for connecting to give, share, and serve. We need to view our health and our relationships as a growing child that, as Drs. Johana and Deane Shapiro suggest, "is valued by both partners as a kind of miracle . . . which one realizes one cannot take credit for, but to which one must contribute to the utmost of one's ability, which one marvels at and is privileged to be a part of."[30]

The collective thinking model is one part of the sexual healing formula, but the physical aspects of connection—touch, intimate contact, and sexual interactions—are the ways we express our cognitive coming together. While sex has become a way we try to connect, you will learn in Part II that sexuality can be an expression and celebration of the connection itself.

PART TWO

A NEW
SEXUALITY
FOR A
NEW TIME

The world is not comprehensible, but it is embraceable; through the embracing of one of its beings.

Martin Buber

7

FREEDOM FROM
THE SEX SYNDICATE
The Rediscovery of Significant Sex

My schoolmates would make love to anything that moved,
but I never saw any reason to limit myself.

Emo Phillips

THE JOB OF SEX

They had planned the search for weeks. Ever since the sex experts had discussed it on the Phil Donahue television show, the couple had decided to find it and to discover the sexual bliss they had been told it would guarantee. The kids were at their grandmother's house, the dog was asleep, and they finally had the rare moments of privacy to begin their erotic hunt, but something was wrong. They were becoming frustrated and impatient with one another.

"It was embarrassing enough buying the book from the guy at the bookstore," the wife told her husband. "Now I'm even more embarrassed. Just give me the picture again and I'll look for the thing myself." As her husband tried to study the genital map to the hidden erotic treasure, she abruptly reached over and tore the page from the book. "Let me see the picture of it again. I have to have one in there somewhere."

"*X* marks the spot," said her husband in an effort to defuse the tension that was building from a situation that was supposed to have been, according to the experts who had written the sex manual, one of the most amorous moments of their sexual life. "Maybe you just didn't get one of those G spot things. Maybe that's why you aren't multiple. Maybe you're even lucky to be singular.''

Her husband's attempt at humor was seen as sarcasm, and the wife became hurt and angry. "No way," responded the wife. "If the sex experts say a woman has one, then I have one too. You just don't know how to help me find it. Maybe if you weren't premature, we could have more time and I'd be able to feel where it is.'

"I'm not premature," said the husband, himself hurt and defensive. "You're postmature. You take too long. We should get one of those vibrators so we can buzz you up to speed."

"Let's just forget the whole thing," answered the wife, as tears began to fill her eyes. "I know I have a G spot, but if you want to give up looking, then we'll just forget it. If I find it, I'm not telling you where it is. I'll just enjoy it myself."

"Fine by me," replied her husband, pretending not to see his wife's tears. "Masturbation suits you because it's sex with your favorite person. Our sex together is getting like parallel masturbation anyway. You come, I come, we sleep. The whole thing is getting to be like the job of sex instead of the joy of sex. Remember? You bought that book, too."

For days after the failed search for a magical vaginal site that the sex experts said could lead to guaranteed orgasm, the couple withdrew from each other and barely spoke. Even though there is no evidence of the existence of a G or Graffenberg spot, experts from a powerful sex syndicate that has evolved over the last four decades have said there is, and thousands of women search in vain for a nonexistent part of their sexual anatomy. Weeks passed before the couple attempted sexual intimacy again. When they did, they said very little, and both felt more distant and unfilled than before.

For over twenty years in my own sex therapy clinic, couples came by the thousands to tell stories like this one. They had been influenced by a sex syndicate—an establishment of sex experts who, without strong research to support their claims, proposed the right way to have pleasurable sex and avoid sexual dysfunction. This sex syndicate code of conduct continues to dominate many sex lives. It includes advice on orgasmic thresholds, direct and extensive clitoral contact to hurry women toward orgasm, a technique for squeezing the penis to slow men down, a contortionistic sexual posture that is supposed to make it possible to keep the penis inside the vagina while maintaining its direct contact with the clitoris, and dozens of other "sex facts" that have little basis in sound research. Doing our own thing sexually has often become trying to learn how to do the sex experts' thing.

The media often defer to experts from the sex establishment, seldom questioning their credentials, findings, or advice, and turning to them for direction and clarification of sexual and relationship issues. Publishers still print hundreds of sex books written by these experts, who themselves are often unable or unwilling to maintain intimate relationships as they preach the secrets for finding sexual bliss. They often extend their advice to dating techniques and sly ways to find the right man or woman they themselves have apparently not been able to locate. Almost all the major authors of the most popular sex and marital manuals, including the pioneers of sex research, William Masters and Virginia Johnson, are single, divorced, or serial monogamists.

The result of the sex establishment's firm control over the definition of good sex has created a bondage of self-pleasure. There is little discussion of the meaning of sex or the healing nature of long and enduring relationships, but much about the mechanics of sex. Self-pleasure is the primary goal, followed by skill in turning the partner on in order to be a competent lover and maintain sexual esteem. Turn on rather than tune in seems to be the sex establishment message, and this message has evolved from three major sources.

THE FIRST SEX SPOT

On a beautiful, peaceful, tree-lined campus in conservative Bloomington, Indiana, the faculty at Indiana University was asked by some members of the community to offer a class in human sexuality. It was the late 1940s, men were returning from the war less innocent but still as sexually ignorant as when they had left, and it was becoming apparent that sexual knowledge would be preferable to the myths that were so dominant. There were no sex experts available, so a reluctant entomologist named Alfred Kinsey was recruited to design and teach one of the first sex education classes in the world.

Kinsey had spent his professional life doing what entomologists do—counting, describing, and classifying insects. His wife once told me, "Alfred never saw anything special about the fact that it was sex he was studying. He thought of himself as a scientist and saw sex as little different than any other topic to be studied. If you were going to teach about it, he thought you should first know about it. He couldn't find any books about sex that contained strong scientific data, so he wrote them himself. He never understood all the big excitement about it all, and was very surprised when all the hate mail and threats on his life and mine started coming in or when the government began investigating his work. He thought he was just a scientist doing his job."

Challenged with this assignment, Kinsey began by collecting information. In more than 2,000 interviews, Kinsey and his staff counted, described, and classified human sexual behaviors. The Kinsey Reports awakened a latent public interest in what the neighbors were doing in their bedrooms, and these two reports are still referred to today.

The first "spot" for the study and discussion of sex was now under way. On the third floor of an old building just above where the cadavers were kept for the medical school, the Kinsey Institute was founded. A sex museum of erotica was established, a library of sexual information from throughout the world was set up, and professionals from France, Germany, Italy, and other countries came to midwest America to learn about sex.

I first studied at the Kinsey Institute in the early 1970s, when anthropologist Paul Gebhard, Kinsey's colleague and research team member, had taken over after Kinsey's death. A few years later, I joined the institute staff as director of professional education. I founded my own treatment center for sexual problems and continued to work closely with the institute and its subsequent director, psychologist June Reinisch. I learned much about the careful, scientific approach to sex, but I also learned that our work was often misquoted, misunderstood, and extended far beyond the limits we ourselves placed on our findings.

Although the institute was never a clinical training center, many of the hundreds of people coming to it were anxious not to learn about the current state of sex research but to become sex therapists who would give advice and treatment under the auspices of having been educated at the Kinsey Institute. Many of them came from the humanistic psychology movement, which advocates the primacy of the individual self. Psychologists from this school, such as Carl Rogers and Abraham Maslow, taught about self-actualization and the importance of finding and doing one's own thing. Psychologists now not only stressed doing one's own thing but emphasized that sex was the thing to do.

As an example of the influence of the sex establishment and the misuse of tentative research findings by people who had never studied human sexuality or even read the original research, I remember the first television show I appeared on to discuss our research. I was asked about something a guest had said the week before. This guest, a sex therapist who said she had "trained" at the Kinsey Institute, had stated, "According to the Kinsey Report, most of us are having sex about two and one half times per week." As the talk-show host repeated the woman's words, the studio audience tittered. "She says she has a way to move it up to over three. As a sex expert yourself, how do you suggest we boost our frequency, especially into our later years, when we all begin to lose interest in sex and our ability to do it?"

I was completely puzzled by the question. There is nothing in the Kinsey Reports stating two and one half times a week as a guideline, and there is no evidence that we lose interest in or capacity for sexual enjoyment as we age. Someone from the new sex establishment had made such assertions without understanding the Kinsey research, and a distorted finding had become a media prescription. When I attempted to clarify the data from the Kinsey research and the fact that there is no national sexual average, that frequency of sexual interactions does not relate to the enjoyment of sex, and that the capacity for sexual enjoyment and desire may even increase through life, the host interrupted. "But Dr. Pearsall, surely you're not contradicting the Kinsey Report?"

June Reinisch has retired as director of what is now called the Kinsey Institute for Research in Sex, Gender, and Reproduction, and it is under the temporary directorship of Professor Eugene Eoyang of the Indiana University faculty until a full-time replacement is found. Dr. Eoyang is a Kinsey Board of Trustees member and has strong research and teaching experience. His interest in sexuality grew from biological research that has implications for human sexual behavior and not from a restatement or misstatement of the original Kinsey findings. The legacy of the institute is a set of descriptive data about human sexual behavior that serves as a base for further work and not how-to-do-it-right guidelines. The institute remains a center for serious research and education, not a training center for self-appointed sex experts to use to establish their credibility.

The Kinsey data were extremely helpful in opening the discussion about sex. Unfortunately, though, sexual statistics are like a bikini. What they reveal is interesting, but what they conceal is vital. Kinsey and his team had no way of knowing if what people said they did was what they were really doing. Kinsey did not ask about why people engaged in sex, what love means, or how sex relates to general health. He was concerned with the "what" of sex because he saw his task as teaching a course about what people did and not why they did it or what they should be doing. He intended his admittedly imperfect research to serve as a base for teaching and for future research, and he was not professionally concerned with the meaning or the health aspects of sex, which are so basic to sexual healing.

THE FIRST SEX WATCHERS

In the late 1960s and early 1970s not far from Bloomington, in St. Louis, Missouri, gynecologist William Masters and his secretary, Virginia Johnson, approached the study of sex from their clinical perspective.

They did what doctors and their staffs did and used observation, diagnosis, and prescription. This famous sex research team created sexual response measuring instruments and an artificial penis with a camera on the end to test, describe, and identify normal sexual response and to determine what is dysfunctional.

The Masters and Johnson Reproductive Biology Research Foundation—later the Masters and Johnson Institute—did what Alfred Kinsey would never have done and his institute still does not do. It suggested "how" to have sex the right way. Masters and Johnson designed a two-week sex treatment program for couples in which a male and female therapy team assigned specific homework to correct what they called sexual dysfunctions. The couples then reported back to their therapists on their success at learning the "sensate focus" technique. This approach was designed as a means to help couples concentrate on erotic sensations and ignore mental images and thoughts about the nature of the relationship. It included requiring couples to spread lotions on each other, squeezing the penis just before ejaculation as a means to slow men down, and stimulating the clitoris to speed up female orgasm.

The Masters and Johnson Institute rapidly became a mecca for sex experts seeking the clinical credibility, jargon, and techniques that they could not find at the Kinsey Institute. These fledgling sex syndicate members now had a place to go to learn how to do it and how to teach others how to do it. The names Masters and Johnson became synonymous with what came to be seen as *the* approach to sexual proficiency or problems. Claiming knowledge of their work constituted automatic acceptance into the sex syndicate.

I trained briefly at the Masters and Johnson Institute in the mid-1970s. In my discussions with Bill Masters and Virginia Johnson, I learned a new "sex speak," a way to talk about sex without sounding like you were talking about an intimate human act. They used terms such as *sexual dysfunction, adequate vasocongestion, dilation of the introitus, pulling back of the prepuce, orgasmic platforms,* and *contractive release.* They proposed stages of sexual response, appropriate timing to avoid the labels of prematurity and ejaculatory incompetence, and stimulation techniques strong enough to avoid inorgasmia, induce lubrication, and result in the physiological relief of neuromuscular contractions of vaginal barrels and penile shafts. This sex therapy program reportedly worked well and fast when offered by these two bright, prestigious, authoritative, often authoritarian people. Unfortunately, the approach was seldom tested for effectiveness or workability when attempted by others. These new sex syndicate members spread through the country to save us from sexual dysfunctions and send us into erotic recovery.

The treatment approach and concepts of sex therapy were a forerunner of the current "recovery movement," which focuses on dysfunctional families in which sexual abuse allegedly abounds, unhappy inner children are unable to be sexually self-fulfilled, and what the movement sees as the only two phases of life—denial and recovery (the modern equivalent of sexual dysfunction and sexual joy).

As I had at the Kinsey Institute, I learned much from Masters and Johnson and their research. I learned more about how our sexual system works and that human sexual response can be an extremely vulnerable thing, easily interrupted by emotional states such as anxiety, fear, or anger. I saw the physical changes that block sexual response when a person feels disgust or pressure, and I saw the glow of health in those who feel sexually fulfilled.

In the early 1970s, when Masters and Johnson's work was gaining notoriety, I designed a sexual problems treatment program as a part of my Problems of Daily Living Clinic at Sinai Hospital in Detroit, Michigan. I did not think that sexual problems existed outside the context of all of life's problems, and my program stressed relationship rather than sexual therapy as a means to sexual and general health. When I attended the Masters and Johnson program, they reported almost 80 percent success with their couples. Their cases seemed almost always to work out well and respond to the sensate focus approach, but the clinical teams I trained in my clinic never saw one couple that followed the course of the Masters and Johnson regimen. In fact, I never saw a case of sexual dysfunction. I saw couples struggling not only with a sexual problem but with problems establishing or maintaining intimate connection on many levels.

In my discussions with Virginia Johnson, I heard a person who was caring, warm, and genuinely dedicated to promoting sexual pleasure and alleviating sexual difficulties. In my discussions with Bill Masters, I heard a bright, professionally cautious physician who, like Kinsey, would never make the sweeping generalizations that those who used his work and writings often seemed to make, and who was consistent in his attempts to legitimize the open, medical study of human sexual response. I borrowed some of their ideas and approaches, particularly their team approach and sound medical orientation, for my own program. Unfortunately, the hundreds of psychologists, social workers, nurses, physicians, and people without any professional degree who attended Masters and Johnson's two-week seminars too often considered themselves ready to tell others how sex should be done.

The key to the Masters and Johnson sex problem correction procedure still dominates sex therapy. Through sensate focus and concentration on genital interaction and erotic pleasure rather than thought, reflection, and feelings, it was suggested that all sexual dysfunctions could be reversed. It was even suggested that gay men and women might become straight if they would only learn the sensate focus techniques of body massage, sexual teasing, use of lotions, forming orgasmic platforms, and achieving adequate genital contractions. The assumption was that maximal pleasure is obtained through intense sexual connection and self-distraction from the meaning of what is going on—the mindless sex orientation of the sex syndicate.

In sexual healing, meaning is everything. Sexual healing goes beyond the *what* focus of Kinsey and the *how* focus of Masters and Johnson. There are no established sexual frequency norms in sexual healing because intimate connection results in and is not caused by sexual expression. Sexual healing is based more on the *why* than on the *what* and *how*, but the current sex establishment still uses a model of sexuality norms and methods, not meaning and intimacy.

A key idea in the recovery movement, the concept of codependence, has replaced the term *sexual dysfunction*, implying that too much thinking about or taking care of someone else is not functional and detracts from the ultimate goal of self-sufficiency and pleasure. One meaning of the word *functional* is "operative, serviceable, or utilitarian," and the Masters and Johnson model of sex was designed to help our genitals meet these criteria regardless of why or with whom we're being sexual. The sexual healing concepts of health-enhancing and intimate, codependent connection through sex but on many levels other than the genitals are not commonly a part of the sex syndicate's approach.

Kinsey gave us the ranges of normal sexual frequencies, and Masters and Johnson gave us the clinically healthy way that sex should be done. Despite the warnings of these groundbreaking, courageous, and creative researchers, hundreds of self-appointed sex therapists use their work as their claim to expertise. When I use the term *sex syndicate* or *sex establishment*, I refer to sex experts who base their teachings on their own views, distortions, and misapplications of the original, unreplicated, and now dated work of these early pioneers without attention to the new research done by those who are not insiders in the syndicate.

THE SEXUAL CHEF

By the mid-1970s, we thought we knew how often and how we should be having sex, and we had a sex syndicate to keep reminding us. However, there was a need for a unifying purpose for sex. The new sex therapists were encountering difficulties with their patients. They were asking questions not only about the genitals but about love, caring, and the purpose for being with someone else. They were doing it but didn't seem to be feeling it. Something seemed missing. They were asking about the why of sex. "We will show you how, the why is up to you" was the sex establishment's answer.

In London, England, medical pathologist Alex Comfort provided the answer to the why. According to his sex cookbook modeled after the best-selling *The Joy of Cooking—The Joy of Sex*—sex is for pleasure. His recipes for sexual delight included lotions, postures, and costumes designed to cook up a banquet of sexual bliss, to help us avoid the dreaded sex dysfunctions, and to keep up with the numerical erotic averages. Meaningful loving was at most a fringe issue in sexual health. One interested and interesting partner was stirred up by a dash of sexual adventure, a few drops of variety, and a coating of erotic apparel, all blended together by a combination of sex toys. Even if we did not find our partner desirable, we could fantasize about a person with whom we really wanted to have sex, use the body of the closest available person as a double for our fantasy partner, and thereby be free from the hassles of trying to establish and maintain intense and meaningful relationships. There was no mention of the necessity of a loving and loved partner with whom one was sharing life, meeting crises, combining on many levels of living, and sharing healing.

There has been comparatively little further research in human sexuality. The small amount of research that was done was quickly replaced by the sex survey approach, based on responses to questionnaires appearing in the more liberal women's and men's magazines.

The sex syndicate code is clear and to the point: Sex is natural, the only unnatural sex act is one you cannot do, the more you do sex the better, too much thinking about the meaning of sex gets in the way of the mechanics, and the more you master the secret spots and techniques and keep your mind and concerns with the meaning of sex out of the bedroom, the more sexually functional you will be. "Don't be a sex spectator" was the warning. "Don't think about it, just do it." There is no place for reflection, consideration, and contemplation in sex. Sex is a raging impulse within us all, and it is best to let it out often and in the functional ways suggested by the sex establishment. Feeling love and staying together for a long time are nice and even cute, but such things have little to do with the real meaning of sex—self-pleasure and joy. As in golf and tennis, you can learn to win in the sexual arena by appropriate practice of the sex syndicate guidelines of service and return.

Learning the process of sexual healing requires an understanding of sexual response and intimacy that transcends the old false assumptions of the sex syndicate and being aware of its influence on your life and loving. Here are twenty-four sexual healing principles that contradict the central assumptions of the sex establishment.

Sexual Healing Principles

- Sexual healing is intimacy for the enhancement of the total health of both partners, and, because of its deep meaning and enduring connection, it ultimately enhances the lives of everyone—the family, the society, and the world. The primary purpose of sex is not to fulfill the individual but to promote more caring and intimacy everywhere and for everyone.

- Sexual healing involves mindfulness, or total and complete awareness of who you are with, where you are, the impact of what you are doing on the entire social system, and, most of all, why you are being sexual. Good sex does not require that you try to stop thinking and "just do it."

- There is no evidence that sexual proficiency or happiness is enhanced by erotically "testing the marital waters." Premarital sex almost always results in a learned pattern of tentativeness, avoidance of commitment, and the assumption that sex can be and even should be separated from meaning and intimacy. Sexual surrogacy teaches surrogate love, so sexual experience and proficiency with one person does not generalize to another. While some people apologize for their lack of sexual experience, celibacy or virginity before committed sex is better for health and sex in the long run. Premarital sex does not prevent later sexual problems in marriage.

- The sex syndicate's sex cycle description—including words such as *arousal, plateau, refraction,* and *afterglow*—has not been proved universal. Sexual healing takes place as a result of each relationship unfolding its own response cycle, usually including phases left out of the sex syndicate's vocabulary, such as interest and reflection.

- There are times during sexual activity when sexual stimulation is ineffective and even painful—for both men and women. What feels very good at one moment may hurt at another. The sex syndicate applies the "refractory" or sexual rest period exclusively to males, implying that women, once turned on, are perpetual passion machines. All body parts, including men's and women's genitalia, experience periods of change in their responsivity and sensitivity, but this does not preclude continuing intimate sexual pleasure and mutual physical intimacy.

- Orgasm is more than genital and muscular contraction. It is as much mind as body because mind and body are one. There are many types and degrees of orgasm, irrespective of genital response capacity, and both men and women can have "multiple orgasms." Orgasms are a relatively insignificant part of the overall sexual healing process, not the goal.

- The terms *premature ejaculation, orgasmic distress, vaginismus, impotency,* and *ejaculatory incompetence* are well-known sexual diagnoses. Each of these alleged problems is based on sex-by-the-clock and experiencing orgasmic contractions at the right time to please the self or the partner. Sexual healing defines sexual health in a nongenital and nontiming way and uses personal interaction rather than mechanical means for understanding problems in connecting intimately and sensually.

- Sexual healing cannot progress if the wrong information on sexual response is used in establishing a sexual relationship. Research from psychoneurosexuality and scientists outside the sex establishment, not the dated and still unverified sex syndicate research, serves as the primary basis of sexual healing.

- Rape is a violent crime and a horrendous personal violation. The sex syndicate often asserts that rape has nothing to do with sex, but sexual healing views rape as a dreadful distortion of sex. The sex syndicate denies this because there is no sexual cycle in the act, many of the rapists aren't erect and can't ejaculate, and so on. To take this position mistakes mechanics for meaning and ignores again the significance of the assault for the rapist and the victim. However pathological, the rapist is using sex to damage, demean, and hurt rather than to heal. The victim often has her or his meaning of sexuality severely altered and requires intensive sexual healing. Ignoring the sexual component of rape only interferes with sexual healing of the victim, understanding of the evolution and nature of rape, and rehabilitation of the rapist.

- On the recommendations of sex therapists, many couples rent and watch X-rated videos as a means of enhancing sexual excitement, but these tapes at best show techniques. They do not teach intimate connection, and many of their techniques are distorted, artificial, and even dangerous. The sex syndicate states that erotica is an aphrodisiac, but pornography and X-rated material tend to have an anaphrodisiac effect in the sexual healing context because they detract from all five levels of intimate connection.

- There is no G spot or magical area in the vagina that is guaranteed to turn a woman on. If you are looking for a turn-on switch, you are working on a machine to make it function right and not connecting with a person. The "spot" and "zone" approach is typical of the mechanical outlook of the sex syndicate, but the whole-person, intimate approach is the way of sexual healing.

- The squeeze technique is the sex syndicate's strategy for delaying ejaculation until the "right time." This approach is potentially harmful, doesn't work, focuses the couple on mechanics rather than the relationship, and makes one partner the therapist and the other the patient. Sexual healing emphasizes holding one's partner rather than grabbing the genitals.

- There is no difference in orgasmic thresholds between men and women, and orgasm is not the central objective of sexual healing. Men do not have orgasm more easily or faster than women unless we accept the sex syndicate muscle and genital contraction definition of orgasm. The easier accessibility of the penis compared with the clitoris may result in earlier genital contractions for the male, and many men have years of practice at coming quickly, but the mind is where both men's and women's orgasms take place.

- Masturbation is not good practice for a better sex life with a partner. Masturbation is not physically harmful and can be instructive, but sexual healing is concerned less with individual pleasure, technique, and timing than with shared connection. The sex syndicate sees masturbation as a path to pleasure often equal to, more convenient, and less time consuming than sexual relationships. It can, however, become a sensual shortcut to avoid the effort required to make a meaningful sexual connection.

- Nonsyndicate sex research related to sexual healing shows that men are much more romantic than women, that women seek sexual intimacy more than most men, and that men have sex more often when they don't want to than women do. The sex syndicate teaches the opposite lesson by asserting that women have to be seduced or manipulated into having sex because they are more romantic and less sexual but that men are more romantically impulsive. Women do tend to need a reason to have sex and reflect about the why and the who, but they are at least as sexually driven as men. They are more contemplative and may look for the one man to meet their many needs, but many men can fall in love fast and irrationally with many women in an effort to meet one need. Women in our society almost always send the first sexual signals. The sex syndicate is male dominated, and the research upon which its women members base their work is often male-derived, so the male-as-aggressor hypothesis dominates. Sexual healing does not involve an aggressor or a seducer.

- In the sexual healing philosophy, sex is volitional and not emotional. Sexual control and abstinence are possible if the meaning and healing joy of sexual intimacy are taught openly to our children. At best, giving condoms to students is a stopgap measure, and condoms without sexual concepts and explicit teaching about sex and intimacy are not likely to do much to reduce sexually transmitted disease. Sexual healing does not always include intercourse. Providing an intense sexual curriculum including erotic alternatives to intercourse and the issue of meaning and intimacy in sexual relationship is the long-term answer to stopping the spread of sexually transmissible diseases.

- Ejaculation is *not* the male orgasm. Research in sexual healing shows that most men seldom have orgasm. They have mistaken pleasurable ejaculatory contractions for mindful orgasm and expect women to "come fast" like they do so both partners can go about their stressed and busy lives. Ejaculation has little to do with orgasm and may even distract a man from a full orgasmic experience, but the Type E or ejaculatory personality seems to want to do everything quickly and spurts through life without connection and meaning.

- Women ejaculate. While they do not emit a fluid with the force that men do, women also secrete a substance during sexual intimacy that resembles the male ejaculate. The sex syndicate speaks only of the male ejaculation and trying to time it to be "mature," but the female sexual emission contains phosphatase from the Bartholin's glands, and it is similar in composition to that from the male prostate. Some women emit more of this fluid than others, and some experience a sense of ejaculating.

- Taking tests together can aid mutual learning, but comparing our intimate sexual conduct with arbitrary and often unfounded generalizations about frequencies and techniques can cause disappointment and blame. Sexual healing is first and foremost a self-discovered way of connecting that is free from "the way" and is creatively learned between you and your partner "your way." Taking tests critically and discussing them together is helpful, but comparisons about sex often lead to disappointment and accusations that block rather than enhance sexual intimacy.

- Men have more difficulty ending relationships than women do and tend to be more physically and psychologically devastated by break-ups. The sex syndicate's popular books and therapy often focus on the needful woman who can't deal with the loss of her lover. Breaking up is always difficult, and women may talk about endings more whereas men may avoid dealing with the problem by vanishing and not calling, but it is both men and women who often don't deal well with life's endings.

- Sex therapy almost never works. It is impossible to separate our sex lives from our whole lives. Sex therapy techniques are mechanical methods rather than the means for merging. They are intended to correct a problem which is seen as separate from the rest of our lives, but sex therapists neglect the unity of the five healing connections. Sexual healing is a matter of togetherness and meaning, not techniques and gimmicks.

- You have read that the sex revolution began with "Kinsey counts" and pseudoaverages such as 2.5 acts of coitus per week. Sexual healing is a process free from assigned averages and statistical norms. Your relationship's current sexual frequency is the right frequency for your relationship at this time. It reflects more than sexual drive; it reflects all five levels of your connection and the pressures from all areas of your daily life. How much you have sex has little to do with how good or bad your sex life is.

- The sex syndicate says that men essentially "come" by friction and women by vibration. Sexual healing transcends such limitations and focuses on each partner's awareness of his or her sex style as described later in this book. It is not the rubbing and vibration of the genitals that leads to sexual healing but the shared whole-life rhythm of two loving and committed partners.

- Never begin a relationship because of sexual attraction, and never end a relationship because of sexual problems. Lack of pleasing sex is one of the most frequent reasons given for divorce and ending of relationships, but sexual healing suggests that a sexual problem is not a dysfunction but a challenge to work harder to connect on multiple levels. Sexual healing, not the ending of the relationship, is called for when there is sexual unhappiness. Sex should be the way to save and not the reason to end a relationship. Don't let your sex life lead you.

Sexual healing requires freeing yourself from the sex syndicate influence and learning the most recent findings about sexuality from sources beyond the sex researchers. It requires rediscovering your own sexual values and sexual and loving style.

WHY THE SEX EXPERTS ARE OFTEN WRONG

As you learn to be a sexual healer, you must begin from a different point of view than that advocated by the sex syndicate. Here are twelve reasons why you should be cautious in accepting the advice of sex experts as you consider sex as a healing part of your life:

1. **The Lack of Valid and Current Research:** Sex therapy as a field is not based on replicated research. Many of the classic sex studies were never repeated, and some of the "sex reports" were little more than popular magazine surveys. It is impossible to replicate Masters and Johnson's findings because they say they destroyed all their research protocols and refuse to allow anyone to see their lab or their data. No statistical ranges and graphs were ever published by the St. Louis team. As you will read in Chapter 9, nonsyndicate research has shown that the sexual cycle of arousal-plateau-orgasm-resolution is not accurate. A different sexual cycle exists, and awareness of this cycle promotes sexual healing.

2. **Unfounded Principles of Psychology:** Sex therapy employs psychological principles that are not only without experimental and theoretical foundation but also severely damaging. A great deal of the psychology of sex was developed by untrained, self-appointed experts who based much of their advice on their personal experience and philosophy. Masters and Johnson devised their own psychotherapy system and concepts, but neither had significant training in psychiatry or psychology. They used a genital approach instead of a joining adventure.

3. **False Claims of Value-free Orientation:** While sex therapists claim to be "personal value neutral" and not to teach sex morality, they actively force their selfish, sexual pleasure first values on their pa-

tients. Some sex experts advise divorce as a solution to relationship problems, others suggest affairs as relationship aphrodisiacs, and a few even offer themselves as better and more skilled sexual options to a suffering sexual partner. Sexual healing begins with the assumption that bonding forever is more healthy than serial pairings in search of the perfect partner.

4. Needless Violation of Privacy: Many of the questions asked by sex therapists are asked to meet the sexual curiosity of the therapist and not to gain data to help the patient. There is little therapeutic value in asking about the number of orgasms per week and whether or not someone enjoys oral sex, yet these and other questions are included on almost every sex history. Sex therapists avoid questions about basic life principles, values, religious convictions, or the purpose of sex, life, and love, all of which are central to sexual healing.

5. Facilitating the Spread of Sexually Transmissible Diseases: Because of their encouragement of sexual practice and experience before committing to a relationship so people will not be disappointed or disappointing, sex therapists have helped to spread serious sexual diseases, including the HIV virus, the herpes simplex virus, and papilloma or genital warts associated with cancer. The sex syndicate's response to AIDS and other diseases has been the "shield" focus: Wear a condom. The history of medicine back to the black plague reveals that epidemics are stopped only when the public learn to relate with more concern for one another's health and welfare and more regard for the collective good.[1] Mechanical or physical intervention works only in the short term if at all. Movement from self-gratification to self-restraint and responsibility help stop the spread of disease; vaccines and miracle medicines only help contain diseases once the civilizations that have created them become more civilized.

6. Overemphasis on Intense Genital Stimulation: Sex therapists' emphasis on the use of the vibrator decreased rather than increased women's capacity to have orgasm in sexual interaction with a partner. Sexual healing involves "letting" oneself "come" rather than trying to "make" someone or oneself "have" an orgasm by physical intensity, and insensitivity and raising the orgasmic threshold can result from too intense genital stimulation.

7. Unethical Practices: No one knows exactly how many, but a percentage of sex therapists became sexually involved with their patients, sometimes doing so openly as an alleged means of "in vivo

teaching" and "therapist surrogacy." This problem has become so severe that to date there have been twelve national meetings on dealing with sex between therapist and patient in addition to more than twenty major articles on this topic in professional journals.[2] (Estimates are that more than one of ten psychotherapists have sex with their patients.) Sexual healing is best accomplished *without* intervention by sex experts or surrogacy by learning about your way rather than someone else's way to intimacy.

8. Devaluing of Long-term Relationship: Sex therapists preach a system of loving based on self-fulfillment, gratification, and the use of rather than the protection of marriage and family. They actively promote premarital sex as good practice for later marriage and assume that anyone in the teen years should "try" sex. From 1920 to the middle 1970s, the entire moral structure of our society was stood on its head, and the sex syndicate helped by mocking the Victorianism that had dominated our sexual mores for so long. However large the gap between the Victorian ideal and Victorian practices, it is clear that the Victorians at least tried to work toward social concern, fidelity, self-control, and regard for lasting relationships.[3] The sex establishment still maintains that the natural evolution of the self will often result in divorce and separation as we outgrow one another instead of grow together.

9. Failure to Recognize the Role of Choice: Sex therapists consider thoughtfulness and mindfulness about sex obstacles to the body's sexual pleasure. They see sex as a physical impulse not to be interfered with by the mind. They teach that sexual impulse is uncontrollable, automatic, and overwhelming. Research shows clearly that every sex act is willful—even in the most passionate relationship. Our genitals *do not* have minds of their own; they need our minds and spirits to direct them. When we are sexual with purpose, meaning, and connection, we heal.

10. Negative Side Effects of Sex Therapy Intervention: Several of the techniques for the treatment of premature ejaculation, orgasmic distress, and vaginismus are often physically damaging to patients. Some "sex therapist" urologists and gynecologists maimed their patients with hormonal injections to stiffen the penis or clitoris, the insertion of pumps, pulleys, and mercury-filled testicular balls squeezed through plastic penile tubes to achieve erection, and cutting away the clitoral hood so the clitoris would be more exposed. These practices are still taking place! We gasp in horror at sewing the vagina closed to guarantee fidelity until marriage or cutting off

the clitoris through clitorectomy, both of which are practiced on millions of women in some countries today, yet we ourselves take a more hygienic but still mutilating approach to sexuality. Sexual healing transcends mechanical repair to emphasize interpersonal rapport and caring.

11. Lack of Professional or Legal Regulation: Since no licensing or regulation is required by any state, many frustrated amateur "psychotherapists" elect themselves sex therapists. They have no training in sexual physiology, psychiatry, or psychology. When I sat on the Michigan committee for establishing the ethics of sex therapy, my call for allowing only state-regulated and licensed professionals in nursing, social work, psychology, psychiatry, or medicine to learn and/or practice the "subspecialty" of sexual health was rejected. Sex therapists, with or without degrees or training, are under the protection of the sex syndicate, which offers its own certification and diplomas, given out after two-week "intensive" training programs.

    We now know that many sexual problems are physiological and metabolic, and that comprehensive and experienced history taking is necessary to understanding any sexual problem. But many sex therapists do not take complete medical and psychiatric histories or give a physical exam. The sex surrogates recommended by some sex therapists devastated the lives of their "clients" and their clients' marriages by treating problems that didn't exist, creating others, and mistreating or failing to refer problems that required professional help for physical or psychiatric distress. Sexual healing incorporates the best and most current medical knowledge to help promote and maintain a full, connected life of wellness rather than just a happy sex life.

12. Development of a Cultist Mentality: A "sex cultism" evolved from the sex syndicate, including nude group encounters, masturbatory circles, sex clubs and retreats, and a "self-pleasure at any price" philosophy. At some sex training centers, fledgling sex therapists offered sensual group massages, nude discussion groups, and sometimes sexual intimacy to show that they were free from hang-ups. Client confidentiality was regularly violated by the telling of "case examples." Sexual healing is based on the sacredness and privacy of the two-person interaction, the mutual protection of each other's most personal secrets and feelings, and constant loyalty to the absent—never saying to a person other than your partner anything you would not say to the partner.

As you explore the sexual dimension of sexual healing in Part II, remember that much of what you may now accept as fact may not be fact at all and does not have to direct your sexual life, and that the new research findings from non–sex establishment researchers have much to teach us about more meaningful and healing sex.

8

HEALING THE SEXUALLY WOUNDED
Less Mechanics and More Meaning

There will be sex after death; we just won't be able to feel it.
Lily Tomlin

A terrible thing happened again last night. Nothing!
Phyllis Diller

VICTIMS OF THE SEX SYNDICATE

"I feel like I'm worked on instead of like I'm making love with my husband," said the wife. "My husband seems to do everything right, but there just doesn't seem to be anything behind it all. It seems like there's no meaning to it. I have an orgasm every time, but I don't feel complete."

"We're great lovers," said her husband. "But somehow our love doesn't seem so great. There's something missing."

Sexual healing's five levels of connection—with self, with another, with something more, with the present moment, and with the body of another person—are often neglected when the approach of the sex syndicate described in Chapter 7 is applied. Sex often seems to be separate from any meaning and may come to feel like a task or skill to be mastered rather than an intimate means for joining with another person. Our success may come to be determined merely by rapidity, numbers of orgasms, and the degree of self-relief from built-up sexual tension that we experience.

IS YOUR SEX LIFE YOUR WHOLE LIFE?

Sex by the rules of the sex establishment may become a miniversion of our whole lives, offering a microcosm of how we live day-to-day and a re-creation in bed of how we are at work or during our daily activities. We hurry for fulfillment and seek to do, to get, and to find instant satisfaction with minimal effort, and our sexual interactions often show the same attitude. Our lives are filled with stress and tension from which we seek relief. Through sex establishment sex, we are given the sensate focus techniques of foreplay to build up tension quickly, and special spots for instant stimulation to lead to quick release, followed by relaxation. In a few minutes, we seem to be re-acting our whole urgent quest for self-pleasure, and reflecting on how we make love may teach us much about what we are making of our lives.

For some people, sex seems to become a kind of narcotic, allowing them to fall asleep more easily. Through our sex, we may be trying to retrace our stressful lives one more time before we turn in for the night, and the result is similar to that of stressful living—relief but not fulfillment. We often continue our stress-addictive life patterns through our sex rather than find more meaning, intimacy, and life purpose through our sexuality. We may be left with the wounds of failed intimacy.

Many of the social and sexual problems of our time—including couple conflict, sexual harassment and abuse, rape, abortion, the apparent increase in violent pornography, and the AIDS crisis—are related in part to the mechanistic and self-pleasure sex syndicate approach. This chapter examines a sexual healing approach to the wounds we inflict on ourselves by such an orientation.

In this chapter, I will look at three of the most significant results of the sex establishment's prescription for sexual health and happiness. First, I will discuss wounded couples and the practical problems of mechanical sex that can interfere with their healing connection. Next, I will describe a case of sexual assault, how it resulted in disconnection on all the levels of sexual health, and how the wounds of this trauma may be sexually healed. Finally, I will summarize a healing connection to replace the mechanistic self-pleasure approach to sex by considering one way the AIDS crisis and all its ramifications may be ended by sexual healing and a different view of the cause of AIDS.

SEXUALLY WOUNDED COUPLES: PRACTICAL PROBLEMS OF EVERY-NIGHT ECSTASY

In their attempt to comply with the rules of the sex syndicate, many couples encounter sexual distress, misunderstanding, and even physical pain. The following are examples of moving beyond the sex syndicate limitations in order to heal wounds caused by the mechanical approach.

"Passion Pains"

Problem: "I'm just not as limber as I used to be. I read about all these postures, but I get cramps in my feet just from being on top of my husband. When I groan because of the cramps, he thinks I'm turned on. If I tell him I'm in pain, it turns him off. When we try him on top, he likes to push my legs back to my head like in the videotapes. I feel like I'm a wishbone about to crack in half. What can we do?"

Sexual Healing Solution: Sex and Substance P

Couples have been taught that sexual arousal depends on proper posturing or the most stimulating and unique "sex stance." It is typical in so-called advanced cultures for one partner get on top of or put his or her weight on the other during coitus. In more primitive cultures, without sex manuals and X-rated videotapes, the partners most often lie side by side or select postures in which no weight is placed on either partner. During sexual arousal, blood flows to the genitalia and the abdominal area. If weight is placed on the extremities or a sexual posture blocks the flow of blood to the extremities even more, cramps and pain can result. Side-by-side postures usually prevent this. Taking a warm shower before sexual activity also decreases blood flow problems. If the problem persists, "sexual limbering" exercises done alone or with your partner while clothed can condition muscles and open circulation to limbs unaccustomed to a seldom-used posture. Lying on the bed, raising your legs to a coital position, moving your pelvis in the motions of coital thrusting, holding yourself up using only your arms, squatting over a pillow as if in a coital position, approximating any other postures you may use in sexual intimacy, and going through the motions of sexual intercourse without actually having intercourse stretch those muscles that may be used primarily in coitus. Any posture you seldom attempt is likely to result in some cramping or discomfort, so practice makes for painless passion.

It has also been found that one reason women can bear the pain of childbirth is that pressure on the vaginal walls causes a substance to be released that inhibits or blocks a spinal neurotransmitter called Substance P, which conveys body pain to the brain. Dr. Barry Kamasurik, a neurobiologist at Rutgers Medical School, has found that touch of the vagina or penis which is perceived as pleasurable results in measurable pain reduction and a form of eroto-anesthesia. In some hospitals in Europe and Japan, the genitals of patients in severe and chronic pain are rubbed and the pain is profoundly reduced. The tolerance of pain increases 70 to 100 percent during sexual stimulation which is perceived as pleasurable. If a cramp occurs during intercourse, resisting the urge to disengage and holding still and pressing on the genitals while kissing might help, assuming you love the kisser.

"I've Fallen and I Can't Get It Up."

Problem: "I know all about the impotence thing. I've heard all the experts. My wife knows all about it too, so she becomes a sex therapist every time I've fallen and can't get it up. She goes into this 'It's OK, I understand, it happens to everyone sometimes' thing, and that really knocks the wind out of my sails and the firmness out of my penis. I feel like her patient instead of her lover. Isn't there some other way to deal with this?"

Sexual Healing Solution: Remember the U Area

Sex experts who are eager to treat "impotence" often end up creating even more problems by making four unfounded assumptions:

1. First, they assume that the erect penis is a prerequisite for sexual pleasure. There is much more clitoral ignorance than penis envy, and you hear very little about clitoral impotence, but both penis and clitoris are capable of erection. While transudation or lubrication of the vagina is often emphasized as the equivalent of the male erection response, clitoral erection also takes place when a woman is sexually aroused. Some men and women encounter difficulties in experiencing erection as fast as or to the extent that they would like, but complete sexual pleasure can be obtained without erection of the penis or clitoris and without lubrication of the vagina.

2. The sex experts assume that the penis or—if they pay any attention to it at all, the clitoris—is almost always fully erect when a person is sexually aroused. In fact, the penis and clitoris vary in erection throughout the sexual response, and firmness is not an indicator of sexual pleasure unless your genitals are the measure of your joy.

3. They assume that erection problems are in the mind instead of the genitals. Most difficulties with clitoral or penile erection and lack of sufficient lubrication are caused by physical problems such as diabetes, poor circulation to the genitals, or other disease processes.

4. It is wrongly assumed that the penis cannot ejaculate when it is not erect. But men and women can ejaculate or emit fluid whether or not the penis or clitoris is erect.

Research at Northwestern University Medical School reveals that tiny nerves around the urethra, or the tube through which urine passes, are the true source of the neurological sensations that lead to physical orgasm. Pleasurable pressure on these nerves results in a turning off of the switch holding back the orgasm generator in our lower back. Erection of the penis or clitoris has little to do with this phenomenon. These urethral nerves are now called the U area (nothing in our neurology exists in one spot), which exists in both men and women. This research also shows that it is not the degree of stimulation but the source and the recipient's feelings about the source that really determine the reaction.

Like all body systems, the clitoris or penis erection ebbs and peaks. Trying to "maintain an erection" only causes a neurohormonal reaction that blocks erection (more epinephrine because of overactivation of the SAM system). The entire body and mind is a sexual organ, not just the genitals. Sexual posturing without erection, moving in sexual rhythms together without erection, and possibly experiencing ejaculation and orgasm not only have been reported to be very exciting but also often allow erection to take place spontaneously once the penile or clitoral focus is off and the SAM system's influence reduced.

"Doing It or Letting It?"

"I know you have to stimulate your clitoris to come. Now, the more he stimulates or I stimulate it, the longer it seems to take. I just get to the edge, but I can't quite get over it. Even the fastest speed on my vibrator doesn't do it anymore. When I masturbate, I can come easier, but even then it's harder to come than before. What's wrong with me?"

Sexual Healing Solution: Tremors from the "Epicenter of Orgasm"

Perhaps one of the most serious errors to come from the sex syndicate was the focus on trying to "have" an orgasm by intense sex spot stimulation rather than "letting" an orgasm happen. New work by neurophysiologist Keven McKenna at Northwestern University Medical School shows that the "epicenter of orgasm" is somewhere in the lower spine. It is like a sex generator humming on idle all the time. We would experience orgasm constantly if the base of the brain didn't inhibit the orgasm generator. A chemical called serotonin acts like a switch that prevents the orgasm generator from operating constantly. If we let go, love, trust, relax, and allow things to happen, the control switch is turned off, serotonin is reduced, the idling and humming orgasm generator is allowed to run at full speed, and orgasm happens. Trying to force and vibrate an orgasm into happening is going against the way orgasm works. Sexual orgasm is something we let happen rather than something we do to or for each other.

"Why Does He Close His Eyes When He Kisses Me?"

Problem: "Every time he kisses me, he closes his eyes. Is that because he doesn't want to see me or look at me? Doesn't he think I'm pretty anymore? I close mine, too. Maybe we just don't want to see each other anymore. Maybe we're fantasizing about someone else. Maybe we're not made for each other anymore."

Sexual Healing Solution: Kissing Is Sniffing

We close our eyes when we kiss because we prefer to smell our lover rather than see him or her. You will read later about keeping your eyes open during sex as a means for intensifying feelings of intimacy and closeness, but there are also advantages to keeping them closed occasionally. There are hundreds of tiny apoline glands near the surface of the skin on the face. When we kiss, we close our eyes instinctively because they are so dominant in our senses (they collect more than 70 percent of the incoming stimulation for our bodies). By closing our eyes, we are free to take sensuous sniffs of our partner. In this way, we can respond to the touch of his or her lips and whiff the apoline aroma mist of his or her cheeks.

Author Eve Glickman writes, "Ancient lovers believed that a kiss would literally unite their souls because the spirit was said to be carried in our breath."[1] It is likely that kissing is a relic gesture from our evolutional history and a means of giving each other the breath of love and life. The Hawaiian culture is based on the sacredness of the human breath as a gift from the gods. It is the responsibility of every Hawaiian to perpetuate the breath—their most important inheritance. When a Hawaiian dies, he or she often calls a loved one to the deathbed to breathe his or her last breath into the mouth and soul of the loved one. This is a sacred way of continuing the culture. (*Aloha* means "love" in Hawaiian; *alo* means "to give" and *ha* means "breath.")[2] We can learn much from this hundreds-of-years-old tradition that applies to our own sexual healing by remembering the sacredness of human connection and our responsibility for maintaining intimacy, and by seeing even the simple act of kissing as a most loving form of connection.

Birds and some animals chew food for their young and then pass it to them. It is possible that we find some comfort from our early nurturing in the act of deep kissing.[3] I tell my patients in our sexual healing program that slowly and gently circling the fingers around each other's lips, cheeks, and forehead while kissing and stopping occasionally to feel each other's breath on the lips and cheeks can lead to a feeling of increased intimacy. We often forget to use our hands when we are using our genitals, so I remind my patients of author Carole Wade's statement "Sex is not a soccer game. The use of hands is permitted."[4] Alternating closed eyes and eye-to-eye contact during sex can enhance sexual healing by promoting different types and levels of connection.

"One Need, Many Wants"

Problem: "I think I can never be happy sexually with one woman. Men just aren't made that way. You can fantasize all you want, but a man needs different women. Women don't need variety like men do. One man for life is fine for them. I don't want to cheat, but it's like I have to. I just want a different woman now and then, but I still need my wife."

Sexual Healing Solution: Quiet Your Impulse for Your Values

Research now shows that men's and women's brains are wired differently when it comes to sexual arousal. Although there are some exceptions, which I will discuss later, a woman is neurologically prewired to need a reason to have sex and a man is neurologically prewired to need just a place. The sexually dimorphic nucleus (SDN) is a little bundle of cells in the hypothalamus at the base of the brain. This is one part of the brain that influences—to a degree not yet completely determined—our sexual responsiveness and preferences. In part because of about eight times as much testosterone soaking the male fetus's brain at eight weeks after conception, the SDN is more than two and one half times larger in most men than in most women. There is evidence, then, for a neurophysiological basis for male promiscuity. (Jackie Mason said, "Eighty percent of men cheat in America. The rest cheat in Europe.") Sexual healing involves developing our ability not to be reactive to our brains but to be proactive or mindful of our values. Quieting a genetically predetermined physical impulse in favor of intimate connection is one of the most necessary acts for lasting love and mutual sexual fulfillment.

Our higher and new brain can tell the lower brain what to do and how to think. Realizing, accepting, and then moving beyond our passionate predispositions is the first step to a creative healing relationship. Once we are aware of the power of our inclinations, we are free to make our own choices as to how these inclinations will play themselves out.

"I Can't Make Love If I Don't Love"

Problem: "I have to feel in love before I can make love. I don't really love him anymore. The books say to communicate about it. So we've talked about it and talked about it, but I can't help it. I just don't love him."

Sexual Healing Solution: "We Feel as Loving as We Behave"

You read earlier that if you want to love someone, you must do it to feel it. The two of you can't talk your way out of a problem you behaved yourselves into, but you can behave your way out of a problem you talked yourselves into. Affirm, care, protect, nurture, forgive, sacrifice, and do random acts of caring. Make what is important to your lover as important to you as your lover is. If love is what you want to feel, love is what you will have to do. Lust happens to you, but when you *do* love, loving feelings result.

Behaving lovingly involves toleration, forgiveness, and assuming responsibility for your relationship rather than criticizing it or your lover. We like "because." We love "although." There is nothing wrong with telling your partner what you prefer in terms of hygiene and appearance. However, sexually healing love requires toleration and acceptance. We don't have to feel love because we are attracted. We can learn to become attracted because we have created a loving bond. You form a relationship when you are ready to love and not because you are already in it. Contrary to the popular myths of modern psychology, we *can* love someone we don't always like by deciding to behave lovingly toward him or her. Whether or not we like someone depends on many things, particularly how much we are willing to put up with and how much effort we put into being the partner we would like to have—modeling the behaviors and demeanor we hope for. Remember, your lover loves a fool, and so do you. None of us is perfect.

THE HEALING POWER OF ANDROGYNY

In addition to the sexual issues just discussed, the sexual healing of relationships includes the principle of androgynous loving, or the combination of what society sees as the male and female ways of expressing love physically. The sex syndicate often tends to feminize what is considered a loving act, stressing tenderness, openness, vulnerability, caring, and emotional expressiveness. While these are important ways of expressing intimacy, they are sometimes emphasized over the traditionally more masculine ways of expressing intimacy, such as doing, acting, showing, and taking responsibility for the sexual encounter. Certainly neither sex has a monopoly on either of these sets of behaviors, but generally the feminine way of loving gets most of the attention. Being a good provider and offering security as a love symbol are often less stressed than being romantic, communicative, and verbal about feelings. Sexual healing combines these styles.

Researchers have shown that our culture views the instrumental or "doing" approach as male and the expressional or "telling" approach as female.[5] When a woman washes a man's shirt, it may be interpreted as an expression of love because our culture sees women's behavior as primarily expressive. If a man washes his wife's car, it is less likely to be interpreted as a loving act and more likely to be seen as something that "men just do." We feminize and therefore halve the potential of love when we see it only as expressional. Talking about and doing about love are equally important to sexual intimacy.

In a study of sex styles by James Rosenzweig and Donald Dailey, couples reported more sexual pleasure and satisfaction in their relationship if what the researchers defined as feminine coupling behaviors (being sexy and exciting, gentleness, and vulnerability) were combined with what they defined as more masculine styles (assertiveness, control, and performance). They concluded that these androgynous relationships were more stable and mutually fulfilling in their sexuality and general life than those which were less balanced and leaned toward the more traditional general sex behavior.[6]

In addition to an effort to establish an androgynous sexual pattern, sexual healing emphasizes transcending romanticized notions of loving. Sexual healing suggests that you don't try to find someone you can't live without but try instead to find someone you can live with. Find someone who is willing to join with you in a mutual and ongoing effort to connect on all the five levels of sexual healing and not someone who seems to steal your heart. After her sexual healing program, one of my patients said, "I finally learned to not look for a man who would knock my socks off but for a man who would help me organize my sock drawer."

SEXUALLY WOUNDED PEOPLE

There is much sexual suffering in the world. Thousands of women and men are raped and sexually abused, and children are sexually assaulted. Even our most sacred institutions have not escaped sexual damage. The

Catholic Church spent more than $50 million in 1992 defending priests against charges of sexual molestation, and at least 2,000 priests have been found guilty of sexual misconduct. While most of us are appalled at the psychological damage such crises cause, the physical health destruction and damage to our healing capacity are also severe.

I describe here one example of the sexual wounding of an individual. She is a patient I treated more than ten years ago, and her case illustrates the depth of the wounds of our sexually misled society and the need for sexual healing.

The Rape of Immunity

When she entered my office, her hands were shaking. She had been referred to me because of her severe rheumatoid arthritis. Her fingers were curled and twisted, and, as she slowly sat down, she groaned in pain. It seemed to hurt her to lift her head to look at me. She appeared to be about fifty years old. I checked her record to be sure there was not a mistake, because she was only twenty-six. Her own immune system had begun to attack her, and her joints were inflamed.

Thousands of people in this country suffer from rheumatoid arthritis. It is the most common of the autoimmune diseases (when the immune system attacks its own body). The doctors had tried everything to ease this patient's pain, but she suffered almost every minute. Her pain had resulted in her withdrawal from others, placement on medical disability, and a life of almost total isolation. She had been sent to me to see if I could offer any help on a psychoneuroimmunological level.

As I began to take her history, I asked about her sexual health. "No one's asked me about that before," she said. "What does that have to do with my pain and my arthritis? I haven't had sex in more than five years."

"If we want to look at your total health, we have to look at your total life," I answered. "Your sexual health cannot be separated from your general health, and it may influence your healing capacity."

She broke into tears as she told the story of being raped by two men at college. She had never discussed her experience with anyone, but the violence had done much more than violate her body and her psyche. Her sexual trauma had, as it does for every woman and man who experiences it, caused a disconnection on all the five levels of connection. It cost this victim much of her connection with her self and her self-esteem, and it resulted in self-blame and loss of much of her sexual identity. She commented, "I feel dirty, used, and unattractive. The assault had turned me off to anything that even resembles sex. Who would want to make love to me? I can't even look at myself naked, so how could I ever let anyone look at me? Every time I do look at my body, it all comes back to me, and

I start remembering what happened. Even when I feel another woman look at me, it's like they know what happened and think that I'm dirty."

The sexual attack on my patient had also torn away her sense of coherence and meaning by resulting in feelings that life's fairness, comprehensibility, and manageability had been banished in one senseless, random, degrading, brutal act. She cried, "There is no sense in it all. It's all so unfair, so needless, so terribly cruel. They were just looking for anybody—any woman. I just happened to be there and they took me. What sense does it all make?"

The woman described her sense of distance from the present moment saying, "I live in a kind of trance. I'm not here. I'm kind of going through life in a daze. If I pay too much attention and think too much, I start to think about what happened. I hate them." She slammed her hand on the arm of the chair and grimaced in pain as she described her separation from life's sensuality. "I don't want to touch anyone, and I don't want anyone to touch me. My body only gives me pain and never pleasure. They stole the pleasure from my life."

As you read in Part I, how we think and feel translates directly to a neurochemical immune profile within our body. The fear and internal rage this woman felt had caused neurohormonal effects. Her mind had been raped as well as her body. From the hypothalamus in her brain to her pituitary gland to her adrenal glands to the immune cells agitated by the epinephrine and corticosteroids pouring almost constantly through her body, the pain of the sexual assault had been imprinted on her immune system. It responded with the blind rage of a frightened, angry child, but, like a child having a tantrum, it was hurting itself more than the appropriate target. She had been violated down to the marrow of her bones, and the result was the autoimmune disorder rheumatoid arthritis.

I reconfirmed my diagnosis through laboratory tests. Her immune system was in severe imbalance, and the SAM system was running almost constantly, causing her immune cells to overreact against her. There are many causes for arthritis, and we all have our own bodily stress targets or organ systems that are most affected when we are stressed beyond our coping capacity. Some of us may develop heart disease or cancer, but our bodies and our healing systems reflect what happens to us and the meaning we give to our lives through our experiences.

The sexual healing approach with this woman was to help her reestablish intimate connection and meaning in her life on all five levels of intimate connection. She joined our ongoing group for women who have been victims of sexual assault and started treatment with one of the female psychiatrists on my staff. She began to speak more openly about her feelings, connected with the other women with whom she was finally able to share her feelings and thoughts about her trauma, and started slowly to rebuild connections in her life. We helped her find a part-time job in our hospital library, where she began to talk with a man in a safer environment for the first time since her attack.

The psychiatrist helped her with her body image, eventually standing at her side as she looked at her naked body, touched it, and reconnected with it by reclaiming her physical identity and remembering that her body could be a source of pleasure. The group helped her deal with her rage by realizing it was a natural emotion that, if held within, would only destroy her. She was helped to direct the heat of her anger into activity such as volunteer work in the rape crisis center at our hospital.

Her therapist helped her resume relationships with others and finally with men. I encouraged her to bring the man she was dating to her therapy to take part in the sexual healing. The consequences of rape not only metastasize or spread through the body of the victim but also spill out to the health of those who relate with the victim. Sexual healing is systems repair, and when possible it is helpful to treat sexual wounds in a couple setting.

In my own clinical meetings with this woman, I helped her in sessions of mindfulness or learning to be intensely aware of her life now rather than lingering in the pain of the past or fearfully cowering from the threats she projected to her future. Through meditation and shared connective imagery with her partner, I helped her to see her immune system back in balance and soothing her body as a protective but loving parent rather than an angry warrior attacking the wrong enemy. I helped her to focus on the present moment as under her control and in relaxed synchronization with her new partner.

Tests showed that her autoimmune condition slightly but measurably improved. Her T cells were moving back into balance. I asked her to meet with the minister at her church, and she decided to return to church on a regular basis with her male friend. With him, she seemed to find meaning and coherence—the connection with something more. Her joint pain gradually reduced to such an extent that yoga exercises were possible. Today, she has returned to her job as an English teacher, working part-time as the school's tennis coach, and is married with two children.

I received a card from her as I was writing this chapter, and that is why her story is included here. On the front of the card is a picture of her and her husband on their bicycles with their children in seats attached to the back. It reads, "Remember me? Remember him? Remember us? More gain, much less pain. Loving and loved again. Not yet totally cured, but feeling very healed. God bless you and everyone there."

THE HEALING OF AIDS?

The viruses—HIV 1 and HIV 2—that cause AIDS are often described as new deadly viruses that are spreading out of control. In fact, researchers now suspect that HIV is one of the oldest viruses and that it has only recently acquired its deadly tendencies. Further, they suggest that our sexual conduct has contributed to the development and strengthening of these deadly viruses and that a change in our sexual behaviors may help control or even kill them.[7] The principles of sexual healing may play an important role in that process.

Dr. Brett Tindall of the University of New South Wales examined survivors of HIV infection who had lived ten or more years. One of his patients is an eighty-one-year-old man who contracted the HIV virus via transfusion ten years ago and is in perfect health, having shown no symptoms of AIDS. Dr. Tindall reports that this man and other long survivors may have been infected by an ancestor of the recent virulent strain of HIV that scientists think mutated in part because of the social and sexual upheavals of the 1960s.

Viruses follow the same laws of evolution and survival that we do, and those viruses that spread themselves the most survive the longest. Perhaps the HIV viruses were less virulent when our sexual behaviors were less open and more meaningful, social constrictions against promiscuity stronger, and prostitution and the free sex market of pornography and sexual titillation more limited. When people had fewer partners, the virus had to survive in one person if it wanted to survive, but with more partners, a more virulent virus can kill off its host and survive in the body of its host's partner. As sex became less intimate and meaningful and more mechanical and self-pleasure focused, the virus had far more hosts to choose from. Now that the virus was traveling from host to host, it had little "motivation" for keeping any one host alive for long.

Evolutionary biologist Dr. Paul Ewald at Amherst College emphasizes the importance of the nature of the HIV viruses. They insinuate themselves into our white blood cells and destroy our immunity. They are not spread like other viruses—by coughing, sneezing, or hand-to-eye contact and by finding as many new hosts as possible in whom to spread themselves. Viruses that show restraint and replicate slowly typically don't survive and evolve, but those that spread fast have more of a chance of surviving. A mere influenza virus in 1918 killed 20 million people worldwide, and scientists now think that World War I and the sick and numerous available hosts huddled in trenches provided good replicating ground and conditions for the development of a virus that virulently replicated through many hosts. In other words, the availability of many hosts helped the virus evolve to a more virulent strain.

Our sexual behavior may have helped the HIV viruses develop to what they are today, and therefore it is a major contributor, cause, and possibly a potential healing factor of AIDS itself. Changing back to more meaningful, exclusive relationships may help slow or even end the AIDS crisis by regressing the virus back to its less virulent form. This is what some scientists at Harvard Medical School are trying to do in a test tube by chemical hyperstimulation, or challenging the virus to reproduce itself constantly through its natural replicative and adaptive powers. When confronted by a drug or an immune system reaction, the HIV viruses readily mutate and can do so tens of thousands of times faster than plants or animals. By hyperstimulation, the hope is that the viruses will mutate out of their range to a point where they can no longer adapt or function. This work looks promising, and if it is validated, condoms and clean needles may do more than prevent new infections. Used widely enough, they might help drive the virulent form of HIV back to its more benign state and eventually weaken it out of existence. While it may be prudent to pass out condoms in schools and clean needles on the streets, it is equally if not more important to consider a paradigm shift, a new way of seeing sex as more than a mechanical means for personal ecstasy.

In order to return to more meaningful sexual connection, a new model of human sexual response and a new psychology of sexuality will be required. This is the focus of the last two chapters of this part.

9

ENCHANTED INSTRUMENTS OF LOVE
The Physiology of Sexual Healing

If the arrangement of the whole universe is some kind of
musical harmony . . . in human nature, the whole music of
the universe can be discerned.

Gregory of Nyssa
(ca. A.D. 330–395)

ATOMIC SEX

"We have nuclear sex," said the wife. "Sometimes we create such heat
that we have an orgasmic explosion."

This woman's statement reflects the impact of years of sex syndicate
domination of the understanding of sexual response, which stresses release rather than connection. Sex researchers have tended to view sexual
response in terms of physical energy buildup, discharge, and tension
relief. Sex therapists have seen sex as more hot than healing and more
exciting than soothing. Sexual healing requires a new model of the physiology of human sexual response based on connection and intimacy and
taken from research in many fields.

EROTIC ENTROPY AND SEXUAL PHYSICS

Most sex experts view the act of sex as a process of erotic entropy or
"spending" of sexual energy through massage or body rubbing against
body until sufficiently intense stimulation is generated for release and

discharge. The friction of fornication is seen as resulting in relief from the intentional buildup of erotic tension. Sex becomes a juxtapositioning of body matter against matter. Metaphors of getting hot, flames of passion, spouting of sex fluids, and various contractions and spasms fill many sex manuals.

Like their medical forerunners, sex experts have tended to view the body in traditional physics terms. The body and genitals are the "matter" and the erotic zones the key contact points or turn-on switches for the sexual machine. The mind, where the meaning of sex—our thoughts and consciousness—is located, and the matter of the body, where physical sensations are collected and expressed, are seen as two separate entities with little relationship beyond predictable sexual mechanics and hedonistic hydraulic principles. The sex syndicate teaches that a breakdown in the sex system results from mental interference with natural physical sex processes; the mind gets in the body's way. The sex experts' idea is to let the body be a sex machine that, when properly turned on, will do its energy generating without mind interference. "Just let your body go" and "get your mind off your own body and on someone else's" are the credos of the sex syndicate. Sexual meaning, purpose, and healing are seen as "soft science" concerns. Letting your sex energy get blocked by thoughts could result in bluing of the testicles or dystrophy of the vagina. The goal is to "let it all hang out and don't be hung up" by asking questions like why and for what and with whom, and never to let a message get in the way of a massage.

As medicine sees the body in mechanical terms, the body is seen by the sex establishment in terms of mechanical metaphors. Copying from their physicist heroes, doctors had long used such terms as hammertoe, trigger finger, sickle-cell disease, clubbing of the fingers, aortic bridges, heart valves, lockjaw, windpipes, bypasses, ruptures, chambers, cavities, and vessel blowouts. Sex experts describe the genitals as interlocking mechanical parts and speak of the penile shaft, coronal ridge, clitoral hood, vaginal barrel, and, most recently coital alignment techniques, which prescribe an almost impossible posture designed to result in perfect genital connection. Masters and Johnson describe "effective" intercourse as "inserting the penile shaft into the vaginal barrel, thereby resulting in the retraction of the clitoral hood by active thrusting and pulling by the coronal ridge."[1] It hardly seems that these sex "parts" are attached to a living, thinking, and feeling being! If the hood has gone up and the shaft has gone in, you are sexually engaged and the sex machines are ready to run.

"I don't know what stage I'm at when we make love," said one husband trying to learn the sex dance of the sex syndicate. "Just when I think I'm in the excitement phase, I end up in refraction."

This man's statement illustrates another feature of the sex establishment model of sexual response. Medicine and psychology have bought into the idea of boundaries and separations, and sexual response too is seen as a stage-by-stage, unidirectional reflexive reaction that, once started, seems to go on without input from our minds or regard for our relationships and who and why we are loving. Sexual response in the sexual healing view is an evolving, multidirectional response, shared uniquely by two partners, and influenced by the meaning given it by the partners, capable of being stopped, reversed, and started again.

Popular books describe the stages of life, passages, and the ever-present stage of "midlife crisis." (In my experience, midlife crisis is really an all-life crisis finally recognized!) Doctors assign stages to cancer and heart disease. Freud's first three psychosexual stages—the oral, anal, and phallic—became a menu offered up by the sex experts for selection by their "clients" as possible sexual approaches. Stages of courtship, seduction, marriage, and even dying are proposed.

Just as medical tests can help us understand and communicate about our health, stages can help us comprehend and converse about our life and loving. However, putting too much emphasis on staging or mistaking stages for real life development can lead us into the illusion that human and sexual experience is made up of cutoffs and distinct and separate phases. This is exactly what happened in the case of human sexual response.

In 1942, Austrian-American psychologist Wilhelm Reich first proposed a four-stage model of human sexual response. He described mechanical tension buildup, followed by the establishment of a bioelectric charge. Orgasm followed in the form of electrical discharge, itself followed by what he called a mechanical discharge. Two decades later, Masters and Johnson described their own version of this model—arousal, plateau, orgasm, and resolution. Several other versions of the "sex cycle" were proposed by various sex experts, yet these arbitrary "stages" have never actually been observed by the St. Louis team or any other sex researcher. In spite of the lack of supporting data, the Masters and Johnson description became the map for sex for millions of couples.[2] No one knew exactly how you could tell when you had gone out of arousal and into plateau, but the sex experts said that it happened, so it must be so. Sexual healing requires that these theoretical stages be completely ignored.

THE COITAL CURVE AND THE GOLDEN ARCHES

In Masters and Johnson's first book, *Human Sexual Response,* there is a line graph showing arousal building in a curving arch toward a peak at orgasm and then falling off into resolution. This "sex arch" is an unquestioned and key part of most sex education and therapy. The huge Gateway Arch on the riverside in St. Louis seems to resemble perfectly the "sex arch" proposed by the hometown team at the Masters and Johnson Institute.

There are two key ways in which the sex arch theory blocks sexual healing and intimate and meaningful physical connection between two people. First, sexual response is not a one-way-only system. Sexual responsivity with another person is a reverberating system that can oscillate between arousal, excitement, and orgasm. It is as possible to feel relief *before* or without orgasm as with it, and no matter what one's age or physical condition, there is no need to try to proceed through a cycle.

Second, the idea that there is an inevitable buildup of erotic energy is inaccurate. The Reichian model of sexual response, which postulated electro-erotic energy buildup and discharge, was wrong. Orgasm is more tenderness than tissue and more meaning than mechanics. Both men and women are capable of experiencing multiple orgasms and orgasms by fantasy alone.[3]

As discussed in Chapter 7, ejaculation is not orgasm, so the male's inability to ejaculate immediately after an ejaculation in no way impairs his ability to respond to thoughts and fantasies.[4] The meaningful sex of sexual healing is not possible if it is artificially limited by one-way sexual cycles and myths of eroto-electric buildup and release.

THE MALE PERIOD

According to Masters and Johnson and other sex establishment experts, all men have a "sex period." This is a uniquely male "stage" just after orgasm that the sex experts call refraction. During this stage, say Masters and Johnson, "no sexual arousal is again possible for an age-dependent period of time."[5] This was Masters-and-Johnson-ese for the idea that men temporarily wear out into a penile numbness after a sexual encounter, and the older the man gets, the more quickly he behaves like a sexually beached whale. Men, not women, have their "period" of sexual "men-pause."

According to Masters and Johnson and the other leading sex experts, women can go on reverberating from orgasm to orgasm into infinity—a situation they describe as a type of sensual seizure called "status orgasmus." Sexism and negative attitudes about women have often resulted in a view of the female as a mysterious "witch" capable of things far beyond the power of the male, and the male-dominated sex syndicate perpetuates this myth. Women, they suggest, are perpetual passion machines that, once properly "turned on," are difficult to turn off. A woman has to lay there pulsating with passion while eagerly awaiting her male partner's recharging.

I suggested in Chapter 8 that there has been a tendency to feminize love by focusing on the expressional rather than instrumental ways of loving. The sex syndicate has masculinized sex through its instrumental approach, which often views women as sex objects.

Like most of the "facts" from the sex syndicate, all this male pause information is completely false. While the penis may experience a refraction (an age-dependent and neurologically based period of transitional insensitivity), the brain does not. A numb penis does not have to mean a numbed mind. Both men and women experience neurophysiological changes that lessen their genital responsivity after a period of sexual stimulation. That's the way all the neurons in the human body work, and the genitals are no exception. There can be little meaningful and intimate sexual healing if we cling to the myth of male virile-pause and divide sexual partners into the always ready and the getting ready.

The unfortunate result of all this sex mythology is that many women tried to endure the near erasure of their genitals painfully rubbed and vibrated by sexually exhausted men trying to distract their idling partners while they "waited out" their unique refractory period. Even the best of men were viewed as "good a few times," but the sex experts believe and teach that not only could women shop until they dropped but they could have sex that way too.

THE "THIRD THING" OF SEX

An unlikely figure altered medicine forever. Albert Einstein proved that medicine's idol—the heralded physical sciences—had been wrong all along! Matter and energy are *not* separate things. They are united by a third entity: the speed of light. Not only was physics shaken to its quantum roots by this discovery but modern medicine was also forced to abandon its idea that mind (energy) and body (matter) are separate. They too are connected by a third thing—meaning—and the meaning we give to our lives translates to our body chemistry, our health, and our healing.

What came to be called *holistic medicine*—the trinity of mind, body, and spirit—has begun to assert itself. New fields of research outside the medical establishment are showing that the relationship between the immune system, the brain, and the body is as strong, complex, and often paradoxical as the quantum world of quarks, atoms, and electrons. We don't only have to go to the doctor to get our prescriptions. Our own minds are apothecaries of healing substances thousands of times more powerful than any drug. The research you read about in Part I showed that our thoughts and feelings can result in the release of these powerful wonder drugs from within our own brains. We still have much to learn about the mind-body connection, and there are many findings in search of meaning, but it is not too soon to say that, when it comes to health and sexuality, the meaning we give to our life and love influences our health and healing.

IS THE HEALER WITHIN OR BETWEEN?

Physics has demonstrated that, if we could make it go fast enough, a piece of solid rock would "implode" into enough energy to light an entire city. Likewise, the mind is capable of killing or curing us with its energy. The doctor is no longer the healer; the healer is within. Prevention rather than repair is the new focus, and life principle "proaction" or choices rather than impulsive reaction are seen as the new key to health and healing. The mind is now viewed as both healer and slayer.[6] The brain is no longer seen as irrelevant to or separate from health but as something infinitely powerful that has the power to work miracles of the mind. If the brain lost its mind in early medicine, holistic medicine has found it again.

I suggest that we must go one more step beyond this revolution. The healer *within* concept has as much potential to isolate us as to help us get better. Sexual healing looks for the healer *between* and maximizes the power of intimate connection between two people who choose to link their inner healers, to seek meaning in life together, and to express that connection physically.

THE END OF OUR SEX LIFE

The major revolution in medicine continues to unfold. Biofeedback, the importance of attitude, love, meditation, chanting, the relaxation response, the reemergence of issues of religion, beliefs, and spirituality are all a part of the new medicine of meaning. All these techniques depend on connection with another person for their full effect, but they represent a shift away from the mechanical orientation. Why we become ill and the meaning of our illnesses and our lives are now as important as and perhaps more important than the mechanical diagnosis. We now know that we do not die of the disease we have; we die of our whole lives and the meaning we give to them. We are not human beings capable of an occasional spiritual experience. We are spirits having a brief and miraculous human experience that we can share deeply and profoundly with another person. We are not humans capable of love and sex. We are sensuality and love itself expressed in human form. We do not "have a sex life." We "are sexuality."

Unfortunately, the sexual response model of the sex syndicate does not account for the rediscovery of the human spirit, meaning, and principle. The remainder of this chapter explores an entirely new model of the meaning of sex in keeping with the remarkable research findings of scientists from throughout the world. It is their work that is leading the way toward a new physiology of sexual response that serves as the basis for sexual healing. Talented and creative researchers outside the sex syndicate have turned their attention to sex, and their work contradicts most of what the sex experts said and still say. The body is *not a sex machine*. It is not only a self-healing system. It is designed for connection.

Sexual healing is based on the premise that we are each a half person and by our nature codependent. We need someone else to become whole, and the self-fulfilled individual is an oxymoron. Even if we become self-fulfilled or self-healed, we can only be half fulfilled and healed without another person. Sexual healing is maximizing our capacity for connection, and the body is an instrument with which we can establish, promote, and maintain that healing bond.

The physiology of sexual healing views the body as an enchanted, resonating musical instrument on which our minds play and which can be used as a means of celebrating and actualizing our connection with another person. A *machine* is an apparatus of interrelated parts which is used to do work—in this case sex. An *instrument* is an object through which something is expressed. A car is a machine, but a violin is an instrument. You drive and operate the former, but you play and express with the latter. One of your key decisions on the way to sexual healing is whether you will see your body as a machine or an instrument.

Sexual healing can be so powerful that, when two lovers view their bodies as instruments in a duet of delight rather than machines going through eroto-electric sex circuits, they can actually begin to look like each other. Their bodies are transformed by their connection. Recent research shows that people who intimately connect over time begin to resemble each other in body and face.[7] If our bodies are physically transformed by our intimate connection, then sexual healing is possible through our connection because body changes body by the process of loving merging. This is the power of the physiology of sexual healing.

To fully realize our sexual healing potential, we must play our sensual instrument beyond mere genital interaction. Most of us have been raised to refer to our sex organs as our genitals, but sexual healing views many other body systems as sensual systems.

BEYOND THE SKIN GAME: SOUND SEX

Life, sex, and sound go hand in hand. Bird songs, whale songs, and other life-sustaining mating and reproductive behaviors rely on systems of calls, groans, and whistles sometimes equal in complexity to written musical scores. Sex research tends largely to ignore the sound of sexuality. Sensate focus and its teasing, touching, rubbing, and caressing is an epidermal phenomenon—a matter of skin-to-skin friction. It neglects sound waves and sensations beyond touch. "Feel and make yourself felt" is the mechanical way. It does not teach us how to listen and understand.

Sexology and psychology emphasize self-assertion and making yourself understood. Both movements see our chief responsibility to be the clear verbal expression of our feelings, not detecting subtle meanings and trying to understand and listen with our hearts for the symphony played by the human spirit. In fact, sex therapists warn strongly against "listening for anything other than words." It is the lover's problem to take care of and assert himself or herself. Sexual healing involves sensual listening and understanding before we try to be understood.

THE UNIVERSAL SIGH OF SEX

My own work reveals that sound plays one of the key roles in sexuality. There is something spiritual in sex sounds, and some researchers outside the sex establishment have begun to understand the transcendent aspects of what sex sounds convey. Some go so far as to suggest that they have discovered the "sound" that represents the spirit, soul, or a feeling of total merging and commitment. It is exactly the sound people make when their sexual intimacy has resulted in complete fulfillment, happiness, and release. That sound is "aahhh"—the delightful sigh of total contentment that signals complete union with self, someone else, something more, the present moment, and sensual delight.

The sound "aahhh" is found in almost every language. God, Ra, Jah, Allah, Brahma, Atman, Yahweh, Ram, Baal, Ahura Mazda, Og, Hachiman, Mab, nagual, mana, aumakua, wakan, and huaca are all words that refer to God or the universal spirit.[8] You read in Chapter 8 that in

Hawaiian *aloha* means literally to give and receive the breath of life and love, and this is the goal of sexual healing—to breathe love and life into each other, particularly at times of illness and suffering.

Sonic Sex Chants

The sound "aahhh" represents giving in to what is, just letting go, and relaxing the jaw and the throat. Try it yourself. Lower your shoulders, close your eyes, think of someone you truly and sincerely love, and say "aahhh." Research shows that your blood pressure will drop, your heart slow, and your brain waves change to relaxing patterns called alpha and theta waves.

The ancient Hawaiian chanting of the kahuna or healers was based on the resonance of the roof of the mouth beneath the brain, which—during chanting—was believed to send healthy and healing vibrations through the brain itself. (The limbic or emotional parts of the brain rest just on top of the roof of the mouth.) The kahuna based their medicine on the assumption that our bodies and all of nature are musical and based on vibrations in harmony with all that exists. Remember, these ancient healers were no mere amateurs or new age gurus when it came to the practice of medicine. Thousands of years before we ever thought of it, the kahuna were performing cataract surgery with sharpened blades of grass, doing brain surgery by opening the skull, doing a repair, and then replacing the missing skull piece with a coconut section. It is said that the kahuna were able to arrest cancer![9] Researchers at Johns Hopkins University have found that the kahuna may have taken certain substances from plants, fish, and worms that preliminary findings indicate can retard the growth of cancer cells.

Ritualistic chanting, praying, incantations, affirmations, and the uttering of holy words are worldwide practices. Meditative chanting has been shown to correct serious health problems including irregular heart rate.[10] When I began to teach the patients in my sex clinic to chant, they felt uncomfortable. They believed the lessons of the sex syndicate that sex sounds result *from* sex touching and do not result *in* sensual feelings, but I emphasized that going through the motions triggers the emotions. I suggested that making sex sounds *is* a way of making love and learning to feel love. I suggested that couples could learn to feel more love by chanting lovingly.

Porno-sound

The sex syndicate thinks that the sound of music could be somewhat helpful in "setting the mood"—preludes to passion. Sex therapists often suggest the playing of "romantic" music. In the 1960s a string instrument called the sitar dominated many water bed sexcapades, and almost all explicit sexual instructional movies, and X-rated videotapes contain "sex tracks" of some of the most annoying, distracting, and intrusive music. Pornographic movies often use music in place of a live sound track because of the expense involved in recording the sex sounds made by the demonstration "lovers," or because the "lovers" make no sex sounds because they are acting. The current popularity of amateur X-rated videos attests to the fact that it is the real sound of sex that is truly arousing.

In my clinic, I asked couples who wanted to rent erotic tapes to rent only the "amateur" type. I asked them *not* to watch the tape but to just listen to the sound track. Every couple who tried what they called this "porno-sound" approach reported more arousal by natural and spontaneous sex sounds than by the explicit visual images. Their minds were giving the meaning to the sounds of sex rather than their brains reacting to imprinted and meaningful visual sex images.

A CELLULAR SYMPHONY AND DNA DUETS

Most of us are emotionally moved by music. While preferences vary, music seems to have a powerful effect on us. It can make us cry, feel joy, and experience sexual arousal. As you listen to your radio today, count the number of songs you hear that really move you. What melodies seem to have a strong effect on you? Do any have a sexually arousing effect? What melodies might arouse your lover? There is something within all of us that responds and reacts to rhythm and melody.

Researchers have discovered that the body itself is intrinsically musical, right down to the DNA that makes up our genes. Geneticist Susumu Ohno has translated the strands of DNA that are inside each of us to musical notes.[11] There are four nucleotides or genetic markers on each strand of DNA. Dr. Ohno and his wife, Midori, assigned the musical note do to the nucleotide cytosine, re and mi to adenine, fa and so to guanine, and la and ti to thymine. When a musical key and timing were added, the resulting music was majestic and inspiring. People who have heard these "human symphonies" mistake them for Mozart, Bach, Brahms, and Chopin, and they are often moved to tears. It is possible that each of us has our own song within that actually "is us." In terms of sexual healing, the survival of the fittest translates not to the strongest or most competitive but to the most harmonious.

IN TUNE TOGETHER?

Einstein, famous for his love of the violin, proposed theories that come close to offering a "music and beat" for our universe. He spoke of the dance of electrons and reverberation between wave and particle. At a meeting in the 1940s attended by almost all the great scientists and Nobel Prize laureates in the world, it was reported that—for recreation and relaxation from the hours of deep thinking—most of the group brought along their favorite musical instruments. They formed their own orchestra, which those who heard them compared favorably with the New York Philharmonic. Einstein said, "Music and scientific research are nourished by the same source of longing, and they complement one another in the release they offer."[12]

My clinical experience indicates that most therapists who tune into the rhythmic dancing between the lovers who come to them for help can "hear" dissonance or missed beats in couples having sexual problems. The most sensitive and therefore the best therapists are not touch technicians but conductors of connections who help restore rhythm to a relationship. The result is new symphonies between lovers to replace the solos that can cause emotional arrhythmia. Like experienced maestros, these therapists can sense disharmony beyond words. They seem to hear that the songs of some couples are incompatible and that they have been unable to learn to sing together. These therapists can change a couple feud to a healing fugue.

The sex experts tend to focus on sexual proficiency and skill. Much like the violinist who is technically proficient but somehow seems unable to make her instrument sing, the sex therapists emphasize the mechanics and the machine over the inspiration, the performance instead of the feeling, and the solo rather than the duet.

SEXUAL SYNCHRONICITY

Sexual healing involves interactional synchrony, or mirroring of each other's body motions and rhythms. By observing people in courtship, scientists have documented the fact that intimate human connection is signaled by the establishment of a gentle mutual rhythm.[13] A dance of connection takes place in which heads are tilted in the same direction, bodies move easily and in the same direction, and the people connecting seem to sway and rock in unison. Sexual healers recognize these connection compositions and learn to maximize them.

As I work with couples in sexual healing, I can hear them coming into tune together and playing and moving in synchronous harmony. Rather than using the typical "talk and teach" approach to therapy, I often try to illustrate this sensuous synchronicity by playing excerpts from pieces of classical music while my technician videotapes each partner and the couple together. Judging from their facial and bodily reactions, some husbands were "Mozart" while their wives were "Bach." Other husbands were "Brahms" while their partners were "Chopin." Some couples seemed to smile, relax, move toward each other, and merge when a piece of music combined their inner compositions. When I showed the couples these tapes, they often reacted with hope and insight into their potential to make new and better music together. They would learn how to stop trying to put the moves *on* each other and how to move *with* each other.

A child psychologist recently reported a fascinating case of healing sound to physician Larry Dossey. It involved an eleven-year-old autistic boy who had never uttered a word and was diagnosed with catatonic schizophrenia or a mental state of stupor. The psychologist played Bach's "Jesu, Joy of Man's Desiring," and the boy began to weep. When the music ended, the boy spoke the first words of his life. "That is the most powerful music I have ever heard; now I can speak," he whimpered.[14] If the body can respond so powerfully to music, it must indeed "be" music. It is an enchanted and erotic instrument on which powerful sexual intimacy can be played in unison with another enchanted instrument we choose to love.

Sexual healing requires our awareness that it is our genes and not our genitals that are really making love to each other. When any two of us make love, in a sense all of us have made love because we are all of the same genetic stuff. Sexual healing does not involve an individual set of sex glands calling out to another set. It is the process of merging our personal identities and sharing our songs with another singer so that we may all sing better together. Sexual healing includes spending time chanting together, sensing each other beyond words, singing together, sitting together listening to the same music, and, possibly, listening to your own music composed from the scores of your very souls.

One sexual healer in my clinic gave a musical description to his therapy experience. "We used to be on different parts of the same song. I was in the prelude, and he was already at the finale. Then we realized that we were both playing the wrong song. Now we seem to be in sync with one another. After we have made love, it is like the allegro is over and we are resting together in perfect harmony. It's like we made something together—like an orgasmic duet. It wasn't his orgasm or mine. It seemed more like it was ours and everybody's. It's like when the orchestra finishes a wonderful performance and the audience feels like it really was a part of it all."

Talk with your lover about sexual sound. Here are six questions and suggestions that may lead to a different way to understand sex problems and solutions:

Sex-ercises for Making Music Together

1. What is your own "sex song"? By this I am not talking about a favorite romantic ballad; I am referring to the piece of music that best seems to represent your sexual style and the rhythm of your relationship. How has the composition changed over the years? Have you lost the beat?

2. Instead of using the usual psychological jargon, such as *hostile, angry, defensive, depressed,* or *withdrawn,* use songs or music to describe your mood. Sit together and listen to a selected piece of your own "mood music" to help your partner "feel" what you feel beyond words.

3. What is your partner's "song of life"—a piece of music that seems to reflect his or her sexual style? How does it compare and combine with yours? How do the tone, the key, the melody, the harmony, and the rhythm compare?

4. What musical work best represents the type of sensual interaction you would both like to have together now?

5. As a new form of foreplay, lie nude together in bed, side by side, not quite touching. Look into each other's eyes and listen to the music you have selected that represents the sex life you both want. Feel the music, and "rehearse" your sexual interaction in your minds and to the music. When the music is over, the rest of the evening is up to you.

6. Try a new type of "oral love" by learning to chant together. Find a sound that you both find soothing—perhaps the "aahhh" sound I mentioned earlier. Repeat this sound quietly together in private. This may be uncomfortable at first, but it can lead to new feelings of closeness.

CEREBRAL COUPLING

Sexual healing is not only melodic it is electronic. I am not referring to the type of individual energy buildup and discharge suggested by the sex establishment but to the actual exchange of body energy between two people who are meaningfully and intimately connected on the five healing levels. Modern medicine bases much of its diagnosis on the electrical impulses given off by the human body. The activities of the heart and the brain are often measured by electronic recording devices—the electrocardiogram and the electroencephalogram respectively. The sex syndicate focus has been on the flesh and fluids of the body and genitals. It missed completely the point that the sex act is also an electronic event!

As startling as it may seem, the electronic impulses of our brains can be transmitted from person to person in ways we do not yet understand. Researchers placed subjects in soundproof and darkened Faraday cages. These are devices made of a lead screen that filters out all outside electromagnetic activity. Each subject was instructed to close his eyes and to try to communicate with another subject using his brain. The EEG analysis showed that during the periods the subjects said they were trying to send their "brain waves," the electrical impulse patterns in the brains of the "receivers" began to match and parallel those of the senders.[15]

In this same study, one set of subjects reported feeling that their "brains had totally blended." The EEG patterns verified that when the couple tried to communicate cerebrally, the electrophysiological patterns had become identical.[16] Psychologist Jeanne Achterberg refers to "transpersonal imagery," or the ability of the consciousness of one person to affect the body of another.[17] Mutual meditation and intimate shared imagery are examples of transpersonal connection that help promote sexual healing. Attempts to verify communication beyond physical communication have been consistently successful.[18] Lovers who say they can communicate beyond words and bodies are not hopeless romantics or new age gurus. They are describing verifiable scientific facts about cerebral electronic loving.

When we connect intimately with someone, our brains fall into a cerebral synchronicity. We connect on an eroto-electrical level beyond our present measurement devices.[19] You can identify people who are relating in cerebral synchronization by observing their interaction, how they seem to move and sway together bodily and how their glances and words seem to create a new composition. Use your hand to mark the beat of their connection and to conduct the rhythm of their relationship as you sense it. In effect, you have become an eroto-encephalograph, registering their connection beyond the capacities of modern medical recording devices.

Try "cerebral synchronization" with your own relationship. It will take some practice, because you have been well indoctrinated by the sex syndicate to rely on your words and your bodies rather than your sixth sense related to your immune and healing system. You are more used to trying different postures than looking for a different way to connect on different levels in your sex life, but try a new way to "come together."

Sex-ercises for the Feeling Mind

1. Sit in separate rooms. Close your eyes and try to sense the communication from your partner. Turn off your inner dialogue, focus on your breathing, and relax your muscles. It will be a "sense" and not a verbal communication that comes to you, because it is likely that your brain waves are synchronizing. Don't try to use your ears. It is your mind that is merging.

2. Pay attention to those times when it just seems like the wrong or right time to have sex. Trust, don't reject your senses. Rely on your "sex sense" for a month, and you will see that when you do have sex, it is much more fulfilling. It is often helpful to hold, touch, and embrace sensually even when you don't feel like it; such activity can result in sexual feelings as often as sexual feelings result in the desire for such behaviors. It is also important, however, to pay attention when something between you seems to be saying that it is not the right time to be physically intimate or that physical connection is urgently needed.

3. Try to seduce your partner with brain power. Sexual healing accepts the existence of human magnetism, so try to feel its pull. Don't dress up in a sexy costume or plan a romantic evening, as sex therapists often recommend. Instead, spend one whole day sending mental sex messages silently to your partner, wherever he or she may be. When you get in bed together that night, lie still and send some more "sex waves." You will be surprised how seductive your brain can be.

4. Have sex with your partner when he or she isn't home. Lie in bed or on the couch, close your eyes, put on sensual music or your "combined love concert." Go through your couple composition with your brain. Use your brain, not your vibrator or your hand. Don't expect the same type of reaction you may have when you masturbate. Although you may experience genital arousal and even physical orgasms, this will be a unique but very fulfilling experience beyond genital sensations.

5. Try to "feel" your partner when he or she is not near you. To do this, you must open your mind. You can't be open to learning about the unknown when your mind is full of the known. Free yourself from "cognitive clutter" and ruminations about daily details and stress. Sit down, breathe deeply, and just try to feel what your partner might be sending. You may be surprised at the love thoughts you intercept on your FM, or "feeling mind," station.

THE DANGERS OF DESYNCHRONIZED SEX

Current research on the natural rhythms of bodily processes supports my contention that there is something much more than biomechanical processes at work when we are being sexually intimate. The music of our genes, if played with the wrong instrument or without commitment to the theme of lasting love, can kill a relationship and maybe even kill you instantly! Drs. Martin S. Gizzi and Bernard Gitler of the New Rochelle Hospital Medical Center have discovered that even the contemplation of unfaithful or illicit sex is a major risk for coronary artery disease.[20] Their research has revealed that what they call "chaotic sex" with multiple partners or even thinking about such activity can result in heart disease or even sudden "sex death." They speak of "bigamy death" caused by sexual guilt and shame as a major heart attack risk, and they present several case studies to back up their assertions. Desynchronized sex may cause a potentially lethal desynchronization of heartbeat so that when you come, you go!

Death during intercourse is rare. It accounts for about 6 percent of all heart attacks. However, when it does happen, it happens more than 90 percent of the time in extramarital sex. Typically, it is the man who expires. He is usually more than thirteen years older than his extramarital partner and is usually inebriated.[21] While the stress of the alcohol, perhaps a rich meal, and the presence of a young and new partner contributes to the unhealthy situation, the cheating or violation of a committed bond also exacts a price on the heart. There is something in our center, a universal principle of sexual fidelity that is programmed into us. It is not learned or optional. Illicit and nonconnected sex is a potentially fatal attraction and exactly the opposite of sexual healing.

MANY PASSIONS, ONE LOVE:
THE NEED FOR SEXUAL VARIETY

But if faithful attraction and sexual fidelity are in our genes and are healthier for us than less committed sex, why is the thought of having different partners so appealing to us? Why is there so much infidelity? I suggest that our desire for multiple partners is preprogrammed into us *not* so we will sexually experiment outside committed relationships to widen the range and variability of the gene pool. Instead, we have a propensity for variety in partners so we can tolerate and enjoy the multiple personalities and life changes within our *one* partner and all the variations on his or her genetically programmed main theme.

Since each of us has many facets of personality, if we are loved for only one of them, we are in jeopardy of losing our lover. When we seek to meet our need for variety by finding actual multiple partners, we are distorting and corrupting our more natural adaptive capacity to enjoy all the personalities of and changes in our own elected life partner. The good guilt I described in Part I can freeze us in our tracks when we are tempted to cheat. It can send us back where we belong—having sex with all the different partners within our one partner and using our desire for sexual variety to adapt to and learn to tolerate and/or appreciate the variations of our partner's genetically programmed main theme. Our desire for variety is only a longing for variations on a theme of lasting love with our sexual healing partner, not a natural inclination for serial relationships.

IN TIME AND IN TUNE TOGETHER

Medical researchers are finally looking beyond the machine to the healthy and unhealthy rhythms of our connection with life. Some physicians are now considering Type A and Type B behaviors as related to differences in tone and volume of voice, tempo of speech and behavior, phrasing of sentences, timbre of voice, and pace of lifestyle. Other researchers are studying the health and healing implications of the conflict between *chronos,* or outside and imposed clock time (*chronos* as in chronic illness) and inside or personal time, called *kairos,* which stems from the natural rhythms of the body.[22] When we are out of sync, we may be more prone to illness, and when our intimacy is governed by imposed mechanical timing, stages, and measures of body response rather than tuned to our own internal rhythms, we may be vulnerable to sexual and health problems.

Artist Michel Foucault wrote, ''But couldn't everyone's life become a work of art? Why should the lamp or the house be an art object, but not our life?''[23] The sexual response model of sexual healing is based on the art of sex and the process of creating beauty and meaning together by merging not only our bodies but our most personal inner healers.

10

THE NEW SOCIAL PSYCHOLOGY OF SEXUAL HEALING
Responsible Intimacy and World Transformation

We have committed the Golden Rule to memory; let us now commit it to life.

Edwin Markham

Love can be found only in action, which is relationship.
J. Krishnamurti

THE QUESTION OF SEX

Why do you have sex? When you make love, what is the purpose of your intimacy? Do you have sex to get turned on, to get relief from being turned on, to turn someone else on, or to help him or her relieve sexual tension? Perhaps you have sex to express your love, to try to feel more loving, or to "get away from it all" and relieve stress. Maybe you have sex because it just seems like the thing to do or something you haven't done enough lately or because your lover expects it or you feel he or she deserves it. In addition to the new physiology of sexual response presented in Chapter 9, sexual healing requires a new social psychology of sex that sees the purpose of intimacy as unrelated to any of these reasons.

From the sexual healing perspective, sex is not just an expression of love. It is a means of expressing your sense of connection—the totality of your awareness of your feelings of oneness with everything and everyone. When you are a sexual healer, you don't have sex to get turned on, you have sex to become more tuned in. You don't try to turn someone else on but to help him or her tune in with you. You don't try to relieve tension but to increase tenderness and togetherness. The sex of sexual healing is not an escape, it is a physical celebration of connection on all five levels of intimacy.

SEXUAL ESCAPE

Seeing sex as an escape from the suffering self creates the sexual problems identified and treated by the sex establishment. Sex is often used like an erotic amphetamine or an ''upper'' drug of delight and a means to shut out the world rather than as the realization that we *are* the world. Sex has become extraordinarily complex, confused, and difficult over the last decades because we have focused more on how to do it than why.

Philosopher J. Krishnamurti writes, ''Sex is the ultimate escape—self forgetfulness—everything else is always 'me.' That there is only one act [sex] in which there is no emphasis on 'me,' so it becomes a problem.''[1] Sexual healing is intimate connection with another person and complete loss of one's selfish ego through the process of two becoming one. Since all healing requires connection, sex is a wonderful way to heal through one act that simultaneously allows freedom from selfishness, connection with another person, and connection with something more, the present moment, and a sensuality beyond the selfish me. Krishnamurti continues, ''Love is not the search for self gratification. Love exists only when there is self forgiveness, when there is complete communion [connection].''[2] This self-forgetfulness and complete union can be a way of life and loving that *leads* to sexual intimacy; it is not just a *consequence of* good sex.

The sex establishment has it wrong. You don't have sex so you can have a good life and good feeling. You can have sex because life and love feel so good that you want to share these feelings with someone else. As long as sex is the sole escape from selfishness, it remains a hiding place rather than a loving place for joining intimately. When we lead a life of less selfishness, sex is *another*—not the *only*—way we find connection.

THREE GOOD REASONS TO HAVE SEX

Sexual healing's three reasons for having sex are to heal oneself, to heal someone else, and to help heal the world. I described in Chapter 5 the psychoneuroimmunology of relationships other than healing bonds; each of these primarily biomechanical-driven interactions posits a purpose for sex that is not one of healing.

The thrill seeker is motivated by sexual attraction and under the influence of stress chemicals which can overstimulate the immune system. His or her primary purpose for having sex is to turn on and maintain the high from the addictive epinephrine that causes the thrill. The love junkie is fixated on falling into love rather than reflectively electing to love, and the result is addiction to elevations of phenylethylamine, which can cause imbalance in the immune system. The love junkie's primary reason for relating sexually is to avoid turning off and getting down or depressed because of a fall in the level of PEA. The love-sick attachment oriented are lulled into a sedated sexual dependence by the soothing of their endorphins. Their primary reason for having sex is to avoid being deserted and losing what they see as their sole source of the comforting chemicals that result in a sense of security. The love-blind and detached person suffers from a depletion of almost all the psychochemical associated with arousal to intimacy, perhaps because the pituitary gland functions inadequately (hypopituitarism), producing too little ACTH to continue to stimulate the adrenal glands. These people's primary reason for having sex is to find peace at any price and to keep their partners content. They may also cycle back through attraction and infatuation in an attempt to restimulate their psychochemistry by contacts with new and more exciting partners. All these sexual psychologies fall short of intimate bonding and the immune-balancing oxytocin release that leads to sexual healing. The psychology of sexual healing is volitional, rational, socially responsible merging with our lover to find meaning together on all five levels of the pentamerous model of sexual healing.

In Chapter 1, I suggested that the objectives of sexual healing are enhanced self-esteem, increased sense of intimacy, shared sense of life coherence, mindfulness of the present moment, and sensual expression of loving caring. Modern psychology has focused almost exclusively on only the first of these levels of connection—self-esteem and self-actualization. The new psychology of sexual healing allows a way to employ all five healing connections.

First, meaningful sexual intimacy allows us to connect with our higher self—the self that is shared by all of us. Sexual healing also allows us to connect with another person, to experience a sense of intimacy and sharing, to sense how he or she feels and thinks and how to give the gift of sensing these things from us. Sexual healing allows us to connect with someone else in finding higher meaning and purpose in life and in developing a shared sense of manageability and comprehensibility of life's endless chaos. It helps us combine with someone we love to be intensely aware of the present moment. Finally, sexual healing is thinking, behaving, and responding sensuously with another person. Much more challenging than ego or self-fulfillment psychology and the instrumental approach of the sex syndicate, the new psychology of sexual healing offers the higher reward of a more purposeful, giving, and caring life constructive rather than detrimental to society.

A more collective approach to social psychology is in keeping with the thinking of Krishnamurti. He writes, "The relationship between two people creates society; society is not independent of you and me; the mass is not by itself a separate entity but you and I in relationship to each other create the mass, the group, the society."[3] Sexual healing is the one human act that can integrate the five connections of healing at one time and also result in the most blissful and splendid of sensations. The most powerful healing act in the world also feels the best, and I suggest that the intense pleasure of meaningful physical intimacy is God's signal that it is intended as one of life's most healthy acts.

SEX IN ITS PLACE

Krishnamurti writes, "Sex has its place; but when the mind gives it the predominant place, then it becomes a problem."[4] Because sex can be so powerful, can accomplish so many connections at one time, and can be so intensely intimate, we have become dependent on sex as our sole means of self-forgetfulness. Sexual healing requires that we practice selflessness as often out of the bed as we do in bed so that when we make love, we love like we live. The twenty-five psychosocial factors from the Psychosocial Inventory described in Chapter 1 illustrate the range of connections necessary to be a sexual healer in a social and full life context.

Psychologist Jack Panksepp of Bowling Green State University states that his research and others shows that "it is just about proven that it is our own natural opiates, the endorphins, that produce the good feeling that arise during social contact with others."[5] Anthropologist Helen Fisher writes, "One fact is becoming undeniable. Infatuation is a physical as well as a psychological event."[6] Sexual healing is the ultimate mind-body event because it merges the altruistic mind with the sensuous body, and the result is a remarkably powerful healing event.

The ego or private self we call "I" has been the focus of sex syndicate psychology. The self-help movement is not too concerned with the larger or collective Self we all sense when we help someone or do something that brings more love and caring to the world. Listen to the self-involved, and you will hear personal pronouns, demands for space, things, and "my" way. Our society and its psychosocial policies have largely become the "I" policies of the ego and our conscious, aware, always striving "self."

A sexually healing marriage is first and foremost cooperative and dedicated to mutual caring. When I ask my patients who and for what they married, they reflect the sex syndicate psychology of "me." "Marriage is for my happiness, my fulfillment, for me to find love, or for my comfort and safety" are some of their answers. In the new psychology of sexual healing, we marry when we are ready to start loving and not because we think we have fallen in love. We marry not because we are ready to take a lover *for* ourselves but because we are ready to make a lover *of* ourselves with someone else.

TEACHING TO DEVELOP PERSONALITY OR CHARACTER

During the reign of the sex syndicate for the past forty years, a sexual psychology emerged to match the dominant sexual physiology model. This psychology is based on the assumption that one's sexual "personality" or self-identity is the single most important element in personal health and well-being.

One assumption of this psychology is that sex education is a strong positive influence on our children. John Dewey and other leading educational theorists asserted that schools should teach a life-enhancement and life-related curriculum. They believed that sex education should be a system for enhancing and protecting the sexual life of the individual as a means of developing his or her personality. Issues of caring, connection, and intimacy were almost ignored in favor of a focus on menstrual films, medical drawings of the genitals, and dire warnings of what were called the venereal diseases.

Some people believe that sex education has been influential and effective, and that it is now firmly entrenched in our schools. Others believe that it has been a powerfully corrupting force. They are all wrong. Now, even the most basic mechanical sex education is *not* found in most of our schools. The assumption that "school-based sex education" is the source of much of our sex knowledge—or many of our problems—is without foundation.

Very little of what could be defined as sex education has survived in our school curriculum.[7] Through the 1960s, sex education did not exist for most students. *Playboy* magazine and its imitators were the "texts" for young people. Hugh Hefner, according to former Director of the Kinsey Institute Paul Gebbard, had the "genius to associate sex with upward mobility."[8] Like the first school sex curricula, the Playboy philosophy was "me first and the best." Sexual prowess and sports car ownership were seen by our children as related, and adults became aware that what the young people were seeing in their magazines would have been illegal just years before. Immediate pressure for more publicly accountable sex education began.

Hundreds of "sex programs" were considered and attempted in the schools through the later 1960s and into the 1970s. Liberals wanted more explicit programs, and conservatives resisted any educational programs other than strict warnings about the danger of sex. Both groups ignored the issue of sexual meaning and healing. Sex was seen as an inevitable force that either could be used for self-recreation, enhancement, or escape or had to be contained, resisted, and controlled. The result was a watered-down mix of charts and chat that portrayed sex as a powerful and almost irresistible mechanical impulse surging through the loins. Sex was not seen as a form of meaningful connection; it was a biological threat to conservatives or an erotic ego entitlement to liberals. Our children were taught to be careful with this impulse so that "Mr. Sperm and Ms. Egg" wouldn't meet.

Even our youngest sex students laughed and secretly mocked our inadequate, awkward, and clearly uncomfortable approach. Teachers never seemed this nervous when they were teaching history! Most students already knew the mechanics. They wanted to know the meaning. They knew how, but they wanted to learn about why. Sex education still ignores these important healing issues.

When reactionaries cry foul and point to the "corruption of our young by sex education," their argument cannot be supported by the facts.[9] Whatever corruption is taking place is related more to the almost complete lack of sex knowledge. The sexual liberals failed to get their "erotic and selfish" version of sex into the schools, and the conservatives prevented any meaningful teaching about the role of values in sexuality in our lives. The real sex education that has had the most influence on our developing young adults is not offered by qualified teachers but by popular media, the sex syndicate's magazines, and the various sources of soft-core and hard-core pornography.

The real sex teachers of our children are other children. I overheard a kindergarten boy teaching sex to one of his classmates. His "text" was a torn sex magazine centerfold. "Look at those," he exclaimed in awe. "They're amazing. I wouldn't want to be a woman, because then I couldn't have a job. I would just stay home all day and play with my tits. That's what all men want to do all the time and that's what all women want them to do all the time."

It is the *lack* of character- and value-based explicit and comprehensive sexuality programs related to the everyday life decisions we all face that is a major cause of our sexual dilemma. We need such education if it includes the issues of meaning, caring, connection, and sexual altruism. Sex education on mechanics and sexual prowess results in more sexual suffering, not more sexual healing.

Films on menstruation, genital structure, and the danger of AIDS do not teach about sexuality in the context of life and love. They do not teach tolerance of various sexual orientations and lifestyles. Whatever sex education is taking place has very little influence in teaching the key point about sexual expression—what you do sexually is not just a matter of self-fulfillment. When you have sex, not only must you take self-responsibility but you must also take social responsibility. It is an issue of mutual responsibility for your lover and for all of us. If we think that sex education is already being offered and is influential, we can't begin to provide a sensitive and effective sex education to our children. If we think it should not be taught in our schools, we leave our children to the corrupt, covert curriculum of myth and pornography. Sexual healing can be taught, but first we must teach our children how to find tolerance, reflection, mutual responsibility, and meaning in their sexuality.

The new psychology of sexual healing suggests that there should be no sex classes in our schools. We need a comprehensive and principle-based sexuality program interwoven with the entire curriculum. We need to understand the sexuality involved in politics, marriage, families, parenting, history, science, and all of life. Every class on every topic should include material on intimacy, sexuality, and connection.

THE PENDULUM OF SEXUAL EXPRESSION

Another assumption of the sex establishment psychology is that the evolution of sexuality has always moved from repression to more freedom, so we should count on freedom winning out. The sex syndicate is committed to encouraging the inevitable movement away from our repressive past. Reactionaries warn that we move toward more and more sexual freedom until we kill ourselves with the inevitable social and physical consequences. Again, both the liberals and the reactionaries are wrong. We are lost in sexual confusion, in search of meaning with only the mechanics and looking to our genitals rather than contemplating with our minds. Philosopher Krishnamurti writes, "Sex becomes an extraordinarily difficult and complex problem so long as you do not understand the mind which is thinking about the problem."[10]

History teaches that there has always been a swing of the sexual pendulum between extreme control and repression and overreactive freedom.[11] We will not get out of our current sexual confusion by assuming that freedom will develop on its own. Nor will we solve our sexual problems through an attempt to stop sexual freedom through censorship, restriction, and denial of individual dignity. We can't fight the pendulum. Some warn that there is a growing resistance to sexual and individual freedom that could drive us back to sexual fear and ignorance. Others warn that blind striving to ride the wave of sexual freedom will result in the collapse of our most basic institution—the strong and lasting family. While the sex syndicate tries to push the line of sexual freedom and the sex cynics try to draw the line to stop it, basic and central principles and new meanings for our sexuality continue to be neglected.

THE DISASTER OF DIVORCE

The sex syndicate psychology teaches that divorce is one good way of finding self-fulfillment and can be done without very serious consequences and often with positive results for everyone concerned. The sex syndicate, in its eagerness to promote self-fulfillment and self-sexual gratification, is a major supporter of divorce. An entire industry has grown to aid the process of bailing out of a marriage and finding self-happiness and a new and better sex partner. At the other end of the spectrum are some cynics who say that marriage and loving can be "sexless." Again, both these orientations are wrong.

The fact is that divorce is almost always a disaster. The majority of our children will spend at least a portion of their lives without one of their parents to raise them. A majority will spend a part of their childhood with no father. The emotional and physical consequences of divorce for the adults and their children are devastating. Daughters of divorce are likely to be sexually unhappy, are more anxious and depressed, and tend to feel a profound sense of lack of control over their lives. They tend to make irrational and destructive marital choices themselves.[12] Sons of divorce tend to become more sexually aggressive and less socially responsible, have more learning problems, and break the law. Sexual healing requires serious reexamination of the consequences of ending our intimate relationships.[13] While some children of divorce may do well under optimal conditions (a divorce that leaves the children in a situation closely resembling a two-parent home), conditions are almost always far from optimal or there would not have been a divorce in the first place!

The sex syndicate thinks nothing of recommending divorce for the welfare of the self. It teaches the myth that divorce can be for the good of the children. Except in cases of actual abuse, this is almost never true. Neither is it true that a loveless marriage is good for the children or the spouses. What is needed is a new way to heal broken love. Classes on "fair fighting" are likely to be less helpful than mutual learning of intimate connection, sensual communication, and caring.

Sexual healing psychology teaches that divorce is almost always the beginning of trouble, not the end of it. The sex syndicate has discredited the idea of staying together for the children as surrender of self-fulfillment, but it is time to reexamine this idea. It takes at least four years for the biology of bonding to take hold, yet it is at about four years after marriage that most divorces take place. People who divorce before that time for reasons other than personal safety or the safety of the children do so because of lack of patience, effort, self-sacrifice, or the fact that they are thrill seekers, love junkies, or love-blind. We *should* consider staying together for our children, growing up, stopping fighting, and putting our efforts into a realistic and responsible healing of love. Sacrificing a part of our dream for the dreams of our children is one of the basic principles of sexual healing.

THE CRISIS OF PATERNAL DEPRIVATION

The sex syndicate social psychology suggests that a single parent can raise a child as successfully as two parents, so if you want to "find yourself" or your relationship does not seem to make you feel fulfilled, the children can always be raised by one parent.

The research, unfortunately, does not support the contention that single parenthood works very well for either the parents or the children, and being a healing parent is related to sexual healing and the maintenance of intimacy and connection in the family system. The feminist movement needed the assumption that the female could do without the male not only financially but in terms of team parenting. The sex establishment and males abdicating their family and financial responsibilities needed the assumption that women (since most single-parent homes are female run) could do parenting alone. Since editors, authors, and therapists were often single parents too, they also needed the assumption that single parenting is as good as and sometimes better than two-parent homes. They were all wrong.

Henry B. Biller, the leading authority on what he calls "paternal deprivation," warns that *single parent* means "mother parent alone." Statistically, single-parent homes are almost always woman-run homes. Studies on the effects on children of homes without a dad have yielded what Dr. Biller calls "a dramatic explosion of the data" regarding the dangers for children from paternal deprivation. Biller reviewed more than

1,000 studies documenting these dangers.[14] My own experience with single-parent homes over decades of clinical work supports Biller's warning that single parenting and paternal deprivation are two of the most dangerous social trends, and without sexual healing or committed and lasting intimacy between two people who can set aside or resolve their egotistical differences, these dangers can only worsen.

The evidence is clear. On almost every measure, children of two-parent homes do better than children of one-parent homes. Biller writes, "There is no longer a dispute. Well-fathered infants are more curious, more secure, more trusting, better at almost everything."[15] Physical, verbal, and sexual abuse are more common in single-parent homes, and crime is more likely to happen to and to be committed by the parent and children in such homes. A recent study of fifty-seven neighborhoods composed of 11,419 people showed that crime is not associated with race or poverty; it is associated with single-parent homes. The problem is that the only men around are criminals. We are still largely a sexist and patriarchal society, but we are also becoming depaternalized through our neglect of fatherhood.[16]

It is simply not enough for a boy or girl to have one good role model. Our children need a relationship model. When single parenthood is imposed by death or illness, the courage and sacrifices of the surviving parent help keep our society together. However, the large majority of single-parent homes occur by the selfish choice or neglect of one or both parents and their inability or unwillingness to work toward sexual healing.

Some men complain that they are prevented from parenting their children by selfish women favored and protected by the courts. Half of all children in the custody of their mothers have little or no contact with their fathers. Andrew Cherlin, a sociologist from Johns Hopkins University, has studied paternal deprivation and writes, "There's a relatively small group of well-educated and sensitive fathers who are prevented by custody arrangements from acting as responsible parents. But their numbers are dwarfed by those who don't give a darn."[17] The selfish sex of the sex syndicate contains the "I don't give a darn, I need what I need" emphasis, and single parenting has been one tragic consequence. The children that may come from our relationships are a component of sexual healing and not necessary obligations that fall to the woman.

Sexual healing psychology teaches that every cell in our bodies must sacrifice itself for the good of the whole. If it doesn't, our bodies mistake growth for health, and cancer results. Much this same "malignant me" growth has happened in family structure. Selfishness is growing so fast that it is crowding out our families. Both men and women have something very special to offer children. Sexual healing includes the goal of enduring and adaptive two-parent homes whenever possible if our loving and sexual health are to become one and the same thing.

PREMARITAL SEX AND PREMATURE DIVORCE

I have pointed out that the sex syndicate social psychology teaches that premarital intercourse is not only unavoidable and self-fulfilling but good romantic technique rehearsal for marriage. In fact, it is very rare in human society for breeding outside of marriage to be allowed. Ira Reiss writes, "The key societal function of marriage is to legitimize parenthood, not to legitimatize sexuality."[18] The key reason to limit premarital intercourse (not necessarily sexual intimacy) is to ensure that children will be raised by two adult parents. A new social psychology of sexual healing proposes that the purpose of marriage is not to guarantee property rights, assure the father that his children are biologically his own, provide readily available sex, or be a tool for self-growth. Sexual healing is based on the premise that marriage is for the collective good and that one important purpose of marriage is to provide for our children's welfare.

Premarital sex is sanctioned by the sex establishment so long as it is "safe," but it is almost always true that children or immature people have sex in childish and often dangerous ways. The result of promiscuity has been a bumper crop of children being raised by teenage girls alone, high divorce rates, widespread institutionalization of our children, and almost complete abandonment of parental responsibility.

The new social psychology of sexual healing proposes that intercourse before the formation of a committed relationship teaches nothing except selfish sexual gratification, and even that is not assured in casual interactions. The increase in premarital sex has not reduced the rate of sexual suffering in marriage and divorce in our society. It does not produce "coparenting," and it does not teach commitment, caring, or healing. Premarital sex is a selfish expression of a sexual need, and it is time that we considered a return to the lesson of "no intercourse unless you are married."

It is important to remember that not having intercourse does not mean not having sex. It is not true that any sex leads to "going all the way." If we keep telling our children that sex is an uncontrollable impulse that, once started, has a life of its own, they will behave according to this self-fulfilling prophecy. Sexual healing is based on the assumption that sex is not an impulse, it is a choice. It doesn't "happen to you," you elect to do what you do and with whom you do it. What you are and what you will become are products of the choices you have made and will make, not the flow of your hormones.

The psychology of sexual healing proposes in the place of premarital intercourse direct and explicit education in "outercourse" or mutual masturbation, sensual massage, mutual verbal arousal, intermammary coitus (penis between the breasts), axillary coitus (penis in the armpit), and numerous other ways to engage in erotic activity short of penis-vagina intercourse and intravaginal ejaculation with or without a condom. Whenever possible, we should teach our children that sexual intercourse is for strong and enduring relationships only.

EXTRAMARITAL PARENTING: THE SURRENDER OF PARENTHOOD

Sex establishment social psychology advocates day-care centers and other surrogate parent arrangements as suitable substitutes for in-home parenting. Surrogacy is a big part of the sex syndicate psychology. Surrogate sex partners are part of the "replaceable parts" approach to sex because sex is seen as something done *to* or *for* but not *with* someone else. Intimacy is viewed as interchangeable. Surrogate lovers teach surrogate love, and mechanically improved but still nonloving partners return from the bedrooms of their "surrogate sex therapists" doing it better but killing their marriages.

The often unrecognized other half of the surrogacy movement of the sex syndicate is parental surrogacy, a more subtle yet more deadly influence on our families. Raising children is one of the most difficult challenges in life. The sex syndicate came very close to embracing the belief that children are the inevitable punishment of careless sex, and if they can't be at least temporarily avoided while the joy of sex is pursued, they should at least not be allowed to get in the way of the pursuit of life, liberty, sex, and our selfish goals.

We seem to have forgotten that parenting is something we do *with* and *for* our children, not *to* them. Good parents do not raise their children, they connect and develop with them. The sex syndicate social psychology suggests that it may not be enough for us to have our careers and our orgasms. The self-fulfillment movement says that if we were too busy fulfilling ourselves when we were young, perhaps now we can try "doing a little parenting" as another way to find ourselves. Artificial insemination of the single woman desiring the "pregnancy and parenting" experience has begun, and many men dump their older wives for younger models so they can have their chance to try parenting. As one wife pointed out, "I think many men owe their success to their first wife and the second wife to their success."

There are four major risks to children in their interaction with their parents. They may be neglected, with most of the upbringing falling to institutions outside the home. They may be deprived, not having enough caring parental contact when the parents are home but too busy and self-involved to provide support and guidance. They may be abused, and suffer physical, verbal, or sexual molestation. Finally, they may be exploited, forced to take care of their immature and selfish parents. Children raised outside the home are more likely to suffer all four of these development setbacks.

U.S. Census figures show that only 30 percent of preschool children are cared for in their own homes. Forty-one percent of them are in another home, 15 percent have some form of group care, 14 percent go to work with their mothers, and 5 percent are "unaccounted for"—thousands of children simply left without adult supervision.[19] If the trend continues, sex syndicate psychology will have encouraged us to accept not only extramarital sex but also extramarital parenting.

Today, most children spend more time watching television than they do interacting with their parents. Because of the impact of the sex syndicate social philosophy, most homes are characterized by one tired and stressed mother wanting only to get her children fed and to bed so she can find just a little time for herself in front of the television, fix the lunches for tomorrow, and collapse in bed to ready herself for the next day. America's children spend twice as much time in institutions as interacting with their own families.[20] If healing is lasting connection, this institutionalization of our families is a major health risk.

Much of the research conducted on day care and its impact on children shows that good quality day-care does not appear to have any adverse impact on most aspects of young children's development. However, is that all we ask for our children, the absence of adverse effects? The sex syndicate's psychology urges us to avoid adverse sex effects, dysfunctions, and hang-ups, and their avoidance of "dysfunction" extends to our parenting philosophy. Do we want more for our children than the absence of negative experiences during their growing years? If so, we must consider the power of lasting intimacy with one person as the antidote to their institutionalization. One of my patients illustrated the dilemma of responsibility when she said, "I spend more time picking my kids up, dropping them off, and watching them do something like play soccer and dance than I do just being with them. I feel like their guardian more than their mother and like I'm standing by as they grow up rather than growing with them."

Moreover, most of the research on day-care centers is done on the more expensive, higher quality, and more closely supervised centers, not the more abundant marginal ones that most Americans can afford. Researchers without an investment in the "selfish sex" approach are worried about the principle behind the day-care movement—the intentional disruption of the mother-child bond.[21] (Remember, statistically the father-child bond has already been almost completely destroyed by the paternal deprivation syndrome.) I have seen in my practice the sad impact of "career women" regretting and despairing that not only their children but they themselves have missed most of one of the most beautiful and important parts of human life—loving and raising a child through the growing years.

Census data collected by the U.S. government over the last ten years show that there has been a doubling of teens killing teens, a 20 percent increase in teen pregnancy, and a 14 percent decrease in percentage of students finishing high school.[22] Maybe more of us should be wondering if we aren't failing in our roles as healers and our healing responsibilities to our society.

Sexual healing social psychology suggests that we have yet to see the "sleeper effects" of the surrender of our parenting to institutions. All the data are not in. We do not know enough about day care to accept it as an alternative to traditional parenting. Parenting is not something you "do" that can be assigned to others. Like your role in sexual healing and in your intimacy with your lover, parenting is who you are with your children.

Adults have the ability to bond with one another and with their children, but our children can only attach dependently to us. When we sever that attachment, we predispose them to neglect of their most basic emotional needs.

GOING HOME AGAIN

The sexual healing social psychology I propose suggests that one parent stay home as primary caretaker of the children. Unfortunately, in a society in which men make more money than women, for many families, it will make more financial sense for the woman to stay home. We desperately need a paradigm shift that does not allow such financial discrimination, but we still cannot afford the increasing negative effects of the institutionalization of child care. Meaningful, ritualistic, consistent family life is lacking, and the effects are potentially devastating. If there is a decision to have children in a still sexist society, sexual healing begins with more women considering staying home to raise children for a part of their lives. Sexual healing also requires that men consider staying with their families as the primary source of support for most of their lives.

When we have a career, we live to work. When we have a job, we work to live. Most men and women do *not* have careers in the sense of total personal commitment to their work as the core of their lives. Nor do they want them. Careers following the definition I offer here constitute about 2 percent of the working population, and this figure includes almost every occupation that could be close to being considered a "life career."[23] Fewer than one in four of us are on the "career track" rather than the "job track," and there is absolutely nothing wrong with this. Our worth is not measured by our accomplishments, achievements, or career status but by our loving commitment to others. Most of us work at the ordinary and necessary jobs that keep society running—filing, working in stockrooms, driving trucks, preparing food, running the cash register, and delivering the mail. Most women and men could easily move in and out of jobs without destroying their "careers."

Some feminists protest that men have careers and therefore women should, too. But statistics show that most men don't have careers as I have defined them either. Particularly those men who have chosen to take responsibility for their families have usually had to take one of the key steps in sexual healing and give up a huge chunk of their selfish dream for the dream of enduring intimacy and a happy, healthy family. The Hopi Indians have a saying that pertains here: "A man cannot get rich if he takes proper care of his family." Getting yours and getting rich are imperatives of the social psychology of the sex syndicate, but these motives have led to much of our parental neglect.

If we truly want careers, then what is our purpose in having children? Do we really want to have it all while everyone around us gets less because of it? There are rare people who may be able to handle a career and a family and be good, loving, present parents, but as painful, difficult, and unpopular as it may be, most of us must make a sexual healing decision: "me first" or "my family first"? Until we confront that choice, we will continue to try to have it all and end up with unhappy families and children.

Sexual healing social psychology also suggests that women who work and use day care are themselves at health risk. Despite claims of increasing equality and opportunity, most women have not the opportunity to change their lives but only to add more work to them. It is often the mother who carries the responsibility for finding the day-care center, carrying on her career, maintaining the home, and often "parenting" the husband, whose job is still seen as more important. I suggest that day-care centers can represent a covert if unintentional means for continuing the subservience of women by offering the illusion that their work is lessened and opportunities increased.

PERSONAL PROFIT AND PARENTAL DEFAULT

You have seen how complex sexual healing is and what difficult choices and sacrifices it requires. Much of the argument for parental default and the necessity of institutionalizing our child care is based on the assumption that times are tough and it takes two incomes to survive. Even allowing for inflation, per capita disposable income is twice as high now as it was forty years ago and three times as high as it was sixty years ago.[24] Complain as we might, it is not a more expensive world we *must* live in. Again, it is our selfishness and the more expensive life *we have chosen* that are our problem. Contrary to the poverty cries of many, most of today's parents *can* live much better on one income than their own parents could. Because of acquisitiveness masked as necessity, they choose *not* to do so.

The sex syndicate's social psychology seems to have forgotten that our parents and our parents' parents made much less selfish choices than we are making. Our grandparents accepted the fact that they would begin their marital lives residing with their own parents or in cramped tenement apartments. Many of our parents and we ourselves did the same. Our great-grandparents raised their children without electricity, running water, or central heating. This does not, of course, mean that we should return to such hardship. Many of us have heard our parents tell us how much more difficult their lives were than ours, and we have become skeptical of these war stories. It is true, however, that our parents' goals were most often "for their children." Sexual healing requires a return to this sense of obligation and responsibility.

Partly because our own parents did and gave so much for us, today's parents have been taught to view the word *necessity* much differently than their grandparents did. New cars and VCRs are now items we have to have. We buy a lot of time-saving devices but seem to have less time than ever before. We seem to desire more "stuff" so we can experience more, but sexual healing involves a joy in the simplicity of "just being together." Author Geoffrey Godbey wrote, "Own less, do less, and say no." We can say no more easily if we are constantly reminded of the urgent *yes* of commitment to our relationships that overrides all else.

It is almost always our *choice* to seek two incomes. Most (certainly not all) fathers or mothers could make enough money to support their families if there were two-parent homes governed by less selfishness and a lower threshold for "necessity." We must overcome the scarcity hypotheses that there is just so much of the essential in this world and that we have to compete rather than connect to get it.

Sexual healing psychology says that the sins of the parents are being visited upon our children. Our current abandonment of parental responsibility in the name of self-fulfillment or our helpless surrender to overwhelming and unavoidable sexual impulse is unmatched in human history. If we continue to follow the sex syndicate ego psychology, we remain romantic reactionaries rather than reasoned reflectors about the meaning of our sexuality.

CELEBRATING SNEAKINESS

Another sex syndicate implication is that the individual right to happiness overrides all other rights. Perhaps the central theme of this social philosophy is erotic ego entitlement or the presumed right to the pursuit of a sex life, career, our piece of the pie, sexual freedom, and sexual joy at almost any cost. "My right to swing my arm ends where your nose begins" is a popular quotation. Such a philosophy ignores the general and collective welfare that is the context of sexual healing.

I remember the large sign hanging in a hotel lobby welcoming members of the annual get-together of the American Society of Sexologists. The sign read "Welcome ASS." When other guests at the hotel protested, the desk clerk said that he was afraid to ask them to take it down because "these people know their rights" and "we don't want to look like we are not liberal and tolerant. Whether we like it or not, I guess we'll have to look at their *ASS* for a few days." As humorous as this seemed to many, it was offensive to others. The sign remained untouched. The sex syndicate can be intimidating in their pursuit of their rights.

Most of our laws are necessary, reasonable, and socially healthy, yet most of us break them regularly. A yellow traffic light no longer means prepare to stop. It means, after a quick check in the mirror for the police, hurry up and beat the red. Joggers run in front of cars, cyclists dodge in and out of traffic, we push, shove, use illegal drugs, disregard no-smoking signs, and ignore the most common of courtesies. We have become a pushy, crude, rude society, and even though much of the world envies what we have, few envy who and how we are.

A Harris poll recently reported that 53 percent of "yuppies" now do their own taxes because they cannot find accountants willing to cheat along with them.[25] "If I can get away with it, I'll do it" seems to be our philosophy, and no society can survive long with such a focus. Sexual healing is collective healing manifested through a responsible two-person intimate connection, not a selfish escape from our obligations to our world.

"Everybody else does, so I have to, too" is another version of the entitlement message. The CYA or cover your ass approach to life has become commonplace. In consideration of the recent concern about the HIV virus, the sexual policy seems to be have sex when, with whom, and how you want to, but cover your genitals.

It is not just the damage to our social system by the "get away with it" approach that is dangerous but the damage to the personal psyche that takes a toll on our health. If a majority of us are sneaky, unprincipled, personality focused rather than character focused, and if most of us are in the "getting away with something" mode, then most of us must be feeling small but nagging twinges of guilt. We must be constantly looking over our shoulders for the law, checking the mailbox for an IRS audit, waiting anxiously for a menstrual period to start (often seen as a blessing rather than the older term "the curse"), or sitting by the phone for a doctor's call with the results of an HIV test. Like spoiled children fearing we have gone too far, we wait fearfully for our punishment.

Fathers who have deserted their children must, at least in some times of quiet reflection, wonder about their children's welfare and what they themselves may have missed. Mothers must reflect during their workdays about their babies at the day-care center, wondering if caring can be divided into night and day or if it is an all-or-nothing responsibility. They and their work-focused spouses must wonder at least a little if they too are not missing something they can never recover and if their children aren't missing almost everything.

Men and women who are cheating on their spouses must at least once in a while wonder about their husbands or wives at home and maybe feel just a little guilty and ashamed. Only the anonymitization of the rest of the world, the ability to see others as "out there" and not a part of us defends us from the deeper sense that the people we cheat on, cut off in traffic, or take advantage of are really a part of us! I believe that "distance defense" is weakening and an overthrow or provolution against the sex syndicate personality ethic is beginning. If character is composed of a balance between the courage to represent ourselves and the consideration to care for everyone else as much as we care for ourselves, sexual healing requires much more than sex techniques—it requires character.

Sexual healing psychology suggests that the universal principles of collective responsibility rather than individual rights lead to better health for ourselves and our society. The focus on complying to avoid punishment must be replaced by trying to do the right thing because it is right. Perhaps with this new social psychology, we will rediscover the real joy and healing power of sex—the elective physical expression of lasting and committed love—as we teach our children how to find the same joy and moral responsibility. Perhaps then we can help heal the world together.

PART THREE

HOW TO
BE A
SEX
SHAMAN

*It is important to remember that we are,
each of us, angels with only one wing.
And we can only fly embracing each other.*

Luciano de Crescenzo

11

OVERCOMING SEXUAL COMPULSION AND EROTIC ANESTHESIA
Discovering Your Sexual Style

Breathes there a man with hide so tough who says two sexes aren't enough?

Samuel Hoffenstein

Love is a dirty trick played on us to achieve the continuation of the species.

W. Somerset Maugham

THE PROBLEM OF THE MATCH

"How can we come together when we don't seem to go together," said the wife. "We just don't match sexually. He's always hot and ready, and I'm hardly ever interested and take a long time to get ready. He's like the Energizer bunny and keeps on going and going. I'm like a cement wheel. You have to really push and push to get me started, and even then I don't go too far for too long. We're a complete sexual mismatch. Whose kind of sex do you have when you have two different styles?"

Sexual differences between partners such as the ones identified by this woman interfere with sexual healing because, instead of being a means of connection, sex often becomes either a contest or a compromise. Sometimes, the conflict between sexual styles results in one of the partners being assigned the dreaded sex establishment label *dysfunctional* while the other partner feels vindicated in style but unfilled in sexual needs. Other times, a sexual style compromise is established, leaving both partners unhappy as each now has sex more, less, or differently than he or she would like.

Sexual healing requires a view of sexuality free from pejorative labels, contention over the place of sex in a relationship, and expectations of what constitutes the proper way or frequency to have sex. Sexual healing is based on the awareness, understanding, integration, and mutual development of sexual styles. It involves being creative more than compromising and developing a unique couple intimacy style rather than submitting to often self-fulfilling prophecies about how someone is or ought to be sexually.

THE FOUR-YEAR HITCH

The objective of two lovers is almost always the same: to find meaning in their individual lives *and* in their life together. The sexual or intimate expressional styles of two partners are typically much different, and these differences may become more and more apparent as the relationship ages. My research indicates that the objectives of intimacy, mutual pleasure, joyful interaction, and healing through sensual relationship require at least four years to develop fully. The psychoneurosexual system and its psychochemistry also require at least that long for the heat of epinephrine and phenyethylamine to die down, the numbing of endorphins to cease, and the bonding hormone oxytocin to influence the relationship.[1]

This four-year "hitch" corresponds with the four-year "ditch"; infatuation and its psychochemical aphrodisiacs end in about forty-eight months. Many partners abandon their relationships before attachment and bonding can take place.[2] The love-blind prone to detachment typically abandon relationships even before the four-year bonding takes place. All relationships will experience a natural period of romantic withdrawal as the internal passion psychochemicals diminish, and a form of monogamous monotony inevitably occurs in which mental effort is required to give meaning to a bonded relationship that now lacks erotic neurohormonal impetus. The challenge of sexual healing is not to be fooled by the passion punch of attraction and infatuation hormones and not to be discouraged by the comforting but dull soothing neurotransmitters. There will always be a romantic "change of love" in every relationship, and sexual healing requires that our minds take over where biology leaves off.

To be a sexual healer, you must be willing to try to remain calm and reflective during the excitement phase of a relationship, to be self-disciplined and tolerant during the withdrawal period, and to work hard during the entire life of the relationship, taking the time to replace infatuation and attraction with meaning and commitment. God will provide the romantic and procreative pull that will draw us together, but it is up to us to make the effort to translate that attraction to lasting healing love. The act of bonding itself will lead to an internal release of less physically intense and stressful but much more healing and healthy chemicals of connection that will help us through the transition from biology to bonding. Sexual healing requires the work, endurance, and tolerance to pass through the four-year hitch period.

Unfortunately, we often form our relationships to develop ourselves rather than the relationship. We remain individually love-drug dependent and reactive rather than work together to make a new relationship with its own neurochemical mix. Anthropologist Paul Bohannan writes that "Americans marry to enhance their inner, largely secret selves."[3] If we remain selfish, we cannot sexually heal because we seek only a match of or for our own sexual and intimacy style rather than the generation of a creative new style from and for both partners.

TWO SYMPTOMS OF "THE CHANGE OF LOVE"

Clinicians have identified two basic origins of clashes in caring: CSB, or compulsive sexual behavior, and HSD, or hypoactive sexual desire. As discussed in Part II, these diagnoses have replaced impotence, orgasmic dysfunction, and premature ejaculation to become widely accepted by sex therapists as the two most common sexual dysfunctions. Couples now come to the sex clinic less to correct or improve genital proficiency than to deal with differences in sexual drive or to help one of the partners overcome what sex therapists now call a sex addiction or aversion.

But all couples experience a change of love life. Just as "change of life" involves neurohormonal variations, the psychochemical profile in couples changes as their relationship matures. At the four-year hitch or ditch period, the change of life may result in some partners longing for the thrill and infatuation of the early stages of the relationship and compulsively seeking new extramarital excitement (CSB). Other partners pass through this period by surrendering to the security of attachment or the safety and low personal demands of detachment, thus experiencing a reduction in the need for sensual intimacy (HSD). If these adjustments are seen as transitional rather than permanent or symptomatic of a failing relationship, sexual healing can help a couple develop an even stronger bond.

Unfortunately, many couples surrender to this change of loving and end or neglect the relationship rather than rally together to reclaim their love at the time it needs them as much as they needed it when it was primarily biological rather than intimately interactional. Alertness to the "change of love" period may help more couples learn to stick it out and grow through this period together.

Sex therapists estimate that more than 38 million people experience "insufficient" or extremely low interest in sex. No one seems clear about how to measure "sufficient" sex interest, but apparently the therapist knows it when he or she sees it. This vagueness usually means that anyone wanting less sex than the therapist is seen as undersexed. The hypoactive sexual desire disabled are seen as those with a slower and less impulsive and energetic approach to sensuality than the sex syndicate deems "normal" or the partner finds acceptable.

Many people suffering from HSD find themselves in relationships with partners who are sexually eager, energetic, and more urgently and erotically driven. Sex experts estimate that more than 45 million people are driven by extraordinarily powerful sexual compulsions that lead them to promiscuity, sexual experimentation, and endless fornication frustration.

From the point of view of sexual healing, CSB and HSD are less two sexual personas than reactions to the natural changes within all relationships—challenging couple problems rather than personal flaws. Remember, the sex syndicate tends to see almost everything as being for and from the self and not evolving within and from a relationship.

While we all bring our unique sexual styles to an intimate relationship, we are also affected by our partners' style and the nature of our developing relationship. Our relationship makes us as much as we make our relationship. An erotic pattern of intimate relationship develops in every relationship as lovers teach and learn from each other. A new whole is formed that is more than the sum of the lovers' individual styles. This environment is created by and can contain the style and meaning of each partner's caring and sexual style.

Compulsive Coitus and the Sexaholics

"I'm Dave, and I'm hooked on horniness," says the middle-aged man as he stands to give his testimony about his crippling addiction to sex. "I'm Marcia, and I'm a must-urbator. I masturbate because I must, and I masturbate compulsively," responds the next group member. The confessions continue around the circle, ending with the group leader saying, "I'm Tom, and I'm a recovering sexaholic like all of you." Introductory confessions and testimonies completed, the rest of the evening is spent discussing various aspects of the famous twelve-step program of Alcoholics Anonymous as they apply to sex addiction and several references to discovering the higher inner power and other new age jargon.

Much as in the sex therapy of the 1970s, there is little reference to the meaning of two-person sexual intimacy in the new recovery movement. There is almost no attention to the fact that the definition of addiction has been distorted and grossly overextended, for to raise such doubts is certain evidence of being "in denial" and not ready for recovery. One must "confess" that he or she is in denial before recovery—life's only other stage—is possible. (There does not seem to be a life period of celebration and being here "now.") All the recovering or denying members are well read in the male and female self-fulfillment literature, feminist philosophy, and the more recent male bonding books. Sex researcher names such as Kinsey, Comfort, and Masters and Johnson have been replaced by recovery movement names such as Beattie, Bradshaw, and Schaef.[4]

Sex addiction, according to the currently popular view, occurs when someone becomes dominated by almost insatiable sexual needs. Nymphomania in sexually starved women and satyriasis or Don Juanism in sexually famished men are concepts that have been around since the first time someone wanted more or less sex than someone else. It is only in recent times that a therapeutic and publishing industry has grown based on this dysfunction.

In terms of psychoneurosexuality, true addiction to sex is impossible because sexual compulsions are not distinguishable from more common, general forms of compulsion such as eating and gambling.[5] People who engage in sexual promiscuity almost always experience a compulsive personality pattern, and their sex lives match their whole lives. They are not sex addicts; they go through life addicted to almost everything, dependent and overreactive. As a clinical psychologist, I have never seen a patient who experienced a balanced and healthy life in every regard except his or her sex life. There is no way that our sex lives can be separated from the rest of our lives.

People suffering from CSB experience disconnection on one or more of the five levels of intimate sexual healing. They often lose track of who they are because of fixation on external sources for identity. They tend to view others as objects to abuse and be addicted to. They lack a sense of coherence or an adaptive explanatory system with which to find meaning in life, and they escape into the distraction of turn-ons to avoid tuning in with someone else. They have little sense of the present moment, typically distracted by guilt from the past or delusions regarding the future. While they may engage in a high frequency of sexual activity, sensuality and intimacy in their physical connections are lacking.

Researcher Eli Coleman has shown that people for whom sex seems the dominant and distracting force in life experience what he calls an "intimacy dysfunction."[6] Dr. Coleman suggests that, because of abuse or neglect as children, people with intimacy dysfunction feel shame, loneliness, and low self-esteem in association with sexual intimacy. To escape these feelings, they seek a distracting sexual high. The high is always short-lived, more shame and guilt result, and a higher high is sought to mask the deep disgust with self. From a sexual healing point of view, the problem is not addiction to sex but difficulty connecting with someone else over time on many levels. Intimacy is replaced by a compulsion to escape the despair of a lack of intimacy and nagging feelings of isolation. The result is "carnal connection" rather than the caring connection of sexual healing.

Too Little of a Good Thing

Hypoactive sexual desire is at the other end of the sex therapist's diagnostic scale. The concept of "sexual appetite" is clinically misleading because intimate connection does not involve ingesting, digesting, or devouring someone or something. While we can be nurtured by someone, we don't feed on each other. Sexual healing is based on sharing the life energy generated by a fully connected life. It is not possible when we draw from the core of our partners' life energy or give energy from our own core. In *Stress Without Distress,* psychologist Hans Selye referred to the concept of egoistic altruism, giving and sharing without giving our lives away.

Sexual healing views HSD as a general health and relationship issue. In our sex clinic, the first step in dealing with a patient's report of not wanting sex enough is to conduct a complete physical exam. Lack of interest is often found to be related to hormonal deficiencies and other metabolic problems and can be corrected by diet, exercise, and sometimes medications. Occasionally, the hypopituitarism of the love-blind is a factor. More often, the problem rests in a lack of desire for sensual body contact because of disconnection on one of the other pentamerous levels of sexual intimacy.

When interviewed in depth from a sexual healing perspective, people reporting HSD often speak of feeling unworthy of love and lacking the energy to be intimate because their energy is spent in self-protection and self-enhancement. They see their own skill rather than social support as most important to their survival, and they are frustrated by having great responsibility but little power. Psychologist David McClelland called this the "inhibited power syndrome" and demonstrated that it results in the lowering of an important immune factor called IgA or immunoglobulin A, which helps fight off respiratory infections.[7]

My patients experiencing what they call HSD often describe distance and alienation from their partners, sometimes feeling that they have been pressured so often to desire sex that they're no longer sure what their own level of desire is. Such patients also often reported being distracted by events such as exploitation, deprivation, neglect, or even abuse in their childhood or earlier relationships, and they dread repeating one or more of these negative experiences in any future attempts to be intimate. They are often disconnected from a sense of meaning in their lives and have become cynical and distrusting. The prospect of sensual intimacy seems incongruous with their sense of distance and lack of purpose; it becomes a source of pressure rather than an opportunity for pleasurable connection.

CONNECTIVE STYLES

To be a sexual healer or shaman, it is helpful to understand these descriptions of CSB and HSD. More important, however, is to be aware of differences in the cognitive styles of the partners in a relationship and the relationship pattern that results from these love maps.

All of us think in our own distinctive ways, and there are many theories that identify styles of cognition and "intelligences."[8] During my decades of work with patients attempting to improve their sexual lives and survive relationship problems, I have discovered basic lovemaking styles that relate to how my patients connect with life in general. These cognitive connection styles transcend gender orientation and the sex diagnosis manuals. I have found that these lovers are showing how they are thinking—broadcasting their cognitive bonding orientations—through the erotic and genital interactional styles they use with their partners. Sex seems to be a form through which a cognitive connective style is expressed physically.

RECOGNIZING YOUR LOVING EROTIC STYLE

Rather than speaking only of sexaholics, sexual compulsions, and hypoactive sexual desire, sexual healing involves the recognition of your own, your partner's, and your relationship's variations on the sexual intimacy theme. Over almost three decades of interviewing patients about their sexual lives, I have developed the following system of erotic style classification to help partners talk about sex without blame and with hopes of recognition, integration, and mutual development of their own couple erotic style.

Rather than use terms which accuse or diagnose, I use a primary color system, which represents a palette for painting the couple's own passion portrait and establishing their sexual style. The primary colors —red, yellow, and blue—represent the basic erotic styles that evolve because of how we were raised, who we are interacting with, our psychoneurosexual systems, and many factors we do not yet understand.

The Pearsall Psychosocial Inventory you took with Chapter 1 measures twenty-five areas of life through which connective cognitive style is manifested. We each work, parent, make friends, shop, and love as a whole person, and our loving erotic style is reflected in all we do, feel, and think. We do not have sex or work lives, and we do not *lead* our lives, we *are* our lives. A key lesson of sexual healing is to understand that we *are* love; we do *not* do it as a separate part of our living.

It is also important to remember that we can alter our loving erotic styles and are not trapped in them. Behavior precedes motivation, so once you understand how to recognize your style, you can decide what aspects of it you want to continue, what aspects contribute to the growth of your relationship, and what aspects you want to change. You can learn to modify your style, blend it differently with others', and shade it to your couple colors.

Each of the three primary intimate connection styles is related to the psychoneuroimmunological patterns of loving I described in Chapter 5—the thrill seeker, the love junkie, the love-sick, and the love-blind. They blend into one another, so most of us are more orange, purple, or green than pure red, yellow, or blue, but understanding of these styles can serve as a starting point for becoming a more sensitive sexual healer.

THE RED SEXUAL STYLE: THE CONTROLLER

The red sexual style is characterized by a tendency toward high sexual interest, extensive and elaborate sex fantasies, desire for frequent sexual interaction, eagerness to talk about and experiment with sex, desire to engage in such activities as watching X-rated videotapes, wearing or preferring that the partner wear sexually provocative clothing and lingerie, and enjoying the incorporation of adventure and mystery into sexual encounters. In the red style a person is seldom embarrassed about open discussions of sex or public demonstrations of intimacy. The red-style person enjoys "doing it" with the lights on and mirrors in place, and he or she is a sex director attempting paradoxically to remain in control in order to lose control. He or she typically functions in the "getting mine" and "seeing that you get yours" mode—a coital commander.

The red-style person often learned about sex from peers, siblings, or pornography. He or she can be tender, but because this style may also be related to the thrill seeker or love junkie patterns, in which attraction, infatuation, and epinephrine and phenylethylamine can be dominant, he or she can distance the partner by a tendency to focus on excitement, variety, sensations, postures, images, and fun rather than meaning, caring, and tenderness. The red-style person emphasizes technique over tenderness and may want to use sex toys and gimmicks.

The red style is processed through the 500-million-year-old parts of the brain, including the cerebellum (our memory center for bodily sensations), thalamus (the brain's relay center for incoming stimulation), and RAS (the reticular activating system, or the on and off switch of the human brain). It is turned on or turned off with little modulation, moderation, or in-between arousal states. The red style is characterized by SAM system activation and the resulting hyperarousal of the body systems. A sexual encounter in the red mode is typically one of get ready, do it in as many ways as possible, and fall into a postorgasmic nap.

Because of the excess SAM or sympathetic fight-or-flight status of the red style, sexual problems are often caused by stress and "mechanical breakdowns," such as early ejaculation and difficulty experiencing orgasm, and the red-style person may be prone to the CSB pattern. The primary strength of the red style is sexual energy, willingness to try anything, and ability to set aside distractions by getting lost in sexual intensity.

THE YELLOW SEXUAL STYLE: THE COMPTROLLER

The yellow sexual style is characterized by cautious experimentation with sexuality. The person of the yellow style can be talked into sexual experimentation but is more reluctant, cautious, and private about it. Easily embarrassed even by his or her own fantasies, the yellow-style person often has to be encouraged or even seduced into sexual encounters and may speak of the "appropriate frequency" or "time and place to do it" rather than spontaneity. The yellow-style person has sex if absolutely necessary to keep the partner happy—with a little light from the bathroom door slightly ajar and no mirrors unless the partner "really has to have that." The yellow style is the sex respondent or the accountant keeping tabs on how often and who does what and how to whom and making sure that sexual quotas are met. Yellow is the sexual turn-taker style.

The yellow-style person learned about sex from intellectualized discussions with his or her parents, from strict religious teaching, or from films, television, videotapes, or technical rather than titillating books and has developed a more rigid and intellectual approach to sex.

The yellow style is also related to the psychoneurosexuality of the love-blind or more detached person. Sometimes because of inadequate adrenocoticotropic hormone (ACTH) from the pituitary gland (hypopituitarism), the yellow-style lover seems to detach easily or distance him- or herself from intimacy. The yellow style involves the 300-million-year-old parts of the brain—the hypothalamus (basic body and life functions), pituitary gland (the master gland so involved with the SAM and PAC systems), amygdala (center for recognizing what is new or old), and hippocampus (one reward center of the brain). This is the brain area concerned with what's old or new, protecting one's turf, and maintaining life balance and the status quo. The SAM and PAC systems combine to form a psychochemical balance, and agitation or depression is rare. The sexual style resulting from this neurobiology is maintenance and survival oriented—getting it done, done right, and on schedule.

Sexual problems for the yellow-style person are often related to fatigue, distraction, lack of interest, or boredom, and he or she may show elements of the HSD pattern. The yellow-style sex partner may be passionately proficient but at times seemingly uninvolved and "just going through the motions" and feeling unfulfilled even after orgasm. The primary sexual strength of the yellow style is attention to sexual details, responsibility, accountability, timing, and knowing what to do when and how often. The yellow-style person is often more skilled than enraptured.

THE BLUE SEXUAL STYLE: THE CAJOLER

The blue style is characterized by romantic reflection, reluctance, and a dash of suspicion. For the person of the blue style, sex is "OK sometimes," but he or she can't understand why it is "such a big deal." The blue style reflects sex as resulting from loving passion and seldom sex for sex's sake. The blue style is the surrenderer who goes along with sex and often enjoys it but usually only when intense emotional closeness has preceded the intimate encounter or may result from it. Sexual interest ebbs and flows with the closeness and intimacy of the general relationship, and he or she may attempt to cajole the partner into sex by trying to be "worthy" of being made love to—by buying gifts, sacrificing, and doing favors. The blue style is primarily compliance.

The blue-style person typically learned about sex from stern or sexually uncomfortable parents, a close friend, or very early and sometimes abusive sexual encounters with other children or adults. There is an underlying guilt about sex often caused by perceived personal violation of real or personally constructed religious edicts. The blue-style person is parental in his or her approach to sex; he or she takes responsibility for and feels protective of the satisfaction and sexual self-esteem of the partner. The blue-style person functions as a nurturer of the partner and the sexual life of the relationship and is associated with strong emphasis on interdependence.

The blue style is related to the attraction-oriented lover—the love-sick whose addiction to endorphins can result in overdependency on the lover rather than interdependency. The blue style is less associated with the CSB or HSD patterns than what I call the RAS syndrome, or reactive accommodative sexuality, in which the lover tries to match his or her desires to what are perceived to be those of the partner.

The blue style is related primarily to the neocortex or higher and newer brain, with dominance by the right hemisphere, where images and feelings are processed. The parasympathetic and PAC systems dominate. The neocortical blue sexual style is one of why and now what instead of let's get turned on or let's do our sexual duty.

Red-style lovers react, yellow-style lovers calculate, and blue-style lovers reflect. Red get angry, yellow get confused, and blue get depressed. Because of his or her emotional reactions, primary sexual problems for the blue-style person are postcoital remorse, distraction during sex by emotional issues associated with the relationship, and difficulty having orgasm or becoming aroused because of "not being there" mentally or looking too often to the partner for approval. The primary strength of the blue-style person is to bring emotion and meaning to sexual encounters.

If many of the attributes of these three erotic styles seem negative, it is because I am focusing here on understanding sexual problems. All three styles bring their unique energies to the sexual relationships. The erotic energy of the red style, the hard work and performance energy of the yellow style, and the emotional energy of the blue style are all keys to sensual fulfillment. All of us have a little of the red, yellow, and blue sexual styles, and our styles change throughout our lives and even throughout the year. But sexual healing requires that we become aware of our more typical and dominant sexual color—our sexual character. The perfectly whole sexual healer would be the person who possesses all of the above characteristics in complete balance and none of the problems associated with each style. No one meets these caring criteria, so one purpose of a sexually healing relationship is to maximize the strengths of the style brought by each partner and to attempt to recognize and diminish the risks for problems that each style brings to a relationship.

Once you and your lover have learned how to recognize your respective sexual styles, the next step is to integrate them. None of us can combine all three styles into a perfect blended loving style suited to lasting bonding and the healthy psychoneurosexual patterns this can bring; we need someone else to bond and blend with. The purpose of sexual healing is to make the always incomplete individual more complete by bonding with another person, being strengthened by his or her positive healing energy, and accepting and forgiving his or her weaknesses.

Deep Red: Conflict-habituated Couples

The combination of two red styles results in the deep red style of hot and passionate sex as often as possible. The couple's hobby might be sex, and there is the expectation that sexual intimacy will occur almost every night or at least whenever possible. There may be conflict in the relationship, and the couple may use sex as a means of distraction from the relationship problems or to establish a mutual system of denying deeper feelings of alienation or pain. One woman in a deep red sexual style relationship said, "Our sex is as intense as I wish our relationship was."

Orange: Passive-Congenial Couples

Relationships are shaded orange when one partner is red in style and the other yellow. The orange couple style is typically complementary, in that one partner is responsible for the sexual and erotic life of the relationship and the other for the details and execution of that life. The red-style spouse may urge an erotic adventure in the hot tub, but it is the yellow-style partner who checks and prewarms the water and makes sure there are towels. One spouse tries to stay turned on and to turn the other spouse on while the other keeps track of earned erotic points or sexual debts. One husband in an orange relationship said, "She's the yellow style. She's into the details. She gets the lotion, lights the candles, and sees that the tissues are by the bed. I decide what postures we use and how we do it. She's the stage manager, but I'm the director."

Bright Yellow: Administrative Couples

When two yellow partners combine, the couple's bright yellow style is indicated by their tendency to "go through the motions" to keep their sexual life alive. There seems to be a sexual quota system, planning replaces spontaneity, and proficiency replaces passion. One wife in a bright yellow couple said, "We know that Wednesday and Saturday nights are our sex nights. We plan on it, and we don't even have to talk

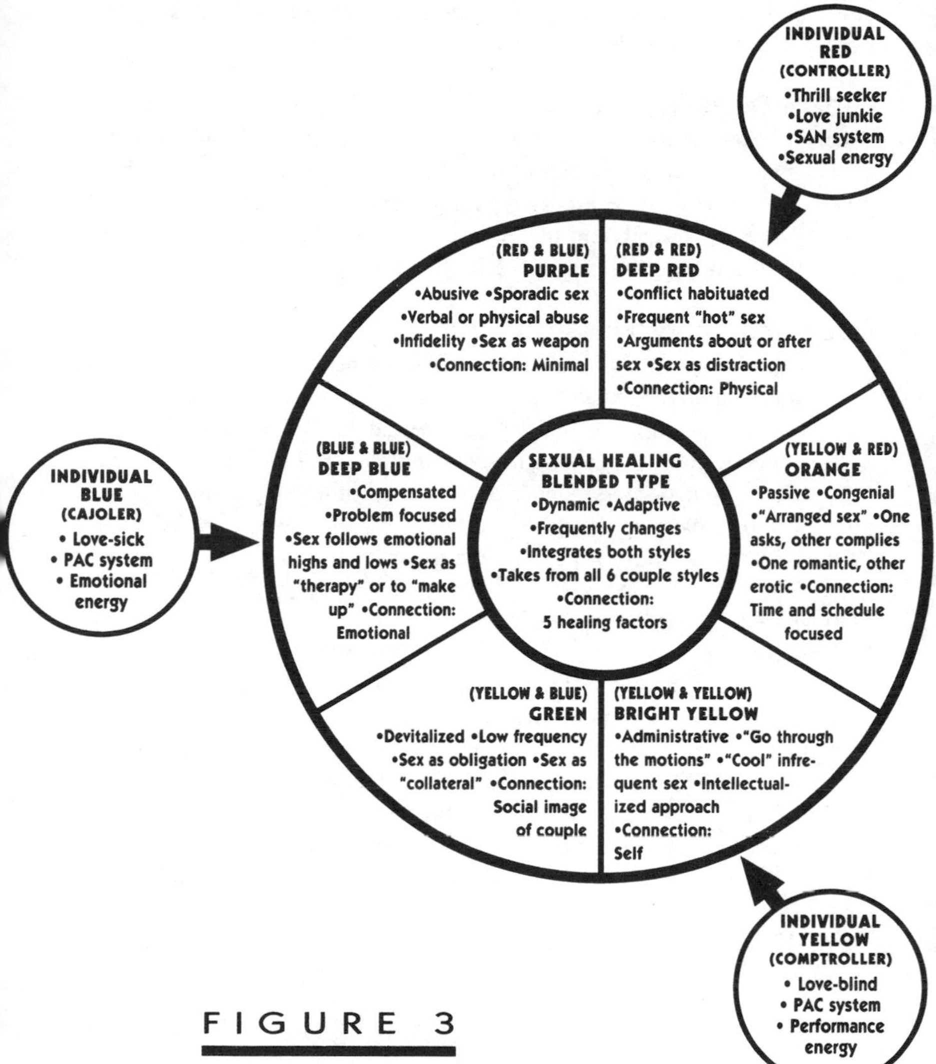

INDIVIDUAL RED (CONTROLLER)
•Thrill seeker
•Love junkie
•SAN system
•Sexual energy

INDIVIDUAL BLUE (CAJOLER)
• Love-sick
• PAC system
• Emotional energy

INDIVIDUAL YELLOW (COMPTROLLER)
• Love-blind
• PAC system
• Performance energy

(RED & BLUE) PURPLE
•Abusive •Sporadic sex
•Verbal or physical abuse
•Infidelity •Sex as weapon
•Connection: Minimal

(RED & RED) DEEP RED
•Conflict habituated
•Frequent "hot" sex
•Arguments about or after sex •Sex as distraction
•Connection: Physical

(BLUE & BLUE) DEEP BLUE
•Compensated
•Problem focused
•Sex follows emotional highs and lows •Sex as "therapy" or to "make up" •Connection: Emotional

SEXUAL HEALING BLENDED TYPE
•Dynamic •Adaptive
•Frequently changes
•Integrates both styles
•Takes from all 6 couple styles
•Connection: 5 healing factors

(YELLOW & RED) ORANGE
•Passive •Congenial
•"Arranged sex" •One asks, other complies
•One romantic, other erotic •Connection: Time and schedule focused

(YELLOW & BLUE) GREEN
•Devitalized •Low frequency
•Sex as obligation •Sex as "collateral" •Connection: Social image of couple

(YELLOW & YELLOW) BRIGHT YELLOW
•Administrative •"Go through the motions" •"Cool" infrequent sex •Intellectualized approach
•Connection: Self

FIGURE 3

Blending of Individual Erotic Styles

about it. It's like an erotic appointment, and we can start making love even while we're watching television.''

Green: Devitalized Couples

When yellow and blue combine, the result is the green style of alternation between sex for release or relaxation and occasional quality moments of romance. One blue-style husband in a green-style couple said, "I really need to be held, kissed, and make love. She just likes to get it done. We do it, but it isn't anything to write home about for either of us.''

Deep Blue: Compensated Couples

When two blue styles combine, the result is the deep blue style of rare but emotionally intense sexual encounters. Sex often becomes a means of mutual emotional support, making up after an argument, or escape from personal depression by merging in sensual intensity. Long discussion may follow the sex encounters. One wife in a deep blue couple said, "Sometimes we don't have sex because we know that after we make love we'll be up for hours talking or crying or arguing.''

Purple: Abusive Couples

When red and blue styles combine, one of the partners often finds his or her needs ignored or sensitivities regularly violated. The red-style partner, because of his or her more instrumental approach, feels frustrated by being unable to meet the emotional needs of the blue-style partner. Verbal and even physical clashes can result from feelings of futility. The red partner feels unappreciated, and the blue partner feels misunderstood. One wife in a purple couple said, "I feel like it doesn't make any difference who I am. He's having sex because he needs a woman and I'm the closest available one." Her husband responded, "She makes sex such a big deal and gets so emotional about it that I just want to get it over with or forget the whole thing.''

Blended Style: The Sexually Healing Couple

At the center of the wheel of couple erotic styles is the blended- or sexually healing–style couple. This relationship is aware of all the individual and couple erotic styles; each partner knows his or her contribution to the couple style and how he or she is influenced by and influences the partner. It is a dynamic and always changing couple style that draws from the whole palette of color available.

As you will note in Figure 3, the blended couple is connected on all five levels of sexual healing. The deep red style is connected primarily on the physical, sensual level. Their sex is characterized by two individuals seeking parallel self-pleasure. The orange-style couple is connected on the time or moment-to-moment level, and their sexuality is planned and arranged to meet the pragmatism of the yellow partner and the urgent sexual needs of the red partner. The bright yellow couple is connected self to self but less as a merged unit, and their sexuality is more executional than it is intimate. The green-style couple is concerned with their relationship's social image and connects primarily on that level, and their sexuality tends to be infrequent and obligatory. The blue couple connects on a strong emotional level that can often lead to as much conflict as it does unity. Their sexual interaction often follows arguments, and their sexual frequency reflects emotional intensity rather than sex drive or expectations. The purple couple is the most disconnected because of the controlling and dominant nature of the red partner and the more surrendering style of the blue. Their sexual style is typically sporadic, with long periods of no sex followed by brief periods of hot sex as a sensual shortcut to connection without mental effort. You can use the couple color chart by finding where your relationship seems to fall, studying your individual style and that of your partner, and discussing how you create the portrait of your own loving.

If you have identified your sexual style and the style of your basic intimate relationship, you have completed two steps to being a sexual healer because you are now better able to recognize your own loving erotic style and have reference points for discussing your patterns of intimacy. You can modify your individual color to help change your couple shade of sensuality, help your partner see the color you have created together, and help your lover modify his or her style.

Our erotic connective styles are learned and can be changed. They are not uncontrollable impulse and pure reaction. They can be reflective responses and ways of thinking, and we can change the way we think once we are clear on how and what we are thinking. Becoming a sexual healer involves learning to transcend the strong influence of the psychobiology of attraction, infatuation, attachment, and detachment to attain mental bonding that lasts through the life cycle and the crises of illness.

12

REMOVING BONDING BLOCKS
The Joy of Codependence

*No one has ever loved anyone the way everyone wants to
be loved.*

> *Mignon McLaughlin*

IMPULSE FOR INTIMACY

"When she looked at me, I felt like we had known each other forever,"
said the man. "I don't know what it is, and I never saw her again, but
when our eyes met it was like we were one person."

Most of us have felt the power of connection with a complete
stranger. For a brief moment, all that is human about us seems to unite
with the personhood of someone else. Beyond sexual attraction, infatuation, or the recognition of a familiar face, we seem to sense that we were
all made to connect with one another and that, from time to time, what is
most human about us seems to draw us together. Sexual shamans develop
this connection sense. When the human impulse for intimacy is acted
upon with another person, the moments and meaning of life are shared
and the connection made permanent and sensualized, a sexually healing
bond is forged.

A SENSE FOR CONNECTION

Every one of our senses is tuned not only to the elements of our outside world but to the essence of another person with whom we may bond. Our senses are not just for survival, they are for connection. Unlike the eyes of other animals, our eyes not only see, detect, and interpret but also send messages and convey our feelings, and our eyes seem able to connect with others' eyes to express complex emotions. Our ears, nose, and skin are not nearly as sensitive as those of other animals, but we seem to be able to be drawn together by the sound, smell, and touch of another person in ways far beyond the interaction of other animals.

You have read that the sight, sound, touch, and glance of a lover result in intense psychoneurosexual responses. Researchers have documented the power of this connection by asking male and female volunteers to look into each other's eyes for two minutes. These men and women were total strangers, but after ending their gaze and going to another room, they all reported strong feelings of attraction and affection.[1] We have genetically built-in bonding ability.

George Bernard Shaw wrote, "When two people are under the influence of the most violent, most insane, most delusive, and most transient of passions, they are required to swear that they will remain in that excited, abnormal, and exhausting condition continuously until death do them part."[2] He was referring to the potency of our neurochemical attraction to overwhelm our judgment. The psychochemistry of human attraction, infatuation, and attachment stimulates our body systems, but we cannot remain in the erotic situation of longing passion. If we do, our health suffers. We eventually have to stop being out of our minds in love and put our minds to our loving. To be sexual healers, we must move through these courting stages to the healthiest of human interactions—bonding.

Our intimate relationships are often more stressful to our health than conducive to it. We are too often seduced and hedonistically hypnotized by the intense chemistry of coupling and the flood of erotic psychochemicals, and as a result we become neurochemically fixated at immature stages of relationship. Fortunately, once you have recognized your primary erotic style—your tendency toward thrill seeking, love junkie–hood, love-sickness, or love-blindness—and the primary color reflecting your connection style, you can integrate this information to negotiate the bonding process. By doing so, you can establish better and healthier balance in your PNS chemistry and immunity.

CODEPENDENCE: CURSE OR CURE?

"My name is Mary, and I'm a recovering codependent," said the young wife as the other women in the sex addiction group I mentioned in the previous chapter nodded in empathetic agreement. "My husband is a sexaholic, and I have given up myself to support my husband's addiction. I am a part of his addiction. I am addicted to his addiction. I am addicted to him. I'm dependent on his addiction. I am addicted to having sex with him." The group stood, circled around the weeping wife, and hugged her for what they viewed as a profound insight in full compliance with the recovery movement orientation.

I have mentioned many times the danger of seeing codependence as a flaw. To the recovery movement, any person (but usually a woman) who continues to care for and offer loving support to a troubled spouse or family member is seen as giving up her individual will and lacking mature autonomy, self-sufficiency, confidence, and assertiveness.

But the effort to break free from the dreaded codependence, and the constant struggle to avoid denial and remain in recovery while keeping the self first and foremost in all things is counterproductive to sexual or connective healing. Sexual healing requires a new view of bonding and a concept of connective codependence as a cure—a means of developing and deploying one's loving erotic style to care for and with another no matter how severe the relationship crisis and challenges may be or how hurt and impaired the partner may become.

COLLECTIVISM, SEPARATISM, AND CULTURE

Unlike our own individualistic culture, in which people fear codependence and self-sacrifice, many other cultures are collectivist. The native Hawaiians view life as experienced through connection with the people of the past, present, and future, whom they call the Great Poe Aumakua. There is no self without reference to others and the welfare of everyone. Unlike most other religions, the ancient Hawaiian religion of Huna recognizes only one sin—to disconnect from or do harm to another person.[3] In cultures such as the Hawaiian and Japanese, the individual has little identity without constant reference to interdependence and constant responsibility for and with others.[4]

In collectivist cultures, social attachments are fewer than in our own, but they are much more intense and enduring. These are codependent cultures, which view independence as a weakness. These cultures are founded on lasting commitment, which is basic to sexual healing. When someone in a collectivist culture becomes detached, selfish, or independent, he or she is seen as "sick." Although I know of no "us help" recovery movement in these cultures offering support groups to help cure independence, failure to be codependent does result in social criticism and even rejection and disgrace.[5]

There are many benefits to our hard-earned independence, and we are a culture of strong and proud individualists. Certainly, no one should remain in a relationship in which he or she is physically or mentally abused, but most of our relationships do not fail primarily because we abuse each other. They fail because we know more about how to be selfish than about how to stay connected. We have worked so hard at finding, being, and protecting ourselves that we have often neglected the most important skill for sexual healing—permanent bonding with others.

Those of us in individualistic cultures tend to make more money, have more things, take more pride in personal achievements, be less geographically bound to our core families, and have more freedom and mobility than people in collectivist societies. Unfortunately, all these benefits have failed to offset the alienation, loneliness, divorce, homicide, and vulnerability to illness that come with self-focus and isolation.[6] We have established bonding blocks—learned behaviors, thoughts, and feelings which prevent us from connecting intimately, permanently, and codependently with a significant person for all our lives.

We have failed to learn the Hammarskjöld principle I described in Chapter 1—that "it is more noble to give yourself completely to one individual than to labor diligently for the salvation of the masses." We have lost contact with our inner dyadal drive. We seem better at becoming attracted to, infatuated with, attached to, and detached from each other in short-term relationships used to serve the purpose of self-fulfillment than we are at making a lasting and enduring bond.

THE MOURNING AFTER

We are not only a society of passionate, intense, brief, hot relationships. We are also a society of frequent, sudden, and cold endings to these relationships. We are taught that when a loved one dies, that is the end of the emotional and spiritual bond and we might as well move quickly on because the external stimulus that caused our love is gone. We are supposed to get on with life and sever all ties with the past relationship except fond memories of unreclaimable experiences with the lost loved one.[7] To hold on to the intense emotions of a bond broken by physical absence is to be mired helplessly and dependently in grief. The threat of dreaded codependence apparently extends beyond the grave! To try to stay connected beyond bereavement is a sign of immaturity, indicative of the need for grief therapy to rid us of the "emotional mummification" of the lost lover.[8]

Sexual healing is based on the ideas that meaningful bonds are forever and that emotionally clinging to bonds is healthy. Other cultures emphasize this infinite bond theory and the idea that mourning after loss is healthy even if continued to the point of what psychologist Mary Gergen calls interaction with "social ghosts." These ghosts are images of the lost partner with whom we actually speak and interact.[9] The Hawaiian concept of a loving human relationship is that it lives on forever, changed only in its nature. The relationship moves from a physical interaction (*unihipili*) and mental connection (*uhnae*) to a more spiritual connection (*aumakua*).

If we approach our bonds as capable of transcending physical presence to become a part of our brains, bodies, and souls forever, we remove a major block to bonding—the idea that bonds are only temporary socially serviceable ties rather than infinite connections. This approach to bonding—intentional development and deployment of our loving styles and the permanency of a loving intimate bond beyond time, space, and even death—reduces the immunotrauma of abrupt endings such as those experienced by the widows of the train wreck described in Chapter 6.

Becoming sexual healers involves freeing ourselves from fixation on the biochemically driven stages of attraction, infatuation, and immature attachment and celebrating forever the love of and within relationship. In the language of quantum physics, where particle and wave and energy and matter are one, we are not just people capable of connections, we are connection manifested in human form.

A CURE FOR THE COMMON COLD OF PSYCHIATRY

Depression is the most prevalent form of mental disturbance in our society, and I suggest that it is directly related to our lack of sexual healing. Depression is called the common cold of mental illness, and most of us will experience a significant depression in our lifetimes. As the emotional rebound theory mentioned in Chapter 3 suggests, a little sadness is as natural and necessary a part of life as a little joy. You have read, however, that depression can also be devastating to health and immunity.

Researchers now feel that in addition to genetic, physiological, and neurochemical factors, depression is caused by our selfish focus on life. Psychologist Martin Seligman writes that "rampant individualism carries with it two seeds of its own destruction. First, a society that exalts the individual to the extent ours does will be ridden with depression.

Second, . . . meaninglessness [occurs when there is no] attachment to something larger than you are."[10] Depression, then, is the opposite of the elation of connection—its pervasiveness and pain equaled by the power and joy of intimate bonding. Since sexual healing involves permanent connection and meaning in place of selfish intensity, it is one cure for the depression epidemic in our separateness-oriented culture.

CLOSE ENCOUNTERS OF THE SEVENTH KIND

Almost everyone in our society gets married.[11] Nine of every ten of us will marry, and even though divorce, affairs, and abuse are common, marriage continues to be the one thing men and women do together more often than almost anything else. We have a dyadal drive to be with just one member of the opposite sex. Monogamy means having only one spouse at a time, but it does not necessarily imply fidelity—being monogamous is not the same as being sexually faithful. The estimates that more than half of spouses are breaking the seventh commandment during their marriages are greatly exaggerated, but lack of commitment to marriage is signaled not just by sexual unfaithfulness. An infidelity of time is much more common, with husbands and wives often spending less time with their spouses than with friends or colleagues.[12] Which is stronger, the desire to bond with just one person or the desire to have a variety of partners?

You have read that sexual healing is based on the premise that fidelity is natural and healthy and that adultery and cheating are potentially lethal perversions of our desire to experience all the personalities within one partner. I mentioned earlier that our need for variety is really a built-in ability to embrace all the identities that make up one love. However, it's easier to respond to sexual impulse and seek physical variety than to reflect, contemplate, and work to connect with all the personalities in one lover. It is easier to "go out on" a spouse than to "work things out with" him or her. You read in Part I about the effect on the cardiovascular system of illicit affairs, coition death, and the negative health impact of simply contemplating extramarital sex. Sexual healers know that a faithful attraction is a healthy one.

MONOGAMY IS ONLY NATURAL

Anthropologist Margaret Mead wrote, "No matter how many communes anybody invents, the family always creeps back."[13] Anthropologist Helen Fisher writes, "Pair-bonding is a trademark of the human animal."[14]

Bonding and connecting intimately over time with one person is a necessary component of sexual healing. Sexual healing requires breaking down the barriers to bonding whether in marriage or with someone with whom we can find intimate meaning and close physical contact in our daily life. As painful as it may be for some people to acknowledge, one may live a long life alone, but one cannot live a whole and healthy life as a lonely self.

WHEN BEING FAITHFUL WAS A SIN

To document the power of the two-person bonded unit, consider the case of one of the best-known sex communes. While many experiments in sexual group living have taken place over the last decades, none has survived.[15] Despite the popular idea that wanting and having a variety of sexual partners is only natural, sex communes all eventually evolve rigid rules concerning who can have sex with whom, and it is typically the founder who receives the most copulation choices.

One of the best-known experiments in "free love" was the Oneida community, started in New York in the 1830s by an assertive, religious, and sexually driven man named John Humphrey Noyes.[16] The community was composed of five hundred men, women, and children, and everything was shared. All sexual partners were everyone's sexual partners. Romantic love for one partner was forbidden, and an exclusive sexual relationship was viewed as the ultimate sin.

Despite the strongest sanctions against pair-bonds, almost every member of the community eventually took part in a kind of committed cheating and formed clandestine and lasting intimate relationships. The attraction of intimate connection was stronger than religious and social decree. In a group where extramarital sex was expected, exclusive sexual relationship won out.

BEAUTY IS IN THE BRAIN OF THE BEHOLDER

As you have read, all bonding begins with attraction. We think that something about someone else draws us to him or her. Perhaps one of our biggest mistakes during the attraction stage is to think that what attracts us is external to us. As you read in Chapter 5, we are always turned on by our own brains and see more how we are than how someone else is. Just as the poet-knight in *Don Quixote* saw the whore Dulcinea as a noble and loving woman, we all create our own lovers. We do not come to believe what we see, we see what we believe, and our love and our lover are transformed in the process. As Shakespeare pointed out, "We see with the mind and not the eyes."

What is beautiful changes not only according to social and cultural standards but according to our view of ourselves and our point of view. If we are insecure about our bodies or emphasize our physical appearance as our primary attraction factor, we will look for a projected image that we either think we are or consciously but more often unconsciously wish we were. It is much easier to be unhappy with what we see than with who we are and how we choose to see.

Beauty is in the mind of the beholder and is influenced strongly by the culture in which that mind develops. Psychologist Phyllis Bronstein-Burrows writes, "The thin, narrow-shouldered ectomorph who was yesterday's spinster librarian is today's high fashion model; the plump and buxom endomorph who was a Victorian romantic idol today is eating cottage cheese and grapefruit, and weighing in every Tuesday at Weight Watchers."[17] Sexual healing requires that we constantly remember that we create our own lovers by what we look for and how we look rather than by a universal and permanent criterion of attractiveness.

We may be attracted by a "neotenic" or cute baby face, a certain body shape, a smile, and very likely a certain look in the eyes. Finding someone to court and eventually bond with depends in part on being attracted and attractive by very narrow cultural standards, and people who are judged low in attractiveness by our often viciously discriminatory cultural cuteness scale may be at health risk. They are excluded from the bonding process through the first door—attraction. Being in a wheelchair, having cerebral palsy, or being scarred or deformed can prevent the bonding of sexual healing that could be so helpful to those who are hurt or handicapped. Such people can only hope that their efforts to reach out will result in finding someone who will believe in the Dulcinea effect and see beyond society's love-blindness to discover inner beauty and help bring that beauty to the relationship.

THE CREATION OF BEAUTY THROUGH SEXUAL HEALING

One of my patients was burned severely when he tripped while carrying a pan of hot cooking oil. The oil splashed up and scalded his face and neck and burned away most of his scalp. Even after several surgeries his scars were quite noticeable, his mouth was twisted to one side by the stretching of skin, and his hair had never grown back. People stopped and stared at him. Because of his imposed disconnection and feelings of rejection and isolation, he became severely depressed. He stopped asking women for dates, withdrew at work, then stopped working completely. He finally surrendered to the ultimate physical disconnection and attempted suicide.

When I saw him in the hospital, his wrists were wrapped with bandages, and he sat slumped and inattentive on the edge of his bed. Antidepressant drugs were tried, and it was finally decided to use ECT, electroconvulsive therapy, to shock him back to attention. I asked his psychiatrist to delay that treatment until I tried another approach.

I asked the nurses to bring the man to our single adult group for people with disabilities. He sat as if oblivious to our meeting, but as other people in the group told of their own feelings of rejection because of body appearance, I could see attention in his eyes. Several group meetings passed until one evening I noticed that one of the group members—a woman in a wheelchair who could not move her arms—had moved close to him. At each subsequent meeting, she sat near the man.

The sexual healing began at the end of one group meeting. As one of the blind patients was describing his desperate attempt to connect with women without the use of his eyes, he said, "I could keep saying that I can't connect with a woman, but I have to start reaching out in any way I can. If I can't send a message with my eyes, I'll have to do it with whatever works. I'll have to talk to them or sing to them, and I have a rotten voice. But at least I have a voice, she has ears, so we can have a little auditory intercourse." Everyone in the group laughed but the man with the scars on his face. He began to cry, reached up, touched his own eyes, and then reached over and took the hand of the quadriplegic woman at his side. "You're beautiful," he whispered. After the meeting, they sat together for almost an hour.

The next morning as I did my rounds, I saw the man pushing his new friend down the corridor. As they passed, he smiled at me. No words came from his mouth, but with his lips he formed the words, "Isn't she beautiful?" I smiled back and went to the nurses' station to ask for his chart. I wrote in his record, "Do not disturb this patient when he is alone in his room with Ms. X." They spent most evenings together making love in that room, each of them tuned in to the inner essence of the other and not distracted by outer appearance.

In three weeks, he left the hospital. He is married to the woman in the wheelchair, his depression has lifted, and he is back to work. I saw this couple the other day for a follow-up visit. As he pushed her into the office, he hit her chair against a table and the light fell and shattered. "He's handsome, but he's still very clumsy," said his wife. "She can't walk, so she can't be clumsy," joked her husband. "But she's still the most beautiful woman in the world." This man and woman had both become sexual healers, reconnected with their lives through a meaningful intimate relationship.

We are all Dulcineas, and we are all created by our lovers and our loving. If it is true that sexual healing depends on total system or society healing, then we must learn to see beauty beyond the narrow limits of "sexiness" that seem to dominate today. We must look with love to find love.

THE THREE WINDOWS OF WORTHINESS

My clinical work and interviews with couples in the sexual healing program indicate that there are three windows of opportunity for developing a sense of worthiness—the connection with self—that is one of the five connections of sexual healing.

The first window is in early childhood, when our parents teach us that we are worthy irrespective of skills and abilities. Unlike in adult bonds, which require conditional and reciprocal loving, the young child is needfully dependent and attached to a parent in mutual codependence. He or she requires unconditional love in order to develop connection with self—self-esteem irrespective of accomplishments and feeling like a good boy or girl even when he or she is not. Lovers in sexual healing receive love for loving and for what they do and express, but children must be loved no matter what they do. One of the greatest gifts a parent can give is to help the child separate self-worth from self-success and personhood from power.

The second of the three windows of worthiness takes place when we are teenagers. Between 1 million and 200,000 years ago, a stage in life unique to humans—the teenager—evolved.[18] Probably because our brains began to get too big for the birth canal, children were born in a more and more helpless state, and the childhood of humans began to be longer than that of any animal.[19] Not only did a longer childhood and adolescent period become necessary in order to learn the increasingly complex survival skills of the evolving culture but now there was time for teenage sexual experimentation, courtship, serial attractions, and infatuations. Unfortunately, meaningful connection practice—learning to connect and bond on all five levels of sexual intimacy—too often was replaced by practice in connection on only one level—sensuality.

The second window of self-worth—adolescence—has become clouded by erotic experimentation and competition rather than learning worthiness based on commitment, meaning, tenderness, and significance.

The mistake of intensity for intimacy is carried into adulthood. Another gift a parent can give is to model through his or her own relationship the sacredness of caring deeply and responsibly for another person. Sexual healing grows from the seeds of unqualified personal dignity and a sense of deep caring for another person that can be planted during the first two windows of vulnerability.

Like any human skill, bonding requires the mastery of development tasks as we grow up. The bonding developmental task during the first or childhood window of worthiness is to be able to separate self-worth from self-success. It requires seeing worthiness as the ability to show responsible compassion and connection with others rather than as a passion for self-fulfillment and a life view that one is what one accomplishes. The developmental task of the second or teenage window of worthiness is to see the skills of consideration, intimacy, compassion, and commitment as more important than studsmanship, seductiveness, manipulation, and popularity.

The third window of worthiness occurs in early adulthood. The developmental bonding task at this stage is to see self-worth as related to giving rather than to how much one can get. It requires overcoming the scarcity hypothesis, that there is only so much of the Essential in this world and that one must struggle and compete against others to get one's share.

If we make it through the three windows of worthiness, we move easily and without fixation through our relationship attractions, infatuations, attachments, and detachments to the highest of human skills and the central ability of a sexual healer—the ability to bond.

Our individualistic society stresses nonbonding messages through all three windows of self-worth. Particularly when we are young adults, we are taught that we must go forth and get our piece of the pie before someone else gets it. Competence and self-confidence come to mean coyness, cleverness, and winning. The sexual healing skills of selflessness and cooperation are not stressed.

LIFE'S TWO QUESTIONS

To be a sexual healer, we all must answer two questions: Where am I going? and With whom am I going? When we focus only on the where, individual life direction, we can become attached to partners as a means to our ends. When we feel blocked in our self goals, we become quickly detached. When we focus only on the whom, we can become attracted and infatuated but easily detached when seeking the right partner distracts us from trying to be intimate and giving partners to someone with whom we have chosen to share our whole lives and with whom we work to help heal the world.

The way to bonding worthiness may be seen in terms of three general orientations to sex that can develop during the windows of worthiness. These orientations are erotophobia, paraphilia, and erotophilia. *Philia* means love and sensuality. When we learn to love loving (*erotophilia*) rather than fear love (*erotophobia*) or distort it (*paraphilia*), we are able to be sexual healers, to maintain meaningful bonds, and to rebond when we have to.

THE EROTOPHOBIC PERSONALITY

Because of problems experienced in one of the windows of worthiness, some people develop *erotophobia,* or the fear of erotic intimacy and lasting intimate connection.

Erotophobes seem awkward and uncomfortable about sexual intimacy, about the topic of sex generally, and with demonstrative sensual touching, holding, and hugging. They often mistake "doing for someone" for "loving with" someone and typically show the yellow erotic style described in Chapter 11. My interviews of erotophobes indicate the following twelve characteristics:

1. The SAD Syndrome—Somatosensory Affection Deprivation: Erotophobes typically were deprived of tender, rhythmic, warm physical contact by both a male and a female caretaker. They tend to shun touch, withdraw from intimate interaction, and become embarrassed by intimacy because of SAD, somatosensory affective deprivation syndrome.

2. Instrumental Body Orientation: Erotophobes tend to see their bodies as separate from who they are. In effect, they "have" bodies rather than "are" their bodies. As a result, they often feel awkward about their bodies and body functions, and this awkwardness is shown by a tendency toward low body esteem, feelings of physical inadequacy, and shyness and discomfort about the bodies of others.

3. Intimacy Fear: Erotophobes fear intimacy, perhaps in part because of the SAD syndrome and its related neuroprogramming and also because they have not had the opportunity to practice physical or emotional intimacy during one of the three windows of worthiness.

4. Opposite Gender Fear and Manipulation: Erotophobes have learned

to use rather than respect, protect, and enhance their bodies. They value manipulation over meaning, and calculation over caring. Because of generalized personal feelings of unworthiness and discomfort or unfamiliarity with the opposite sex, erotophobes can use or allow themselves to be used by but not merge and interact comfortably with the opposite sex.

5. Homophobia: Because of insecurities regarding body image, self-esteem and worthiness, and discomfort with the opposite sex, erotophobes often show a fear or even hatred of homosexuality. Perhaps in part because homosexual activity may represent an unconscious means of escape from the pressures of meaningful and intimate heterosexual bonding, erotophobes attempt to purge these covert urges through either publicly stated dislike of and disgust with homosexuality or denial of their own homosexual feelings or identities. All homophobes are not heterosexual.

6. Same Sex Competition: Erotophobes are in competition with their own sex because of feelings of unworthiness. Often consumed by work or career, erotophobes are engaged in chronic compensatory efforts to prove their worthiness by being better than any other man or woman. Just being good at something is not good enough, and erotophobes think about work and love in terms of win-lose rather than win-win.

7. Fast Fantasies: The erotophobe's sexual fantasy life is of quick, anonymous encounters. A walk through the corridors of the mind of an erotophobe reveals only numbers, dates, figures, and an occasional fast and anonymous sex encounter fantasy. Often there is a secret fascination with pornography because of the safe distance such an interest seems to provide from expression of real fantasies and desires.

8. Sex to Show Love: The erotophobes' sexual style is typically yellow. Sex may be a way of *showing* or proving love or meeting perceived relationship obligations but is seldom a means of *sharing* and *expressing* loving feelings. Sex may become habitual or something that is done regularly on certain nights; it is seldom a spontaneous act of caring. Erotophobes often marry people who are quite the opposite in approach to intimacy and sexuality, perhaps because of an unrecognized desire for meaningful connection missed in one of the three windows of worthiness.

9. Constricted Sexual Humor: I will discuss later the role of humor in sexual healing. Erotophobes feel such discomfort with sexual inti-

macy and open intimate sensual expression that sex jokes are avoided entirely, laden with sexism, or in shocking contrast to their own sex lives.

10. Denial and Compensation Defenses: Erotophobes typically deny any "sexual hang-ups" while being critical of others' sexual styles or orientations. They are obviously uncomfortable with direct and sincere discussion of sex but typically claim to be knowledgeable, open, and tolerant in such matters. They also deny the distance they maintain from others and their tendency to be distracted or "too busy to care." Erotophobes compensate for their fear of erotic and intimate sensual connection by working hard, earning a lot of money, or presenting gifts and goods in trade for meaningful and intimate sharing of the self.

11. Lack of Sexual Knowledge: Erotophobes usually had little or no direct sex education from a parent or adult figure, but they may hide defensively behind rigid and often extreme and insincere religious convictions. As a result, they have developed a set of firm and biased sexual beliefs and sexual "common sense" totally without foundation in fact while rejecting further sex education.

12. Sexual Symptoms: Erotophobes typically suffer from "mechanical" problems of premature ejaculation, difficulty having orgasm or diminished intensity of orgasm, and decreasing interest in sexual intimacy. Because the body is separated from the self, it tends to be used for sex rather than experienced as a sexual whole in connection with another body.

THE PARAPHILIAC PERSONALITY

Paraphiliacs see sexual interaction as a diversion, dirty, illicit, or a weapon or item of negotiation, and to be used for escape from feelings of worthlessness and low self-esteem. They often become involved in extramarital affairs or are consumed by an interest in "hard" pornography, such as peep shows and X-rated video tapes, or "soft" pornography, such as erotic novels and television soap operas. They tend to see sex as a release, a distraction, or an escape from stress rather than an expression of intimacy, and they are oriented to the red erotic style.

1. The BAD Syndrome—Bonding and Attachment Displacement: The paraphiliacs' windows of worthiness were typically characterized by exploitive attachment of the primary caretaker to the child rather

than healthy parent-child bonding. Parents of paraphiliacs often either used them sexually or—because of their own immaturity—forced the children to be prematurely independent. Paraphiliacs were typically exploited and often experienced physical or even sexual abuse, resulting in a distortion of physical intimacy for aggression and manipulation rather than joyful and caring connection.

2. Focus on Control: Perhaps because they were so controlled by adults and so consumed and frightened by the regressive needs and apparent helplessness of an immature adult during their own windows of worthiness, paraphiliacs value control over all else. They have sex to control rather than to connect and may use sex to manipulate, coerce, or even hurt.

3. Body as Tool: Paraphiliacs see their bodies as almost irrelevant. At best, the body is a necessary tool to get what they want of and from others. Paraphiliacs show little regard for the "whole" body of someone else but may be fetishistic and imprinted on parts of the body or associated clothing for sexual stimulation.

4. Genitalized Intimacy: Paraphiliacs think that having sex is making love and have difficulty understanding sexuality as a means of expressing loving feelings. Sex is something that can be bought or sold, and paraphiliacs "have" someone and "do it to" someone rather than join with another person intimately.

5. Resentment of the Opposite Sex: Paraphiliacs harbor a deep resentment of the opposite sex. Perhaps because of the treatment they experienced from an immature or overly dependent parent, paraphiliacs are aggressive sexually in both vocabulary and act.

6. Ambivalent to the Same Sex: Paraphiliacs have difficulty establishing and maintaining adult same sex relationships. For them the opposite sex is a source of constant distraction or fixation, so same sex associates are seen as either competitors or possible surrogate sexual objects with whom to act out illicit sex fantasies anonymously.

7. Forbidden Fantasies: A walk through the mind of a paraphiliac is like a stroll through a museum of sexual horrors. Sadomasochistic themes abound, and whips, boots, chains, spike heels, and orgies populate the fantasy life of the paraphiliac.

8. Sexual Depersonalization: Paraphiliacs "have" sex with *a* man or woman and seldom *the* man or woman they are with. The sexual partner comes to represent sex in general and the gender rather than

a specific person worthy of love and care. Paraphiliacs project their own sense of worthlessness onto others and therefore feel free to use others as they see fit. Whether homosexual or heterosexual, paraphiliacs are focused on body rather than relationship and attracted more to bondage than bonding.

9. Sex as Release: While erotophobes may experience sex as an obligation, paraphiliacs see sex as an outlet for pent-up anger, fear, and emotional tension. Sex is a lose-lose proposition because paraphiliacs never seem to find the intensity they so eagerly seek. The partners of paraphiliacs almost always feel distant from and used by the paraphiliacs and may feel trapped into trying what they consider sick or kinky sex.

10. Repression and Projection Defenses: Paraphiliacs have typically repressed much of their childhoods. On occasion, however, they become extremely agitated by flashbacks and breakthroughs to consciousness by associations to a childhood missed, abused, or used up by an inadequate or suffering adult. Paraphiliacs also tend to project onto others their resentment at having been used and exploited and as a result use and exploit others and feel used and exploited by them.

11. Pornographic Knowledge Base: Paraphiliacs have typically been "shocked" into precocious sexual awareness by either sexual abuse during childhood or premature exposure to adult sex scenes. Their sexual knowledge comes from the dark side of sex—the hardest-core pornographic magazines or peep shows—and they attempt to perpetuate sexual mythologies derived from contacts with other paraphiliacs.

12. Sexual Symptoms of Paraphiliacs: Paraphiliacs are typically of the red sexual style, counting sexual conquests or experiments and seeing how many different sexual experiences they can have. The primary sexual complaint of paraphiliacs is lack of arousal and a feeling of doing it more but enjoying it less. They typically deny or project blame for their sexual performance inadequacies, such as lack of or difficulty having erection or vaginal lubrication, inability to have orgasm, or premature ejaculation.

THE EROTOPHILIC PERSONALITY: THE SEXUAL HEALER

The erotophile is the personality profile of the sexual healer, and it represents a model of sexual health rather than just an absence of sexual problems. Erotophiles are comfortable with close and intimate contact, are capable of caring deeply for others, and love to love. Sex is an extension of a need for meaningful connection and a deep and profound sense of loving. Erotophiles feel connected with themselves, with others, and with something more than themselves. They are typically oriented more to the blue sexual style but are capable of developing and deploying the strengths of both yellow and red styles to help the relationship grow.

1. The GLAD Syndrome—"Good Loving Affection Display": Erotophiles received touching, rocking, stroking, and physical contact from both a father and a mother figure. Their dependency as children tends to have been prolonged and may continue far into adulthood in a dependence shared with and given graciously back to the more needful aging parent. Either mother or father was present for most of the prolonged childhood, and erotophiles had experiences being cared for by and caring for others. They regularly experienced a model of two caring people who showed their loving by touching and holding and who never hinted at divorce or separation, even at the most stressful times. To the erotophile, bonds are forever.

2. Bonded Childhood: Erotophiles moved through and beyond the natural attachment of childhood to experience reciprocal bonding with parents. Unconditional acceptance but a strong lesson of conditionally earned love characterized their childhood experiences, and as a result they feel very worthy of bonding as adults and see others as worthy of bonding with.

3. Prototype for Caring: Erotophiles typically have a strong "intimacy imprint" of two loving parents, grandparents, or some other strong, loving, lasting, intimate relationship. They have witnessed a loving couple deal with adversity and illness, and they have witnessed sexual healing in action.

4. Template for Tenderness: Erotophiles, having been touched and rocked gently, have learned how to do the same.

5. Body as Self: To erotophiles, the body, the brain, the genitals, and the "self" are all one. They feel little awkwardness about their own bodies and appreciate the beauty of others in a perspective free from popular social standards.

6. Generalization of Intimacy: Erotophiles score very high on the Pearsall Psychosocial Inventory. They are noncompetitive, cooperative, and gentle in working, playing, and all life activities.

7. Respect for the Opposite Sex: Erotophiles were loved by the oppo-

site sex as children and young adults, tend toward androgyny, and feel a respect and love for the opposite sex as adults.

8. Enriched and Gentle Fantasies: The fantasy life of erotophiles contains a range of fantasies that have evolved from their intimate relationships rather than from pornography or sexist myths.

9. Love Overflows into Sex: Erotophiles engage in sexual intimacy because of profound feelings of love but are so secure in their loving that sexual experimentation and occasional obligatory sex in a bonded relationship are possible without guilt or disappointment. The key words are *development* and *deployment* of a range of loving styles rather than compulsive submission to a fixed love map.

10. Identification and Sublimation Defenses: Erotophiles know how to feel as their partners feel, how to express empathy, how to sublimate sexual needs when necessary, and how to be spontaneous and impetuous at other times.

11. Sexual Knowledge: The sexual knowledge of erotophiles derives primarily from parents and siblings who shared real-life experiences and open discussion of the biology of sex, and who modeled comfort and gentle humor regarding sexuality. Erotophiles' sense of sexual values is clearly established, tied to early childhood, but adaptive to development and changing life situations. Erotophiles are seldom judgmental; they are comfortable with variations of sexual orientation and behaviors.

12. Sexual Symptoms: The sexual problems of erotophiles are disappointment, despair, depression, worry, and concern for the welfare of their partners. At times, erotophiles are distracted from their own pleasure by associations—real or not—to the perceived feelings of others.

TAKING DOWN THE BONDING BLOCKS

The characteristics of the erotophile or sexual healer reveal eight tools for breaking down blocks to bonding.

Bonding Block Breakers

1. See connective codependence as the best kind of shared dependence and realize that sexual healing is as much endurance and toleration as it is erotic sensual intimacy.

2. Be aware that we live in a culture that sees bonds as temporary, but that sexual healing sees all bonds as forever.

3. Remember that attraction, infatuation, and attachment are the psychochemical foreplay of true bonding and not the features of bonding itself.

4. Realize that depression is almost always a symptom of lack of bonding and see depression as a cry for more intense bonding rather than a reason for withdrawal.

5. Know that intimate and lasting sexual exclusivity is what healthy bonds are made of and for.

6. As parents, teachers, therapists, and community members, attend to the vulnerability of the three windows of worthiness or critical bonding developmental periods. Do one's best to protect the sense of self-worth of every human being.

7. Know that bonds don't happen, they are made. Meaningful bonds are not the automatic and inevitable result *of* love but result *from* loving behaviors and intimate caring acts.

8. Realize that all of us possess remnants of individualistic cultural clutter and the erotophobia and paraphilia which it causes. Each of us has traces of the red, blue, and yellow erotic styles. Recognizing these tendencies in ourselves and tolerating, learning from, or forgiving them in others allows us to move beyond their limitations to their potential for creative new ways of bonding.

13

DESIGNING YOUR OWN
SEXUAL HEALING PROGRAM
Fit for Love

Sex is the most fun you can have without laughing.
Woody Allen

THE HEALING SECRET OF THE GREAT KAHUNA

The deep orange sun settled on the dark blue Pacific Ocean horizon, shining like a large operating-room light on the delicate surgery to be performed on the beach. Drums pounded as dancers swayed, and gentle early-evening trade winds blew spray from the surf across the blind man's face as if to help anesthetize him for his operation. Instead of a gallery of medical students, a school of dolphins splashed just offshore. The Hawaiian kahuna healer bent forward, took the edge of a sharpened piece of grass, and gently cut away the cataract from the man's eye. Within days, the old Hawaiian would be looking out to the ocean in the warm glare of the morning sun as he tossed his fishnet with his prior accuracy.

The native Hawaiian kahuna of hundreds of years ago are reported to have performed such delicate surgery as removing cataracts and trepanning or boring through the skull to correct brain infection and then replacing the cut-away pieces of skull with segments of coconut shell or sections of other human skulls. They were able to perform abortions and circumcisions, and administered herbs and extractions from sea animals to cure ulcers, heart trouble, epilepsy, and even cancer.[1] Researchers at our medical schools are now examining some of the potions of the kahuna to find leads to cures for the major diseases of our civilization.

The remarkable feats of the kahuna were related to a single major premise regarding health and healing. Despite their great skills, the kahunas' first concern was to safeguard the soul's connection with everyone and everything. Their remarkable techniques were always based on and secondary to the sacredness of being joyfully connected to nature and the *'ohana* or family. Their first charge was to stay "on the path" and follow the way of *aloha,* or loving connection.

Huna in Hawaiian means "the secret," and the word *kahuna* means "keeper of the secret."[2] Like our own doctors, the kahuna had to master the skills of healing and the techniques and methods of their shamanistic tradition. They were expected to go through more than two decades of training in the ways of natural medicine. All their study was based on "the healing secret" that all health is intimate connection and all illness is a form of disconnection. Healing is reestablishing connection through intense awareness of loving and joyful intimacy with all that is and remembering that the meaning of living and loving is always to connect.

I live on the Hawaiian island of Maui. This island is named after the demigod Maui, a playful trickster who jerked the Hawaiian islands from the sea. When I nearly died from cancer, I went with my wife to our Maui home for our own sexual healing of *huna*—the joy, humor, love, and total connection between life and nature that we found there. This chapter will describe a program for combining joy and physical sensuality like that found in the Hawaiian huna philosophy so that you can be sexually, sensually, and intimately fit for love.

SHAMANISTIC POWERS

Shamanism derives its name from the primitive religion of northern Asia which asserted that shamans or healers can evoke the power of connection with ancient and sacred spirits to perform sometimes miraculous healing. There have been shamans throughout history in all parts of the world. To become a sexual shaman or healer requires learning two special skills practiced by all shamans: playful joy in living with others and sensual activity and movement throughout the life cycle. To be a sexual healing shaman, you must begin to practice these skills in your own daily life.

SEXUAL HEALING PROGRAM
PHASE 1: DETERMINING YOUR SEXUAL FITNESS

There are many ways to measure your physical fitness, but we are not often asked about our sexual fitness. To begin a sexual healing program, I recommend the following four steps:

1. Retake the Pearsall Psychosocial Inventory you took while reading Chapter 1. Assess changes that have taken place now that you have read this book. Your score and your partner's score on this test are every bit as important as the results of a medical test.

2. Schedule an appointment with a doctor for a physical examination with your sexual healing partner. Sexual health and physical well-being are one and the same. Ask the doctor ahead of time if she is willing to do a tandem medical evaluation, with two patients at the same time. Medical histories, blood pressure, and general physical examinations are conducted with both partners present, and information is shared between the couple and the physician. While some doctors will find this idea new, I have taught this procedure to my own medical students for years. Most doctors I know are willing to do such exams and will often find them a good way to get important health information by having the partner present to help with dates, symptoms, and other information. The exam also helps each partner learn about the other's body and physical condition and health issues that need attention.

   Don't be afraid to ask your doctor direct questions about your sexual health. If the doctor is embarrassed, that's her or his problem, not yours. If you feel too embarrassed to ask your doctor questions about your sexual health, that's the doctor's problem, too, because sex is a key part of health and the doctor should be able to make you comfortable enough to discuss this important area. If she or he doesn't seem to be at ease with the topic, find a new doctor.

3. Talk with your partner about your sexual life. Discuss your frequency, what you do, where you do it, how you do it, why you do it, and how you feel after you do it. Try to determine if your relationship is too strongly influenced by the sex syndicate as discussed in Chapter 7. Decide together whether your sex life is your own, in keeping with your desires and feelings.

4. Check your sexual stamina by talking together about these seven components:

- Do we have the ability, skill, knowledge, and energy for the sex life we both desire?

- Do we engage responsibly and with mutual concern and caring in every sexual encounter?

- Do we regularly make time for sexual intimacy, and do both of us take responsibility for making that time?

- Are we still both choosing to show our sexual interest in all areas of our relationship by behaving lovingly and tenderly?

- Are we both happy with what we do sexually and how we feel when we're doing it?

- Is our sexual intimacy congruent with both of our beliefs and values and free from guilt and shame?

- Do we both feel fulfillment and enhanced health and well-being after we have been sexually intimate—even if one or both of us did not experience physical orgasm?

You have high sexual stamina if you both answer yes to all of these questions. The fewer yes answers, the lower your stamina. A little work in the area where you answered no or not sure can help enhance the sexual stamina needed for sexual healing.

SEXUAL HEALING PROGRAM PHASE 2: WORKING OUT

To remain sexually fit and to be able to sexually heal throughout your life, I suggest that you add fifty minutes a week to whatever fitness program you now use to protect and enhance your health. If you're not doing anything to promote your health, check with your doctor about getting started. More attention to diet and more regular exercise are crucial to feeling good, retarding the effects of aging, and reducing the risk of serious disease. The evidence is clear that the closer we get to age fifty and beyond, the more we are at risk of entering the "disability zone" or proneness to illness, weakness, and injury.

There are two reasons for the vulnerability of aging—genetics and lifestyle—and you have control over lifestyle. By adding a fifty-minute-a-week sexual fitness program to your current fitness plan, you can profoundly postpone disability and illness.

If our perceptions and beliefs become our biology, thinking old can make us old. There is no evidence that our brain cells die off as we age.

Using our brains as we get older actually causes the growth of new connections between our brain cells, and when our brains change, so do our immune systems.[3] Since our brains are key to our sex lives, thinking old can slow us down and thinking young can help maintain a more youthful and sensual sexual system that maintains our healing capacity.

By applying the "fifty more sensual minutes around fifty" principle, you can prolong your vitality and even help reverse problems associated with aging such as chronic heart disease, Type II diabetes, vascular disease, hypertension, and osteoporosis.[4] Most fitness programs ignore sexual fitness, but sexual healing is the pleasurable way to get fit for life and love.

In addition to your doctor's dietary and exercise recommendations, your fifty minutes of sexual workout during the week should contain three components: shared laughter, mutual weeping, and couple erotorobics.

ANATOMY OF A "LAUGHGASM"

The etiquette of sexual healing is gentle and mutually enjoyable humor. Etiquette expert Emily Post wrote, "The joy of joys is the person of light but unmalicious humor." One of the best ways of practicing connection is to spend part of your extra fifty minutes a week practicing intentional and regular laughing as a way of coming together in joy.

Kids start to do it before they are ten weeks old. By sixteen weeks, kids do it once every hour. By four years old, kids do it about once every four minutes all day long. Just as when adults do it, every time a child does it, his or her temperature goes up one degree, thereby enhancing resistance to infection. Stress chemicals go down, muscles first tense and then relax to induce a state of relaxation, the whole cardiovascular system pulsates, the chest and abdominal muscles quiver, and air rumbles up the windpipe to smash against the trachea. The result is an explosion of a gust of wind traveling faster than seventy miles per hour! All of this is followed by a wonderful and almost total sense of peaceful and joyful connection.

What is this remarkably pleasurable, intimate, and healing act that has only positive consequences and is completely free? It's laughter, and, like sexual orgasm, a laughter spasm or laughgasm spreads healing effects throughout the body. After years of working with couples, I am convinced that he or she who laughs . . . lasts. Laughter helps us heal by helping us cope and connect, care and relate, and feel as others feel. Our hardiest and "heartiest" laughs come when we share our sense of the absurdity of life.[5] Laughgasms happen when we feel as if we have "come" together in the realization of the joy of living even when life seems ridiculous or harsh and cruel. When we learn to laugh in the gale of the chaos of life, we enhance connection and thereby improve our health.

When we laugh, cortisol—the stress chemical that impairs our immunity—is reduced. Laughter causes an increase in our natural pain-killer—endorphin—and this internal morphine also helps keep our immune systems in balance.[6] Research indicates that twenty seconds of laughter has about the same cardiovascular benefits as three minutes of strenuous rowing. One of my patients observed that "a good guffaw is equal to about two grams of fiber." Laughing involves many of the same physiological mechanisms as sex, and by laughing more, we protect and enhance our sexual health.

Laughter is the catalyst for connection and for making other health behaviors work. Yale psychologist Gary E. Schwartz found that exercise while angry or sad actually had reduced biochemical and cardiovascular benefits, while exercise with humor and a sense of connection increased the benefits of a workout by more than one half![7]

One of the best ways to connect intimately with another person is to learn how to laugh with that person. As Dostoyevsky wrote, "If you wish to glimpse inside a human soul and get to know a man . . . just watch him laugh. If he laughs well, he's a good man." I recommend linking laughs as a means of sexual foreplay, during sex, and as sexual afterplay, but also as an important part of your fifty minutes a week dedicated to enhancing your sexual health.[8]

THE SEARCH FOR APHRODISIACS

Humor and laughter are potential natural aphrodisiacs. The word *aphrodisiac* derives from the name of the Greek goddess of love and beauty, Aphrodite. The world has searched for millennia for aphrodisiacs, and, with few exceptions, the search has been in vain because we were looking outside ourselves. It is our own psychochemicals elicited by our own thoughts that produce the most powerful aphrodisiacs, yet the tendency to seek external stimulation rather than meaningful and joyful connection as a source of arousal has resulted in some funny and sometimes tragic results.

Alcohol and other drugs have been tried for arousal, but in most cases drugs impair sexual arousal and capacity.[9] As a part of your sexual healing fitness program, stay off all drugs as much as possible. Most prescription drugs also have varying degrees of detrimental effects on sex, but these effects are seldom emphasized in discussions between doctor and patient. Ask your doctor about them.

Sexual healing is enhanced by the absence of alcohol, so stop or severely decrease your alcohol intake. Alcohol is the world's most commonly self-prescribed depressant. It detracts from our ability to find meaning and intimacy by lowering inhibitions and inducing a pseudoselflessness that is really a form of withdrawal rather than intimate connection.

In the 1970s, some researchers thought they had found the brain's own Spanish fly. (*Spanish fly* is a substance derived from a Rumanian beetle that has a reputation as a strong aphrodisiac but is actually an irritant of the lining of the bladder and urethra that can result in death.) The suspected natural brain aphrodisiac is a hypothalamic peptide called LHRH (luteinizing hormone-releasing hormone). Researchers identified the composition of this brain chemical, injected it into rats, and the rats assumed the sexual posture called lordosis—in other words they were made instantly ready for a rat orgy. A book was released warning of possible sabotage of our drinking water with LHRH to create sexual havoc. Later research disproved the aphrodisiac power of LHRH in humans.

There is one new substance that researchers feel shows some promise for improving sexual function and enhancing sexual response, particularly in people who experience a chronic illness that interferes with their sexual functioning. This substance is yohimbine hydrochloride, a crystalline alkaloid derived from the sap of the tropical evergreen or yohimbine tree in West Africa. Under a grant from the National Institutes of Health, researchers have found that this substance produces positive effects on both sexual desire and sexual response in people experiencing some physical or health disruption of their sexual systems.[10]

If you intend to practice sexual healing, my work with sexual healers indicates, however, that the cleaner your system is of drugs of all types, the more aroused and healthy you can be. As part of the fifty-fifty sexual fitness program, I recommend avoiding or reducing your intake of caffeine; sugar; salt; tobacco; over-the-counter drugs; prescription drugs when possible; other drugs such as cocaine, marijuana, and alcohol; red meat; and milk and other dairy products. All these substances have some negative effect on most people's health, and the less of them we put in our bodies, the more likely we are to stay well.

Laughter, however, is completely safe, has no known negative side effects, and is excellent sexual practice. Laughter involves the gradual buildup of tension, joyful and shared release of that tension when a connection is made between the joke teller and the joke respondent or when two people discover an insight into absurdity together, and subsequent relaxation. Laughter results from a sense of "getting it" and "coming together" through a shared "aha!" and discussing the cause for the laughter can provide a way to talk about sex in a safe and humorous way.

THE DIRTY DOZEN

As a part of your fifty-fifty sexual fitness program, schedule some time to laugh together and to make laughter a natural aphrodisiac for you. Here are twelve "sex jokes" given to me by my patients. Humor, particularly sex humor, is highly individual. I urge you to collect some laughrodisiacs for your own relationship. You and your partner can probably think of much funnier jokes, but these twelve may serve as a challenge for starting your own collection.

1. "Do you know what a pelvis is?" asked the nurse. "Certainly," said the man. "It's a personal friend of Elvis." "Well, then, do you know what a prostate is?" continued the nurse. "Of course, it's a position when you lay flat on your back." "What does rectum mean?" she asked yet again. "It means she darn near killed him," he answered. "I'll bet you don't know what urine is," she pressed on. "I sure do," he answered confidently. "It's the opposite of 'you're out.' "

2. Rub-a-dub-dub
   Three people in a tub,
   And that's on a slow night.
   —Sign in a Swingers Club

3. "I told my girlfriend that I couldn't please her sexually unless she told me what she wanted. She said, 'OK. Get off of me!' I said, 'All right, but remember it's better to copulate than never.' "

4. "I think sex is natural, but not if it's done right."

5. Advice to anyone who wants to try sexual bondage as a means of arousal: You have to be fit to be tied.

6. "I'm too shy to express my sexual needs except over the phone to people I don't know."

7. The road sign in the mountains warned, "Chains required." Someone had added the words "Whips optional."

8. Bumper Sticker: "Sex Appeal—Give Generously."

9. She said, "The trouble with living in sin is the shortage of closet space." He answered, "Maybe, but the most romantic thing a woman ever said to me is 'Are you sure you're not a cop?' "

10. She said, "Whenever I'm caught between two evils, I take the one I've never tried." (Mae West)

11. Two brothers—one age six and the other age five—walked up hand in hand to the pharmacist's counter. "My little brother needs ten dozen menstrual pads," said the older brother. "What in the world does that little boy want with menstrual pads?" replied the pharmacist. The older brother answered, "It says on television that if you wear those, you can ride a bike and swim, and my little brother can't do either one."

12. On the way home from the drugstore, the two brothers passed a brothel, although they had no idea what it was. They watched as men knocked on the door, the madam answered, took fifty dollars from each man, and ushered him in. An hour later, the men left smiling by the back door. Noting the pleasure the men seemed to show after visiting this strange house, and having no idea what the source of the pleasure might be, the two brothers knocked on the door. The madam look disapprovingly at the little boys as the older brother handed her a quarter and asked if he and his brother could have whatever it was the men were having that seemed to make them so happy. She pulled them in the house by their ears, spanked them several times, and threw them out the back door. As they lay in the dirt with their rear ends stinging, the younger brother said, "Boy, I couldn't take fifty dollars' worth of that!"

The Pearsall Psychosocial Inventory in the Appendix includes an item that deals with the role of humor as related to health, and my clinical work shows clearly that those couples who laugh together stay together and stay healthier longer. Spend a few minutes of your fifty sensual fitness minutes per week laughing together. Remember to include sex jokes that stretch your level of comfort. One purpose of spending part of your sexual fitness program laughing is to prevent sexual sclerosis or hardening of your sexual attitudes.

HEALING TEARS

The evidence is clear. Unlike the tears that flow when we cut onions, tears of emotion contain stress hormone waste products and toxins that are washed out of our systems through our tear ducts. More than 2,000 years ago, Aristotle theorized that tears released at a drama cleanse the mind of suppressed emotions through a process he called catharsis. Researchers have identified endorphins, ACTH, and stress hormones in our tears.[11] Perhaps one function tears perform in our loving relationships is draining the system of the psychochemicals of attraction, infatuation, detachment, and attachment.

Laughing together is a key part of your sexual healing program, but so is crying together. I encourage my sexual healing couples to seek a medical prescription I call "elicitors of psychogenic lacrimation," tear-jerker movies. Having a good cry together can result in feelings of intimacy and often sexual arousal because of the shared closeness and affection. Spend some of your sensual fifty minutes per week crying together.

AGING AND SEXOPENIA

Almost every day I receive announcements about professional meetings throughout the world. These meetings are now including topics related to psychoneuroimmunology, mind-body imagery, stress management, and the latest in meditation, visualization, and imagery approaches to illness and healing. My review of the last twenty programs from 1992 to 1993 indicated not one mention of the sexual aspects of healing.[12] I suggest that there is a major risk to our health that is neglected when we ignore sexual healing or the positive enhancement of our natural healing capacity through intimate connection with someone else.

It is a fact that as we age, we become more prone to illness and disease. We get weaker, more sluggish, more easily tired, and our bodies begin to deteriorate. Tufts University researchers William Evans and Irwin Rosenberg suggest that much of the deterioration we automatically associate with aging is premature and that we enter much too soon into what they call the "zone of disability."[13] They describe "an overall weakening of the body caused by a change in body composition in favor of fat and at the expense of muscle" that often accompanies aging because of unhealthy diet and lack of exercise.[14] They refer to a new disease associated with lack of physical activity they call sarcopenia (*sarco* is Greek for "body" and *penia* is Greek for "reduction in amount or need"). Their prescription for treating and preventing sarcopenia is regular physical activity and prudent diet, but they never mention sex.

I suggest that my older patients, and some of my not-so-old patients, suffer from what I call sexopenia, or failure to remain sexually interested and active that results in deterioration of sexual health and the loss of sexuality's healing potential. Sexopenia is a general weakening of the natural healing system caused by a lack of meaningful sexual and sensual intimacy, and, like sarcopenia, it is best treated by reengagement, in this case in sexual activity.

Our society has become fitness conscious and in some instances fitness consumed. We know that how we eat and exercise are crucial to our life span and our health span. We seem to feel, however, either that our sexual fitness will take care of itself or that general health will guarantee sexual health. The lack of use of the body as a sexual organ can render it less able to be sexual over time. Here are twelve symptoms of sexopenia:

The Sexopenia Syndrome

1. Decrease in degree of penile erection in the male and vaginal lubrication in the female.

2. Genital soreness during or after sex, often accompanied by soreness in other muscle groups.

3. Decreasing sensations in the genitals during sex and numbness and diminishing of response in erotic zones such as the breasts, nipples, neck, and inner thighs.

4. The feeling that sex is becoming a chore or an obligation rather than an expression of intimacy and a source of delightful sensations and mutual pleasure, often accompanied by feeling tired rather than invigorated by sexual activity.

5. Cramps or feelings of tingling or "falling asleep" in the legs, hands, or feet during or after foreplay or coitus.

6. Headaches during or immediately following sexual activity.

7. Decrease in intensity of orgasm and number of orgasmic contractions.

8. A desire to avoid or postpone sexual intimacy even when feeling aroused because being sexually intimate seems to take too much effort.

9. Lack of responsiveness to sexual stimuli, signals, and attempts at seduction from the partner that were previously effective.

10. Lack of interest in sexual imagery, fantasy, stories, erotic novels or movies, or other sources of arousal that were previously exciting.

11. Lack of effort to appear sexually attractive and lack of interest in being viewed as attractive.

12. Lack of dreams and daydreams with sexual content.

Imagine an entirely safe activity with no side effects that can prevent or delay all these symptoms and that feels good, is fun, helps others, and at the same time can help you maintain body strength, muscle mass, aerobic capacity, low blood pressure, and bone density, and even help keep the arteries clean, cholesterol down, and the cholesterol-HDL ratio within healthy limits. Sexual healing can do all of this, yet medicine's general discomfort with the topic of sex has resulted in an emphasis on the low-fat and high-exercise rather than the erotic, joyful, and pleasurable approach to health.

EROTOROBICS

As a part of your extra fifty sensual minutes per week, consider regular erotorobics. Jogging, walking, stair climbing, and sit-ups are fine, but I suggest that the erotic and sensual movements of the body accompanied by sexual arousal and mentioned in Part I are also physical health–enhancing. You may consider these exercises unusual and even embarrassing, but you may also find that you can prevent some of the symptoms of sexopenia by practicing them regularly.

An Erotorobic Workout

Remember that it is as possible to behave yourself into a way of feeling as it is to feel like behaving in a certain manner. Going through the motions of sex whether or not we are having sex can help sustain our sexual interest and feelings, keep us in good sexual condition, and improve our overall health. Try these eight erotorobic exercises either alone or with an interested and interesting partner:

1. Get in and out of bed several times. Roll over in bed, and practice positioning yourself as if someone were sharing the bed with you.

2. Assume various sexual postures, stretching and reaching with your legs and arms. If you have a partner, remember that coitus is only one way to enjoy sex. In Chapter 10 I described axillary coitus, rubbing the penis in the armpit of the partner, and intermammary coitus, or rubbing the penis between the breasts of the partner. Outercourse is rubbing the clitoris or penis on the thigh, calf, arm, or any other part of the body. Go through the motions of coitus without insertion and with clothes on. Many cultures practice these behaviors as often as they do intercourse, and such sexual exercises can help you stay limber and ready for coitus when you choose to have it.

3. Gently caress and massage your own pelvis and genitals. It doesn't matter if they respond in a sexual manner. The purpose is to bring blood into the genital area. It is also a good idea to stretch and warm up before sexual activity and to cool down with slow and relaxing stretching exercises after sexual activity.

4. Practice humping. Using a pillow, move your pelvis in rhythmic thrusts. If your partner is willing, "sex-dance" together to erotic music, swaying your hips and using the muscles you might use in coitus.

5. There is a set of muscles that is almost totally neglected in most workouts. Men and women have sex muscles, and unfortunately they are usually the first to weaken with age. You can learn to exercise them and keep them from becoming loose. There is a floor of these tiny muscles between your legs that forms a kind of sling from front to back. You can feel one group of these muscles when you cease your urine flow in midstream and the other when you contract the muscles used to hold back bowel movements. These muscles support the bladder and part of the rectum, and they help maintain the tone and tenseness of the vagina in women and relate to erection in men.

The major sex muscles are the bulbocavernosus, the urethral sphincter muscle contracted by pelvic muscle uplift and holding, and the levator ani group, including the pubococcygeus, puborectalis, and iliococcygeus muscles, which are contracted in the attempt to hold back a bowel movement.[15] All these muscles can be strengthened and kept in tone and control by voluntarily contracting them several times a day. Pulling the pelvic muscles firmly inward and holding them there for a few seconds strengthens one group, while contracting the muscles that hold back a bowel movement strengthens the other group. Fifty contractions of the sex muscles a day is a good idea, and some of our patients lie next to each other without touching as they do their sex muscle contraction erotorobics.

Once you can recognize and learn to control your sex muscles, contracting them during coitus can be pleasing to the man as the vagina massages the penis and to the woman as the diameter of the penis briefly enlarges. During coitus, pulling up on the pelvic muscles and alternating this contraction with tensing these muscles as if holding back a bowel movement can create a sensual and pleasing genital rhythm.

6. Practice your "flirting" behaviors. Arch your back, sway your hips, stick out your chest, flex your muscles, strut, and practice presenting yourself as sexually attractive. Remember the Mae West warning that it is better to be looked at than to be overlooked. It is all too easy to fall into what comedian George Burns calls the habit of giving old age a bad name by acting and walking "old." Remember to exercise your smile muscles too. Fifty smiles a day strengthens these tiny muscles, makes you look better, and may strengthen your relationship in the process.

7. Practice sexual gazing and sexual smiles. It has been said that by age fifty, we have the face we deserve. Avoid the scowl and frowning that sometimes come as we deeroticize ourselves.

8. Unless your moral or religious principles forbid it, masturbate. One contributing cause to dystrophy of the primary and secondary sexual organs is lack of use, and regular masturbation results in improved blood flow to the genitals, cessation and even reversal of poor circulation to the genitals, and some amount of endogenous secretion of hormones, including oxytocin. As I stated earlier, masturbation is not damaging physically. It is not a means for sexual healing in and of itself, but it can be helpful in keeping up your sex organ tone if your frequency of sexual intimacy is not up to your needs.

I realize that erotorobics may seem strange and spending about ten minutes a week laughing together, ten minutes a week crying together, and thirty minutes a week in erotorobics is not a common health practice. However, I have documented throughout this book that intimate physical responsivity maximizes the healing power of sexuality, and, as in any other human activity, we have to stay sexually fit to be able to heal and be healed sexually. There can be no total fitness without sexual fitness.

To give your later years sexual healing potential, try the steps in this sexual healing program. It may be the most healing fifty minutes you ever spend.

14

INTENSIVE CARING
Sexual Healing and Aging, Heart Disease, and Cancer

Sex isn't the best thing in the world, nor is it the worst thing in the world, but there is nothing quite like it.

W. C. Fields

TO CURE, TO HEAL, TO LOVE

As I walked along the corridors through which I had been rushed on the hospital gurney, I felt a chill and my hands began to shake. After more than three years, I was returning to the same hospital in which I had been dying of cancer. My wife saw me begin to cry and took my hand as we walked past the intensive care unit where our sexual healing had taken place. I had just completed several tests and was coming back to hear if I was free from cancer or cursed again with the disease. We announced our arrival and sat down to wait for my name to be called.

I could not sit still. I paced, knowing that in just a few minutes and with just a few words, my doctor would give me the news that would determine the course of my life. After what seemed like hours, we were called back to wait in one of the exam rooms. We sat down, held hands, and looked quietly at the door. My wife's hand tightened around mine as the door opened and the doctor walked in with my medical records clutched against his chest.

"You're completely clear," he said. "You're in excellent health. You're cured of the cancer."

My wife and I embraced, cried, and said together, "We did it, we did it!" Our sexual healing was confirmed.

It is not so much how long we live but how we live long that is important, and we are only truly cured of any serious disease we experience when we live long enough to die of something else. We are only healed when the length of our lives is matched by the depth of our loving, but the news that I was given a life to love here on earth caused me to cry again. The lessons of sexual healing are not only paths for a longer life span but, more important, a map for the journey through a longer love span.

Drawing on the points made in the first thirteen chapters of this book, this final chapter addresses the three major health challenges of our time. Sexual healing can be of help in all illnesses (and in physical health), but old age, heart disease, and cancer are representative of the disconnection diseases for which sexual healing offers the most hope. Sexual healing offers much in dealing with these life challenges, and, through our confrontation with what hurts, kills, and cripples so many of us so often, we can learn basic lessons from these three illness challenges that apply to all other diseases.

THE THREE MASS KILLERS OF OUR TIME

Before your life is over, you can be certain that you and someone you love will suffer from one of the terrible triad of the diseases of our civilization. The first of these is sarcopenia, mentioned in Chapter 13, the loss of physical and mental stamina that can come with aging. The second is the biggest killer in our society, heart disease. The third is cancer. We can only hope to "cure" or fix a small percentage of the many forms of these three diseases, but we can do much to heal all of them by making sure we maintain our connection with life and loving not only *through* our experience of the illness but *because of* it.

LIFE SPANS AND LOVE SPANS

Almost 40,000 people living in the United States are over one hundred years old, mentally alert, involved in life, and doing well physically. Most of these people have had and still have what most nutritionists would view as terrible diets, rich in fat, low in essential nutrients, and low in fiber. Most of these people have seldom done aerobic workouts, meditation, or mental imagery, and have never heard of new age or holistic medicine or mind-body approaches. Their lives have been filled with as much or more stress and hardship as any. So to what do they attribute their healthy longevity?

Every centenarian uses different words to describe the secret of their durability, but their messages are remarkably similar. They point to four reasons for their long and healthy lives, and recent studies verify four key lifestyle approaches correlated with longevity. These factors are directly related to the principles of sexual healing I have identified throughout this book.[1]

The four long life span fitness factors are engagement, optimism, activity, and the ability to adapt to loss, all of which support key elements of sexual healing—connection, meaningfulness, freedom from shame and guilt, the ability to bond forever and beyond physical loss, and regular use of the body to remain actively engaged with daily life.

FREEDOM FROM THE BLACK DOG SYNDROME

Professors Leonard Poon and Gloria Clayton at the University of Georgia studied ninety-six independent, noninstitutionalized centenarians over five years.[2] They found that the centenarians' optimism was revealed in their almost complete lack of serious and chronic depression. They did not take life too seriously or cynically, and spoke much more of caring for others than "self-fulfillment." Their sentences were filled with "we, us, and ours," and not "I, me, and mine," so they avoid the trap of personalizing negative life events that can lead to depression.[3]

People living long and well talk like sexual shamans. They tend to be free from what Winston Churchill called his "black dog," his nickname for his chronic depression, which often clouded his concern for others as he sank into fits of lonely despair. The black dog syndrome often chases a person to compulsive activity in order to avoid the sad personalization that may accompany quiet moments of intimacy with someone else. People tracked by the black dog of depression avoid intimacy and reflection so they will not have to focus on what "dogs" them every hour of their lives—what they see as the pervasive meaninglessness and permanent bleakness of life.[4]

Sexual healing is ultimate connection and freedom from selfishness and personalization. It involves connecting with rather than turning away from others and learning from shared reflections rather than being frightened by their intensity and meaning. Sexual healing tames the black dog by helping people become involved with others' welfare as much as or more than their own and avoid the personalization of negatives through more shared interpretation of events.

The centenarians tended toward shared rational optimism and much more concern for others than themselves, and they enjoyed personal connection rather than compulsive escape into busyness. When they cried, they cried more often for the loss of a loved one or for the plight of someone else. They were often modest about their accomplishments, and seemed to prefer talking about other people's lives rather than their own, and were seldom hypochondriacal or overly concerned about their health. People who live long and healthy lives do not feel pursued by a black dog of depression barking at their heels.[5]

REMAINING ENGAGED

The second predictive factor identified by Drs. Poon and Clayton was continued connection with and engagement in daily life. The centenarians remained passionately involved in the goings-on around them. They pursued hobbies, visited with friends, reflected happily on the past, and generally led a sensual life of total immersion in the joy of living and celebration of the present moment. They knitted their afghans and tilled their gardens to produce blankets and vegetables for others and not to be the best knitters or gardeners in the world.

You read in Part I about how the selflessness and intimate life engagement in twenty-five key areas that constitute sexual healing may translate to psychoneurosexual healing benefits. It appears that the best way to prevent not being able to do things when we get older is to keep doing things—to stay connected so we will not feel disconnected. To live long and well, consider being less selfish and more altruistically involved.

USE IT OR LOSE IT

In addition to their optimism and engagement, the centenarian sexual healers remained physically active, often stretching, bending, laughing, working in the garden, or walking a mile or two regularly. Most studies of older people neglect their sexual activity, but my own research indicates that the long-living also remain long-loving and erotically involved.[6] Sex researcher Frank Beach writes, "Older folks continue to do sexually what they have always done, but in diminishing amounts."[7] However, ethnographer Alan Merriam reported that African Bala men continue to be sexually active well into their eighties and nineties, with most of the men reporting having intercourse as often as twice a day.[8] It is also possible that these men were reminded of having sex by the fact that researchers were asking them about it. The chief benefit of sex surveys may be more as sensual reminders than as good and reliable sources of sex frequency data.

A recent survey of 200 people ages 80 to 102 showed that 88 percent of the men and 72 percent of the women fantasized regularly about sex.[9] Studies of older people that do not reveal this activity typically fail to ask about it. I have found no difference in sexual interest, masturbation, or fantasy between my middle-aged patients and those over eighty.

While I was consulting with a cardiologist about the ninety-seven-year-old patient he referred to me for help with depression, the doctor was shocked when I told him that the depression was related to his patient's sudden decrease in sexual activity. "He never told me he still had sex," said the physician incredulously. "But you never asked him," I responded. "And you told him to avoid too much excitement. He gets very excited when he has sex, so he stopped having sex. Now that he's back to his usual frequency, his depression has lifted." Older people can ride bikes as well as younger people, but sometimes they have trouble finding a bike that suits them or people laugh at them when they ride. The same goes for sex and older people. It is our agist attitude toward the sexuality of older people and their difficulty finding interested and interesting partners that restrict their sexual freedom and health.

The options for sexual expression in our society generally lessen with aging. Men die sooner than women, and by age sixty-five more than half of married women are widows.[10] Older men, unlike older women, tend to seek younger partners, thus leaving women a smaller pool of potential partners. Masturbation is becoming a more acceptable option among the elderly population, but continued sexual activity of some type is the rule and not the exception for older people when social discrimination and medical ignorance do not block them from sexual healing.[11] Permission for sexual expression throughout the life cycle is an important aspect of total health care.

THE LANGUAGE OF LONGEVITY

In addition to selfless optimism, passionate engagement, and regular activity, the centenarians who so clearly model the ideas of sexual healing were able to maintain the bonds of their lives and loving. Perhaps in part because they had lived so long and therefore had had so much practice in dealing with loss, they were able to adjust well to loss and practice the "good grief" you read about earlier. You also read in Chapter 14 about the sexual healing nature of permanent bonding, moving beyond attraction, infatuation, and attachment to the maintenance of intimate connection even after a relationship ends physically.

Listen to the language of longevity and you will hear references to loving bonds that will never end and regular talks and meetings with the social ghosts I described earlier. You will hear references spoken as if relationships that ended decades ago were real today. These older people have not mummified their past lovers, family, and friends; these relationships and people are fresh in their minds and hearts and not idealized and artificial memories.

Long-living healthy people tend to talk regularly to a deceased partner or spouse for advice, direction, or support. These social ghosts remain an active and real part of their lives. They provide models for action, attitudinal perspectives, esteem, emotional support, and even sexual fantasy.[12] It is the essence of the sexuality of sexual healing that bonding is infinite connection and not merely brief physical contact.

Without one intimate and enduring connection in our lives, we tend to suffer "selfs saturation." We can crowd out and even lose our core identity by overwhelming it with the several "selfs" we use to survive in contemporary society. We feel obligated to be a parent, worker, nurse, financial planner, driver, housekeeper, daughter, caretaker of a parent and so on, and we lose sight of who we are. Whether they were aware of it or not, the centenarians lived in harmony with the essence of their core identities by doing less, having less, and remembering who they really were and the reason for their lives throughout their lives.

HEART DISEASE AND CANCER

Cardiovascular disease is the leading killer in our society. It accounts for 40 percent of all deaths. Decades ago, infectious diseases were the number-one killer, but improved health practices, increased social responsibility, and advancements in medicine have allowed us to control and in many cases eradicate infectious disease as a mass killer. Cancer, in all its forms, is the second leading cause of death. There are more than 600,000 deaths from cancer a year; almost one in three of us will have a form of cancer, and two of three families will be disrupted by this dreaded disease.[13]

Genetics, diet, exercise, and environmental factors are all involved in causing or preventing cardiovascular disease and cell disease. To further illustrate the power of sexual healing, the remainder of this book examines its possible impact—the enhancement of our natural healing and health capacities through intimate and lasting connection—on heart disease and cancer.

AFFECTIVE ANTIGENS

To effectively, sensitively, and rationally employ sexual healing in defense against or for the healing of cardiovascular disease or cancer, it is helpful to understand the personality aspects of these diseases. There is no evidence that any personality causes any disease, and you read earlier about the dangers of sickness shame and guilt. As the editor of the *New England Journal of Medicine,* Marcia Angell, warns, attaching credit to patients for controlling their disease also implies blame for the progression of their disease.[14] Despite many very interesting findings, psychoneuroimmunology does not prove a direct relationship between personality and disease. However, the interesting findings emerging in psychoneuroimmunology and psychoneurosexuality hold great promise for a more complete understanding of the healing potential of the mind and the relationship of personality to healing and illness.

Sexual healing takes a different approach to the potential personality-disease link. It is not just who we are as individuals but also the "type" of person we choose to connect with and the nature of that connection that affect our health and healing. As you read in Chapter 5, thrill seekers (epinephrine), love junkies (too much monamine oxidase, causing a strong dependence on phenylethylamine), the love-sick (endorphins), the love-blind (hypopituitarism and deficiency in ACTH), and lovers who bond (balanced neurohormones and oxytocin) all experience different patterns of psychochemistry. How we love (proneness to a red, yellow, or blue style) and the sexual style of our relationships (various combinations of the primary erotic style colors) also affect our neurochemistry. You read that our lovers can be potential antigens or erotogens, and we ourselves can be antigens or erotogens to our lovers. Our partners, through how they love and how we perceive their loving, present our immune systems with a challenge that can strengthen or impair our immunity as much as anything we do or feel. Psychiatrist Theodor Reik wrote, "Tell me whom you love and I will tell you who you are and, more especially, who you want to be."[15] Our loving is equivalent to our healing and how healthy we hope to be.

Our own personality characteristics are as influential for our partners' disease proneness as they are for us. If sexual healing is "us" rather than "self" healing, it is important to consider the relationship between people's personalities and not just the individual personality's possible etiology in disease. The essence of sexual healing is not only *how* we live but how and with whom we love.

DISEASE-POTENTIATING PARTNERS

Few researchers question the link between poor coping with stress and heart disease. Exactly how that relationship plays itself out within our bodies is less clear, but it is certain that our daily lifestyles influence our cardiovascular systems.[16] In my work with sexual healing, I look not just at the patients but at the personalities of the primary people with whom heart patients live and love, and the nature of their relationships. I have found a "heart irritant" profile of spouses and partners that may contribute to the development of heart disease or augment the chances of engaging in behaviors which make one more prone to heart disease. I have also found partner "cell irritant" profiles that relate to cancer.

Sarcopenia—or experiencing weakness, increased illness, and frailty because of disuse of the mind and body—is sometimes seen as an inevitable result of getting older. We may assume that we have to act our age, that we are losing stamina, that our brains are losing nerve cells, and that we should go gently into the nighttime of life. Much of our society is all too willing to accept this model of aging. Sarcopenia-potentiating partners may have accepted this view. They may fall into a premature caretaker role, protecting and infantalizing their partners by doing *for* instead of *with* them.

There is a common assumption that there is a Type A personality who is so driven, hostile, aggressive, and impatient that he or she cares little about love and relationships. My work with heart patients indicates that they are *very* loving and caring but somehow have walled off their hearts and emotions from the people they should be the closest to.[17] They feel that their worth is what they accomplish rather than who they are. While this is undoubtedly related to the heart patients' own emotions, behaviors, and lifestyles, I have found that they seem to find potentiating partners.

These heart disease–potentiating partners tend to encourage the emotional distance. They may give subtle cues that the patients' successes, accomplishments, and status are more important than personal and intimate identity. By consciously or unconsciously rewarding doing over being and distance over intimacy, the potentiating partners promote rather than prevent or correct the behaviors that become cardiovascular risk factors.

There is also a popular view that cancer patients tend toward depression, are overly accommodating, feel inadequate, and tend to repress their anger, fear, and sadness. Dr. Lydia Temoshok suggests a link between some forms of cancer and the "Type C" personality.[18] She warns, however, that a new age version of mind over matter that simplifies the connection between a complex set of diseases such as cancer and personality is not only wrong but dangerously misleading. In my experience, cancer-prone people have very creative and full emotional lives but can't seem to find the right person, place, or avenue to tell their stories. Potentiating partners tend to discourage such sharing and to diminish the patients' personal potential. They may see the patients as helpmates but not as strong, creative, independent people in their own right.

Dr. Temoshok does not address who the Type C patient chooses to live and love with as a health factor, but I have found that cancer patients' illness and healing are strongly influenced by with whom and how they love and connect.

US OVER ILLNESS

An important warning is in order here. Just as we must avoid the self-sickness shame and guilt that is wrongly associated with the emerging findings on the mind-body link, we must not interpret initial and preliminary findings in sexual healing research regarding the possibility of a "disease-potentiating partner" as an indictment of someone else. If sorting out cause and effect in individual disease etiology is extraordinarily complex, applying these findings to relationships and illness is even more so. Blaming someone else for our illnesses is no more productive and at least as destructive and unfair as blaming ourselves. However, viewing illness and healing in terms of sexual healing connections and relationships instead of focusing exclusively on the individual mind-over-matter approach, adds new ways of understanding the process of healing, sets the stage for new research, and promotes a collective and cooperative approach to understanding illness and healing.

I have focused my research on relationships rather than individual patients. Because of this, I see vulnerabilities and strengths as a dyadal rather than individual issue. Sexual healing requires the view that a new understanding of disease etiology as related to and even promoting intimacy and connection rather than just self-attitude is an opportunity for unique new healing ways.

As evidence of the unifying effect of illness, the divorce rate in couples where one of the spouses is very ill is much lower than that of the general population.[19] There are likely many reasons for this finding, including being too busy dealing with illness to divorce or feeling too guilty and obligated, but my patients and I have found that illness can induce increased intimacy. Cancer can cure neurosis, and a heart attack can cure compulsive rushing to beat the clock. Illness and healing are likely much too complex to ever allow researchers to understand their complete nature. The best we can hope for are some clues that may enhance our healing capacity, and this is my purpose in proposing consideration of the sexual healing or relationship component of these natural life processes.

THE DISEASE-POTENTIATING PARTNER PROFILE

My interviewing of the partners of people with sarcopenia, cancer, and heart disease, the patients themselves, interviewing and analyzing with my clinic teams the videotapes of couples struggling with illness, and analyzing the results of their mutual and individual scores on the Pearsall Psychosocial Inventory indicate the following behavioral patterns of a person relating with someone who is suffering from one of the three major killers.

If you are suffering from sarcopenia, heart disease, or cancer, discuss these profiles with your partner. If you are the partner of someone with one of these three diseases, reflect on your pattern of interaction with your partner. Remember, you're looking for healing leads, not assigning responsibility.

The Sarcopenia-Potentiating Partner
THE CUSTODIAN PATTERN

1. Exploited or neglected as a child, often thrust into the role of parenting his or her own parent. Tends to parent the partner rather than engage in adult interactions and shared responsibility.

2. May have had a parent or grandparent for whom he or she was assigned responsibility, thus learning a nursing pattern of relating to others that encourages dependence and helplessness rather than others' self-care, autonomy, and effort at staying healthy.

3. Lack of outside interests and life involvement. Tends to assume caretaker role as an avocation replacing other interests.

4. Low self-esteem and self-effectiveness compensated for by taking care of the patient in order to establish his or her own identity.

5. Assuming a martyr role, and enjoyment of others' comments about how he or she is sacrificing and forfeiting his or her life for the good of the patient.

6. Strong feelings of guilt for real or imagined transgressions against the patient and for contributing to or causing the illness.

7. Valuing of control and tendency to diminish the preferences and tastes of the patient by attempting to make most decisions about daily living—shopping, decorating, financial management, and so on.

8. May have been or may feel that he or she has been sexually abused or lacking in sexual education and experience. Seeks safety from sex by considering sexual intimacy unimportant, age-inappropriate, or an unnecessary health risk.

9. Because of insecurity in parental role or feelings of rejection, may neglect or deprive children by parenting the patient.

10. Fears the aging process in his or her own life and deals with fear by projecting premature aging onto the patient.

11. Fear of intimacy and use of aging as an escape from adult interactions and ongoing life decisions. Establishes a rest home environment for the patient that is really a safe place of withdrawal for himself or herself.

12. Harboring of unexpressed resentment toward the patient over past real or perceived transgressions, passive-aggressively entrapping him or her in a paternal or maternal or custodial situation.

The sarcopenia-potentiating partner seems to thrive on the adversity of disease. Every new crisis only solidifies the custodial role. By contrast, sexual healing is based on mutual caring, not one-way caretaking.

The Cardiovascular Disease–Potentiating Partner
THE PLEASING PERSON PATTERN

1. Self-sacrificing and deferential to the self-goals of the patient, allowing him or her to set the limits and determine the relationship objectives.

2. Unfailingly pleasant while avoiding confrontations caused by the patient's selfishness or disregard of the relationship.

3. We tend to get more of whatever we reward in our relationships. The partner of the heart patient tends to thrive on the patient's accomplishments, relishing a better lifestyle while verbally denying the importance of accomplishments, goods, and money.

4. Complaints about lack of emotional support while surrendering to its inevitability, withdrawing, and applauding the patient's "doing addiction."

5. Embarrassed by the patient's angry outbursts but seldom addresses this issue directly. May apologize to others for these outbursts but seldom in the presence of the patient.

6. Frightened by the patient's anger and hostility.

7. Infantilization of the patient by attempting to seduce or even trick him or her into taking vacations and rests. Treats the patient as a child, overindulging needs or cleaning up after him or her.

8. Almost always sexually available for the patient and will "take it when he or she can get it," but seldom sexually demanding. Tends to trade sex for intimacy and shows the blue erotic style.

9. Bragging to others about the patient's accomplishments even while complaining about his or her overwork.

10. Worry about the patient's health while often providing an unhealthy diet as a means of "courtship feeding" to win time and attention.

11. Secret worries about the patient's health or sudden death, but more concern with being accepted and not upsetting or worrying the patient by expressing these fears.

12. View of self as a helpmate, source of support, and beneficiary rather than an equal in the relationship. Puts the patient on a pedestal.

In my clinic, the partners of people with heart disease often respond affirmatively to most of these characteristics while joking about "having to put up with all this success." Beneath this thin layer of denial, however, there is often deep worry and sadness when the issues of future health and love are confronted.

The Cancer-Potentiating Partner
THE PASSIVE PERSON PATTERN

1. View of self as superior to and more mature and important than the patient, thereby ignoring his or her unique strengths.

2. Little patience for listening to long, creative, cathartic stories, or tendency to listen sometimes with sympathy (the judgment that a feeling is legitimate) but seldom with empathy (the judgment that a feeling is to be accepted and heard because it is your partner's feeling whether it is intellectually valid or not).

3. Dependence on the patient for almost everything, including keeping of financial records, housekeeping, child management, and particularly emotional support while giving little support in return.

4. Sexual and sensual distance or self-involvement, with little regard for the patient's sexual feelings or needs. Tends to the yellow erotic style.

5. Emotional stoicism or distance but willing to do "what has to be done" when illness or other problems strike.

6. Tendency to dump personal problems on the patient but no receptivity to the patient's problems or view of others' problems as a sign of weakness.

7. Conscious or sometimes unconscious restriction of the patient's emotional, career, and personal growth. Minimizes his or her dreams and goals.

8. Frequent ridicule, mockery, or demeaning of the patient's behaviors, possibly in public.

9. Frequent expressions of disappointment with others, which is turned to frustration with the patient.

10. Typical intense involvement in hobbies or interests that do not involve or interest the patient. Views attempts by the patient to share interests as encroachment on private space.

11. Little sense of humor and failure to find humor in most things.

12. Attention to the patient only when something deemed "important" takes place. Tends to be arbitrary, authoritarian, and narcissistic.

The partners of the cancer patients I have interviewed are unable to see these characteristics until they were documented in clinic videotape vignettes. When confronted by their behaviors, the partners tend to blame the patients for "causing" these behaviors by their own inadequacies.

A CLOUD OVER THE CONNECTION

Correlation is not causation, and all these behaviors can as easily be manifested in the suffering partner as in the caretaker. Sexual healing emphasizes understanding relationship, not individuals, but the focus here is the neglected component of healing—another person.

Sexual healing involves not only looking at the partner as well as the patient but looking at the impact of disease on a relationship and a relationship on disease. Based again on my years of treating couples, here are the stages of the impact of disease on a relationship.

Impact of Disease on the Dyad

Stage 1—Sickness Separation: The first stage of the relationship's re-action to illness is for both partners to draw apart. Because of fear, confusion over what to do or say, anger at the patient for being ill, or the patient's unconscious anger that the partner is not ill, and sometimes the well partner's usually unfounded guilt for having caused or contributed to the illness, there is usually a period of "disease alienation" when sickness strikes.

Stage 2—Drop in Sexual Desire: Accompanying or shortly following the sickness separation stage, there is a period of sexual with-drawal by one or both partners. The sick partner may lack the energy for sex or feel—usually wrongly—that he or she will give the illness to the partner. The well partner may feel that it is too selfish or inconsiderate to continue to seek sexual pleasure.

Stage 3—Total Dependency: Even the most strong and independent patient may become childlike and dependent on the partner beyond the effects of the illness. The well partner is seen as nurse or doctor rather than lover. Sometimes, it is the care-taker who becomes dependent on the patient and begins to need the patient's illness and dependence as a clear definition of his or her role in a relationship that lacked such definition before. Disease can force a decrease in emotional distance, and a new definition of who is strong, who is weak, and who has what responsibilities. It is not always the patient who is dependent on the caretaker.

Stage 4—Rejection: Even in the most caring relationship, the well partner may begin to reject and become impatient and angry with the sick partner, because of the fatigue of being the caretaker or disrespect for the partner's constant childish demands.

Stage 5—Needfulness of the Well Partner: Supporting the caretaker when a patient requires extensive care is one of the most ignored aspects of healing. The well partner may begin to suffer physical symptoms because of the extensive demands and one-way nurturing nature of the relationship.

Stage 6—The Test of Tenderness: The sick partner may send subtle signals of a need for touching and intimacy, and if these signals are missed by the busy and hassled caretaker, the relationship can become desensualized just when closeness can be a healing factor. The many physical maintenance tasks required of a well partner—bathing, feeding, dealing with bowel or urinary problems, and cleaning up after spills or illness—can contribute to distance. The resulting infantilization of the patient or parentalization of the caretaker can seriously affect their mature sexual needs.

Stage 7—Sexual Healing or Lost Love: The couple must now pay attention to the issues raised in this book. Both the sick and the well partner must remember that intimacy heals and that the relationship cannot be surrendered to the sickness. Time spent talking about life in general instead of the illness and holding, touching, and looking into each other's eyes are key to healing at this stage. Because of the burdens of illness and the healing process, it will likely be necessary to "do it to feel it" when it comes to sensual intimacy, but this is one of the best things you can do.

SEXUAL CPR

You have read about the links between immunity, healing, and intimate connection with another person. As a brief review of the findings from psychoneurosexuality, here are some of the healing benefits of a strong intimate relationship—the CPR of sexual healing.

C = Connection

You have read about the powerful impact of meaningful connection with another person on the healing and immune system. There is sufficient research from psychoneurosexuality to suggest that you should pay at least as much attention to meaningful, enduring, and intimate relationship maintenance as you do to exercise and diet. All illness is a form of disconnection within a system—a heart choked off from the body by arterial blockage, overgrowing cells shoving aside and separating organs, or a body disconnecting from a spirit because of premature aging and physical and mental deterioration. One antidote to the isolating nature of illness is personal and caring connection.

P = Passion

While connecting with who we are as individuals and with a higher spiritual purpose and meaning in life are important to our health, the pleasurable, sensual, and passionate aspects of interpersonal connection are often ignored. Sexual healing calls attention to the role sexuality can play in maintaining, protecting, and enhancing our health.

R = Reason

The issue of meaning—a caring reason to be intimate and to find life's meaning through togetherness—has been emphasized throughout this book because sex can as easily kill us as heal us. It is the reason we attach for our lovemaking and our intimate connections that gives them healing power. If our reason is to share and learn through crises, to tolerate and forgive each other's shortcomings, to develop our own loving styles as we learn from the styles of our lover, to try to stay together for each other and the welfare of the world instead of for self-fulfillment, our sexual bond is infused with the most wonderful gift of life—the capacity to be whole together forever.

AN INVITATION TO SEXUAL HEALING

Sexual healing is not possible without a new view—or perhaps a return to an old and often forgotten view—of love and sex. As a review of what you have learned about the five healing connections, I offer the following invitation to a sexual healing.

1. Reconsider what love and sex mean to you—the sensual self-esteem connection of sexual healing. *Love* is a word that now seems to apply to almost everything except a sacred, awesome, inspiring, and

overwhelming need to lessen our deeply felt sense of incompleteness by committing completely and forever to someone else. Sexual healing love is a collective act of merging; not a feeling we have for someone who seems to meet our every need or bolster our self-pride but a feeling shared with someone with whom needs will be met together. You can only love yourself once you are able to love someone else.

The sex of sexual healing is based not on a need for someone else's body or someone to make us feel good but on a desire to join with someone on all of the five intimate connections. In this context, sex with someone else is expressing all that we are willing to give and receiving the same. We do not *have* sex lives, we *are* sexual beings, whose sex is inseparably entwined with all that we are and can be.

2. Reconsider what love and sex mean in your relationship—your connection with another person that makes sexual healing possible. I have used the word *relationship* throughout this book, but it is a tedious and pallid term for the most humane and meaningful of all human acts. A loving relationship is more than contractual commitment *to* someone else, it is surrender *with* someone else. What is surrendered is selfishness, and sexual healing connection requires not that we seek self-satisfaction through our loving with someone else but that we work to create loving together to find mutual joy.

Sex in a healing relationship is tolerant and forgiving, free from mechanical rules and cycles, and motivated by the imagination rather than the activity. It is not about giving or getting greater bodily satisfaction. It is about accepting the disappointment and risks of intimacy, transcending the attraction and infatuation that draw us together to relish the quest for new and healthier bonding.

3. Reconsider what love and sex mean as you connect with something more—the spiritual connection of sexual healing. Sexual healing love is a mutual love that shares and demonstrates a spiritual conviction about what life is for, not a lonely love shared in a vacuum between two people who find little spiritual meaning or coherence in their life together.

Sex is often spoken about now freely in a mechanical and sometimes cynical manner in the media and in most public speech. The sex of sexual healing differentiates between imposed secrecy and the sacredness of inviolable privacy, but it takes into account more than individual freedom and the right to privacy. Even if no one else knows it, our healing sex is moral and an extension of our faith and beliefs. The sex of sexual healing is not something we have to hide, even though we treasure its privacy and uniqueness. It transcends the simple defensive "what we do in our bedroom is our business" to return to virtue, goodness, and gentleness in private life as well as public.

4. Reconsider what love and sex means as you try to live in the present moment—the mindful connection of sexual healing. Love can be the ultimate escape from the constraints of time. When we focus on our loving and our lovers, time doesn't fly—we do. The pressure of time is individual, and by joining intensely with someone else, the pressured self is freed from the regrets of the past and fears of the future to celebrate the joy of the infinite now. When we are loving and loved, we feel liberated from our compulsive concern for time and realize that what really matters is not how much we do or have but how intensely we love and are loved.

   The sex of sexual healing happens *in* rather than *for* the moment. It is based neither on seeking to alter maleness or machismo nor on patriarchal control over women but on working to understanding the dependent relatedness of men and women. Healing sex is not concerned with power, legalism, and self-protection but with merging, sentiment, and the acknowledgment that each of us is a half person who needs someone else to be healed or whole.

5. Finally, reconsider the meaning of sensuality and erotic body to body connection as ways of sexual healing. Reflect on the power of loving touch, sexual intimacy, and demonstrative erotic caring to alter the healing power of the body. Remember that healing is wholeness, and wholeness can only be achieved with another person. Healing love is based on being the lovers we want to be, and loving as we want to be loved. If you want to be loved by a sexual healer, you must work to be a sexual healer.

Healing sex is touching, holding, and joining with another person on all five levels of connection so that, when we face the natural and necessary times of suffering in our lives, we discover even more love. By doing so, no matter how dreadful the disease, we are healed. The sex of sexual healing reclaims sexuality from those who regard it as a means of mechanical self-pleasure. Rather, sex is a means of healing the number-one disease of our time: the individual's lack of profound and prolonged contact with another human being.

APPENDIX

THE PEARSALL PSYCHOSOCIAL INVENTORY

The Pearsall Psychosocial Inventory measures your fitness in twenty-five areas of life connection. This test is designed to be taken by a sexual healing couple. Score yourself, have your partner score you, and total the results.

Each of the twenty-five psychosocial connection factors is discussed in Chapter 1. Sexual healing requires psychosocial health—connection with the self, with others, with something more, with the now, and with the body of another person. Your score on this test reflects your general "connection-ability" in all these areas and therefore is a measure of your sexual healing capacity.

It is important to talk with your partner about each item. Look particularly at those items where you differed on the score assigned and discuss your views on that area of life connection. The closer you are to 200 points, the more "connection-ability" you have and the more likely you are to be a sexual healer.

PEARSALL

PSYCHOSOCIAL

INVENTORY

THE
"25 PSYCHOSOCIAL
FITNESS FACTORS"
SURVEY
"P - F - F"

Paul Pearsall, Ph.D.

Self-Scorer's Name _____

Scoring Partner's Relationship to You _____

Pretest Estimate of Own Score _____
    (SPFF—Self Psychosocial Fitness Factor 0–100)
    (Or Prior Score)

Pretest Estimate of Partner's Score of You _____
    (PPFF—Partner Scoring of PFF 0–100)
    (Or Prior Partner Score of You)

Pretest Estimate of Total Psychosocial Fitness Factor
    (Or Prior TPFF) _____

SCORING SYSTEM

4 = Very Much So	**1** = Rarely
3 = More Than Occasionally	**0** = Never
2 = Occasionally	

SELF   **PARTNER**

1. _____   _____   This person has many close and longtime friends, initiates contacts with these friends, and enjoys being with them at least as much as doing other things.

2. _____   _____   This person feels highly respected, supported, and appreciated at work by fellow workers and supervisors and appreciates and respects them in return.

3. _____   _____   This person eagerly looks forward to going back to work on Monday mornings.

4. _____   _____   This person is very satisfied with his or her job.

5. _____ _____ This person feels in control, effective, challenged by problems, and strongly committed to work and family.

6. _____ _____ This person regularly attends church, synagogue, or another religious institution and has strong and personal religious convictions.

7. _____ _____ This person gets plenty of rest, takes naps sometimes, falls asleep easily, sleeps soundly, and awakes early and refreshed.

8. _____ _____ This person has a loving, supportive spouse.

9. _____ _____ This person enjoys a comfortable, erotic, fulfilling sexual life.

10. _____ _____ This person enjoys touching and being touched.

11. _____ _____ This person seems to feel popular and well-liked and never lonely and isolated.

12. _____ _____ This person is a caring, giving person who is never selfish, self-involved, or self-centered.

13. _____ _____ This person is seldom angry—on the inside *or* the outside.

14. _____ _____ This person does a lot of charity work, helping others, and giving of his or her time for good causes without reward or attention.

15. _____ _____ This person is sincerely optimistic, "up" almost all the time, seldom critical or negative, and is one of the happiest people I know.

16. _____ _____ This is one of the most patient, trusting, and tolerant people I know.

17. _____ _____ This person is free from shame and guilt.

18. _____ _____ This person plays and laughs a lot.

19. _____ _____ This person cries easily in private and public.

20. _____ _____ This person smiles almost all the time.

21. _____ _____ This person is calm and easygoing, and seldom overreacts.

22. _____ _____ This person finds worth in *who* and *how* he or she is rather than in *what* he or she does or possesses.

23. _____ _____ This person expresses his or her emotions easily, honestly, and openly.

24. _____ _____ This person prays, contemplates, or meditates daily.

25. _____ _____ This person makes time every day for family rituals such as dinner together and maintaining family traditions.

Scoring

SPFF _____ **PPFF** _____
   (self)   **(partner)**

SPFF _____ **+ PPFF** _____ **= TPFF**

ITEMS ON TEST THAT REQUIRE ATTENTION:

TOTAL SCORE INTERPRETATION

190–200	ROBUST—A SEXUAL HEALER
170–189	PSYCHOSOCIALLY FIT—GOOD POTENTIAL FOR HEALING
140–169	COMPROMISED—NEED MORE INTIMACY
139 and below	FRAGILE—HEALING URGENT

NOTES

CHAPTER 1

1. For an excellent description of the process by which the brain cells and the bone marrow cells communicate via the neuropeptides and how the monocyte immune cells become a part of the brain, see R. Ornstein and C. Swencionis, "What Is the Healing Brain?" in *The Healing Brain: A Scientific Reader,* ed. by R. Ornstein and C. Swencionis (New York: Guilford Press, 1990), pp. 3–9.

2. For one example of a cautious interpretation of the data emerging from psychoneuroimmunology, see L. Temoshok and H. Dreher, "The Type C Connection, in *Noetic Sciences Review,* Spring 1993, pp. 21–29.

3. As quoted in S. McCammon, D. Knox, and C. Schacht, *Choices in Sexuality* (Minneapolis–St. Paul: West Publishing, 1993), p. 578.

4. The sense of coherence is defined by psychologist Aaron Antonovsky as "a global orientation that expresses the extent to which one has a pervasive, enduring through dynamic feeling of confidence that (1) the stimuli deriving from one's internal and external environments in the course of living are structured, predictable, and explicable; (2) the resources are available to one to meet the demands posed by these stimuli; and (3) these demands are challenges, worthy of investment and engagement." In his *Unraveling the Mystery of Health* (New York: Jossey-Bass, 1987), p. 19.

5. C. G. Jung, *Memories, Dreams, Reflections,* Aniela Jaffé, ed.; Richard Winston and Clara Winston, trans. (New York: Vintage, 1965), p. 340.

6. As quoted in R. Keyes, *Timelock* (New York: Ballantine, 1991), p. 89.

7. Ornstein and Swencionis, "What Is the Healing Brain?" p. 6.

8. For a review of the evidence relating social support and health, see J. S. House et al., "Social Relationships and Health," *Science,* vol. 241 (July 1988), pp. 540–45.

9. D. Ornish, "Changing Life Habits," in B. Moyers, *Healing and the Mind* (New York: Doubleday, 1993), p. 107.

10. S. L. Syme, "Social Support and Risk Reduction," *Mobius,* vol. 4 (1984), pp. 44–54.

11. T. Moore, *Lifespan: Who Lives Longer and Why* (New York: Simon and Schuster, 1993).

12. L. F. Berkman and S. L. Syme, "Social Networks, Host Resistance, and Mortality: A Nine-Year Follow-up Study of Alameda County Residents," *American Journal of Epidemiology,* vol. 109, no. 2 (1979), pp. 186–204.

13. J. G. Bruhn, "An Epidemiological Study of Myocardial Infarction in an Italian-American Community," *Journal of Chronic Diseases,* vol. 18 (1965), pp. 353–65.

14. J. Lynch, *The Broken Heart: The Medical Consequences of Loneliness* (New York: Basic, 1979), p. 13.

15. J. Kiecolt-Glaser, et al., "The Enhancement of Immune Competence by Relaxation and Social Contact," a paper presented at the annual meeting of the Society of Behavioral Medicine, Philadelphia, May 1984.

16. M. Kenny, *Immunological Predictors of Recurrence in Herpes Simplex II,* paper presented at the annual meeting of the American Psychological Association, Toronto, Aug. 1984.

17. As quoted in S. Covey, *The Seven Habits of Effective People* (New York: Simon and Schuster, Fireside Books, 1990), p. 201.

18. For a full discussion of the interactions between well-being, self-fulfillment, and relationship, see J. Shapiro and D. Shapiro, "Well-being and Relationship," in *Beyond Health and Normality,* ed. by R. Walsh and D. Shapiro (New York: Van Nostrand Reinhold, 1983).

19. C. Darwin, *The Origin of Species* (New York: Modern Library, 1959).

20. P. D. Thomas, J. M. Goodwin, and J. S. Goodwin, "Effect of Social Support on Stress-related Changes in Cholesterol Level, Uric Acid Level, and Immune Function in an Elderly Sample," *American Journal of Psychiatry,* vol. 142, no. 6 (1985), pp. 735–37.

21. One example of such studies is research at the Menninger Foundation in Topeka, Kansas, which found that people in intimate loving and romantic relationships had lower levels of stress chemicals in their blood (blood lactate), more immune cells (white cells), and higher levels of endorphins (natural painkillers) and reported feeling less tired (so had less of a neurotransmitter called serotonin). Another study showed lower blood pressure in students who were in loving romantic relationships than in those who had many friends but no single close relationship. See S. Sisca, A. Walsh, and P. Walsh, "Love Deprivation and Blood Pressure Levels Among a College Population," *Psychology,* vol. 22 (1985), pp. 63–70.

22. R. Spitz, "Hospitalism: An Inquiry into the Genesis of Psychiatric Conditions in Early Childhood," *Psychoanalytic Studies of the Child,* vol. 1 (1945), pp. 53–74.

23. I. Eibl-Eibesfeldt, *Ethology: The Biology of Behavior* (New York: Holt, Rinehart and Winston, 1985).

CHAPTER 2

1. Dr. David Spiegel conducted a landmark study on the effect of psychosocial treatment on patients with metastatic breast cancer. For a discussion of his work, see D. Spiegel, "Therapeutic Support Groups," in B. Moyers, ed., *Healing and the Mind* (New York: Doubleday, 1993), pp. 157–70.

2. See T. Friend, "The Placebo Effect: Gauging the Mind's Role in Healing," *USA Today,* June 15, 1993, p. 6D.

CHAPTER 3

1. B. Klopfer, "Psychological Variable in Human Cancer," *Journal of Prospective Techniques,* vol. 31 (1957), pp. 331–40.

2. Y. Ikemi et al., "Psychosomatic Considerations on Cancer Patients Who Have Made a Narrow Escape from Death," *Dynamic Psychiatry,* vol. 8 (1975), pp. 77–93.

3. N. Cousins, *Anatomy of an Illness* (Toronto: Bantam, 1983). See also his *Head First: The Biology of Hope* (New York: E. P. Dutton, 1989).

4. The Benacerraf and Ader quotes are found in S. Locke and D. Colligan. *The Healer Within: The New Medicine of Mind and Body.* (New York: E. P. Dutton, 1986), p. 25.

5. Psychiatrist Scott Peck's book *The Road Less Traveled* is one of the classic discussions of behaving lovingly in order to feel love and loved. New York: Simon and Schuster, 1978.

6. One of the best books about love and healing is J. Borysenko, *Guilt Is the Teacher, Love Is the Lesson* (New York: Warner, 1990).

7. Covey writes about the paradigms of dependence, independence, and interdependence in his *Seven Habits of Highly Effective People* (New York: Simon and Schuster, Fireside Books, 1990), pp. 49–52.

8. Experiments on conditioning immunity are found in Locke and Colligan, *Healer Within.*

9. See M. Rogers, "The Influence of the Psyche and the Brain on Immunity and Disease and Susceptibility: A Critical Review," *Psychosomatic Medicine,* vol. 14 (1979), p. 159.

10. H. Besedovsky, "Hypothalamic Changes During the Immune Response," *European Journal of Immunology,* vol. 7 (1977), p. 232.

11. As quoted in Locke and Colligan, *The Healer Within,* p. 57.

12. J. E. Blalock, "The Immune System as a Sensory Organ," *Journal of Immunology,* vol. 132 (1984), p. 1067.

13. Locke and Colligan, *The Healer Within,* p. 58.

14. Ibid., p. 58.

15. W. B. Cutler et al., "Human Axillary Secretions Influence Women's Menstrual Cycles: The Role of Donor Extract from Men," *Hormone and Behavior,* vol. 20 (1986), pp. 463–73.

16. Ibid.

17. Quoted in my book *Super Marital Sex: Loving for Life* (New York: Doubleday, Ivy Books, 1987), p. 1.

18. Quoted in D. Kline, "The Power of the Placebo," *Hippocrates,* May–June 1988, p. 26.

19. C. B. Pert, "The Wisdom of the Receptors: Neuropeptides, the Emotions, and Bodymind," *Advances,* vol. 3, no. 3 (1986), pp. 8–16.

20. For an interesting discussion of how we share one universal mind rather than being billions of individual brains, see K. Wilbur, *No Boundary: Eastern and Western Approaches to Personal Growth* (Boston: Shambhala, 1985). He writes, "In short, the quantum physicists discovered that reality could no longer be viewed as a complex of distinct things and boundaries. Rather, what were once thought to be bounded 'things' turned out to be interwoven aspects of each other." (p. 38).

21. E. Schrödinger, *What Is Life? and Mind and Matter* (London: Cambridge University Press, 1969), p. 145

22. R. C. Byrd, "Positive Therapeutic Effects of Intercessory Prayer in a Coronary Care Unit Population," *Southern Medical Journal,* vol. 81, no. 7 (1988), pp. 826–29.

23. Dr. Larry Dossey is the pioneer in sound scientific and medical clarification of issues related to healing and connection. See L. Dossey, *Meaning and Medicine* (New York: Bantam, 1991), p. 177.

24. See Locke and Colligan, *The Healer Within.*

25. See L. Dossey, *Recovering the Soul* (New York: Bantam, 1981).

26. For a careful and scientifically valid approach to this topic, see J. Achterberg, *Imagery in Healing* (Boston: Shambhala, 1985).

27. See D. D. Brigman and P. O. Toal, "Designing Imagery for Specific Conditions," Mansfield Center, Conn.: National Institute for the Clinical Application of Behavioral Medicine, 1991.

28. R. Walsh and F. Vaugham, eds., *Paths Beyond Ego: The Transpersonal Vision* (New York: J. P. Tarcher, 1993).

29. P. A. Norris, "Clinical Psychoneuroimmunology," in J. V. Basmajian, ed., *Biofeedback: Principles and Practice for Clinicians* (Baltimore: Williams and Wilkins, 1988).

30. J. Achterberg and G. F. Lewis, *Imagery and Disease* (Champaign, Ill.: IPCA, 1984).

31. For a discussion of the metaphor of illness from an individual perspective, see S. Sontag, *Illness as Metaphor* (New York: Farrar, Straus and Giroux, 1978).

32. B. Siegel, *Love, Medicine, and Miracles* (New York: Harper and Row, 1986).

33. B. Siegel, "Response to Dr. Spiegel," *Advances,* vol. 8, no. 1 (1992), p. 2.

34. Siegel, *Love, Medicine, and Miracles,* p. 181.

35. D. Spiegel, "Reply to Dr. Siegel," *Advances,* vol. 8, no. 1 (1992), p. 3.

36. Dr. Spiegel disagrees so strongly with Dr. Siegel that he writes, "I might add that I bitterly regret the fact that my last name sounds so much like his." In his "A Psychosocial Intervention and Survival Time of Patients with Metastatic Breast Cancer," *Advances,* vol. 7, no. 3 (1991), p. 11.

37. Ibid., p. 13.

38. See A. P. Chesney and W. D. Gentry, "Psychosocial Factors Mediation Health Risk: A Balanced Perspective," *Preventive Medicine,* vol. 11 (1982), pp. 612–17.

39. R. L. Solomon, "The Opponent-Process Theory of Acquired Motivation: The Costs of Pleasure and the Benefits of Pain," *American Psychologist,* vol. 35 (1980), pp. 691–712.

40. This study was done in my own state of Michigan. See C. B. Wortman and R. C. Silver, "Coping with Irrevocable Loss," in *Cataclysms, Crises, and Catastrophes: Psychology in Action,* G. R. VandenBos and Brenda K. Bryant, eds. (Washington, D.C.: American Psychological Association, 1987).

41. I have found a "phoniness factor" in persons with the sickness shame syndrome that prevents them from fully experiencing the natural negative emotions that accompany life catastrophe. My work was with a group of more than 500 seriously ill patients (cancer, heart disease, paraplegia, etc.) over more than twenty years in the Department of Psychiatry at Sinai Hospital of Detroit.

42. T. Friend, "The Placebo Effect: Gauging the Mind's Role in Healing," *USA Today,* June 15, 1993, p. 6D.

CHAPTER 4

1. See K. Von Dreisler, *Redbook,* April 1993. See also K. Von Dreisler, "The Healing Powers of Sex," *Reader's Digest,* June 1993, pp. 17–20.
2. A. Aron and E. N. Arone, "Love and Sexuality," in K. McKinney and S. Sprecher, eds., *Sexuality in Close Relationships* (Hillsdale, N.J.: Erlbaum, 1991), pp. 25–48.
3. For a complete description of the SAM and PAC systems and their impact on our health, see P. Pearsall, *SuperImmunity: Master Your Emotions and Improve Your Health* (New York: McGraw-Hill, 1987).
4. For a critical review of the therapeutic benefits of touch, see C. C. Brown, *The Many Facets of Touch* (Skillman, N.J.: Johnson and Johnson, 1984).
5. G. G. Hayden, "What's in a Name? 'Mechanical' Diagnosis in Clinical Medicine," *Postgraduate Medicine,* vol. 75, no. 1 (1984), pp. 227–32.
6. D. Kreiger, *Foundations of Holistic Health: Nursing Practice* (Philadelphia: J. B. Lippincott, 1981). See also D. Kreiger's *The Therapeutic Touch* (Englewood Cliffs, N.J.: Prentice-Hall, 1979).
7. D. P. Wirth, *Unorthodox Healing: The Effect of Noncontact Therapeutic Touch on the Healing Rate of Full Thickness Dermal Wounds.* Unpublished study. Healing Sciences International, 29 Orinda Way, Box 1888, Orinda, Calif. 94563.
8. See M. J. Meaneuy et al., "Effects of Neonatal Handling on Age-related Impairments Associated with the Hippocampus," *Science,* vol. 239 (1988), pp. 766–68.
9. G. F. Solomon, S. Levine, and J. K. Kraft, "Early Experiences and Immunity," *Nature,* vol. 220 (1968), pp. 821–23.
10. T. J. Fillion, and E. M. Blass, "Infantile Experience with Suckling Odors Determine Adult Sexual Behaviors in Male Rats," *Science,* vol. 231 (1986), pp. 729–31.
11. J. Lynch, *The Broken Heart: The Medical Consequences of Loneliness* (New York: Basic Books, 1979). For a study of the effects of caregiver touch, see S. J. Weiss, "Psychophysiological Effects of Caregiver Touch on Incidence of Cardiac Dysrhythmia," *Heart and Lung,* vol. 15 (1986), pp. 495–506.
12. See V. M. Dreschler et al., "Physiological and Subjective Reactions to Being Touched," *Psychophysiology,* vol. 22 (1985), pp. 96–100.
13. D. Ornish, *Dr. Dean Ornish's Program for Reversing Heart Disease* (New York: Random House, 1991).
14. L. Scherwitz, paper presented at the Clinical Application of Behavioral Medicine third annual conference, Orlando, Fla., Dec. 4, 1992. See also L. Scherwitz et al., "Type A Behavior, Self-involvement, and Coronary Atherosclerosis," *Psychosomatic Medicine,* vol. 45, no. 1 (1983), pp. 45–57.
15. As quoted in H. Dienstfrey, "What Makes the Heart Healthy? A Talk with Dean Ornish," *Advances: The Journal of Mind-Body Health,* vol. 8, no. 2 (1992), p. 34.
16. Ornish, *Reversing Heart Disease,* p. 34.

17. See R. Williams, *The Trusting Heart* (New York: Times Books, 1989). See also L. Scherwitz et al., "Self-involvement and Coronary Heart Disease Incidence in the Multiple-Risk-Factor Intervention Trial," *Psychosomatic Medicine,* vol. 48, nos. 3 and 4 (1987), pp. 187–99.

18. *The American College Dictionary.* New York: Random House, 1960, p. 1102.

19. J. Kiecolt-Glaser et al., "Psychosocial Modifiers of Immunocompetence in Medical Students," *Psychosomatic Medicine,* vol. 46 (1984), pp. 7–14.

20. S. Cohen and G. M. Williamson, "Stress and Infectious Diseases in Humans," *Psychological Bulletin,* vol. 109 (1991), pp. 5–24.

21. S. L. Kimzey, "The Effects of Extended Spaceflight on Hematologic and Immunologic Systems," *Journal of the American Medical Women's Association,* vol. 30, no. 5 (1986), pp. 218–32. See also S. L. Kimzey et al., "Hematology and Immunology Studies: The Second Manned Skylab Mission," *Aviation, Space, and Environmental Medicine,* Apr. 1976, pp. 383–90.

22. J. B. Jemmott and S. E. Locke, "Psychosocial Factors, Immunologic Mediation, and Human Susceptibility to Infectious Diseases: How Much Do We Know?" *Psychological Bulletin,* vol. 95 (1984), pp. 78–108. See also J. B. Jemmott and K. Magloire, "Academic Stress, Social Support, and Secretory Immunoglobulin A," *Journal of Personality and Social Psychology,* vol. 55 (1988), pp. 803–10.

23. B. Dixon, "Dangerous Thoughts: How We Think and Feel Can Make Us Sick," *Science,* vol. 86 (Apr. 1986), pp. 63–66.

24. National Academy of Sciences, *Bereavement: Reactions, Consequences, and Cure* (Washington, D.C.: National Academy Press, 1984).

25. M. E. P. Seligman, "Helplessness and Explanatory Style: Risk Factors for Depression and Disease," paper presented at the annual meeting of the Society of Behavioral Medicine, San Francisco, Calif., 1986.

26. L. S. Sklar and H. Anisman, "Stress and Cancer," *Psychological Bulletin,* vol. 89 (1981), pp. 369–406.

CHAPTER 5

1. E. Berscheid and E. Walster, "A Little Bit about Love," in T. C. Huster, ed., *Foundations of Interpersonal Attraction* (New York: Academic Press, 1974).

2. G. White et al., "Passionate Love and the Misinterpretation of Arousal," *Journal of Personality and Social Psychology,* vol. 41 (1981), pp. 56–62.

3. J. A. Lee, "Love Styles," in R. Sternberg and M. Barnes, eds., *The Psychology of Love* (New Haven: Yale University Press, 1988), pp. 38–67.

4. For a discussion of the two-component theory of emotion, see R. Reisenzein, "The Schacther Theory of Emotion: Two Decades Later," *Psychological Bulletin,* vol. 94 (1983), pp. 239–64.

5. J. Borysenko and M. Borysenko, "On Psychoneuroimmunology: How the Mind Influences Health and Disease . . . and How to Make the Influence Beneficial," *Executive Health,* vol. 19, no. 10 (1983).

6. For a discussion of the physiology of reaction versus response, see J. Kabat-Zinn, *Full Catastrophe Living: Using the Wisdom of Your Body and Mind to Face Stress, Pain, and Illness* (New York: Delta, 1990), pp. 264–82.

7. L. Dossey, "The Role of Consciousness in Health: Emerging Models of the Mind," in *Depth Perspective on Psychoneuroimmunology and the Mind/Body Connection* (Mansfield Center, Conn.: National Institute for the Clinic Application of Behavioral Medicine, 1991), p. 23.

8. Research indicates that there may be "hot" and "cold" reactors and responders. See my *SuperImmunity: Master Your Emotions and Improve Your Health* (New York: McGraw-Hill, 1987).

9. For an excellent description of the relationship between neurohormones and immunity, see M. Borysenko and J. Borysenko, "Stress, Behavior, and Immunity: Animal Models and Mediating Mechanisms," *General Hospital Psychiatry,* vol. 4 (1982).

10. H. Selye, *The Physiology and Pathology of Exposure to Stress* (Montreal: Acta, 1950).

11. Ibid.

12. R. M. Nerem, M. J. Levesque, and J. F. Cornhill, "Social Environment as a Factor in Diet-induced Atherosclerosis," *Science,* vol. 208, no. 1452 (1980), pp. 1475–76.

13. S. J. Whitcher and J. D. Fisher, "Multidimensional Reactions to Therapeutic Touch in a Hospital Setting," *Journal of Personality and Social Psychology,* vol. 37, no. 1 (1979), pp. 87–96.

14. R. Glaser et al., "Stress, Loneliness, and Herpes Virus Latency," paper presented at the meeting of the Society of Behavioral Medicine, Philadelphia, May 1984.

15. See M. Minkler, *Social Networks and Health: People Need People,* series on the Healing Brain, Cassette No. T 57 (Los Altos, Calif.: Institute for the Study of Human Knowledge, 1988).

16. B. Larson, *There's More to Health Than Not Being Sick* (Waco, Tex.: Word Books, 1984).

CHAPTER 6

1. R. W. Barthrop et al., "Depressed Lymphocyte Function After Bereavement," *Lancet,* vol. 1 (1978), pp. 834–39.

2. The view of the immune system as a peripheral receptor organ was coined by H. Besedovsky on the basis of his research showing changes in the brain when the immune system was stimulated. See his "Hypothalamic Changes During the Immune Response," *European Journal of Immunology,* vol. 7 (1977), p. 232.

3. See M. Stein, "Biopsychosocial Approach to Immune Function and Medical Disorders," *Psychiatric Clinics of North America,* vol. 4 (1981), pp. 203–21.

4. Immunologist Robert Ader is a pioneer in establishing the field of psychoneuroimmunology. See his *Psychoneuroimmunology* (New York: Academic Press, 1981).

5. Sherlock Holmes, in A. C. Doyle, *The Adventure of the Mazarine Stone.*

6. E. M. Smith and J. E. Blalock, "Human Lymphocyte Production of Corticotropin and Endorphin-like Substances: Association with Leukocyte Interferon." *Proceedings of the National Academy of Sciences,* vol. 78, no. 12 (1981), 7530–34.

7. D. G. Myers, *Psychology* (New York: Worth Publishers, 1992), p. 522.

8. S. J. Schlieger, S. E. Keller, and M. Stein, "The Influence of Stress and Other Psychosocial Factors on Human Immunity," paper presented at the thirty-sixth annual meeting of the American Psychosomatic Society, 1979.

9. For a well-balanced review of this issue, see D. Grady, "Think Right, Stay Well?" *American Health,* Nov. 1992, pp. 50–54.

10. J. M. Mossey and E. Shapiro, "Self-rated Health: A Predictor of Mortality Among the Elderly," *American Journal of Public Health,* vol. 72 (1982), pp. 800–807.

11. M. Irwin, M. Daniels, T. L. Smith, E. Bloom, and H. Weiner, "Impaired Natural Killer Cell Activity Following Bereavement," *Brain, Behavior, and Immunity,* vol. 1 (1987), pp. 98–104.

12. D. L. Udelman and H. D. Udelman, "A Preliminary Report on Antidepressant Therapy and Its Effects on Hope and Immunity," *Social Science and Medicine,* vol. 20, no. 10 (1985), pp. 1069–72.

13. C. Thomas, "Stamina: The Thread of Human Life," *Journal of Chronic Diseases,* vol. 34 (1981), p. 41.

14. A. Justice, "Review of the Effects of Stress on Cancer in Laboratory Animals: Importance of Time of Stress Application and Type of Tumor." *Psychological Bulletin,* vol. 98 (1985), pp. 108–38.

15. See L. Scherwitz et al., "Type A Behavior, Self-involvement, and Coronary Atherosclerosis," *Psychosomatic Medicine,* vol. 45, no. 1 (1983), pp. 45–57.

16. H. Dienstfrey, "What Makes the Heart Healthy? A Talk with Dean Ornish," *Advances: The Journal of Mind/Body Health,* vol. 8, no. 2 (1992), p. 30.

17. L. Scherwitz, "The Psychology of Health, Immunity, and Disease," paper presented at the Clinical Application of Behavioral Medicine third annual conference, Orlando, Fla., Dec. 4, 1992.

18. Dr. Dean Ornish says, "Behaviors, per se, are generally not the problem. It is the underlying motivation that determines whether the behavior is a problem or not." Quoted in Dienstfrey, "What Makes the Heart Healthy?" p. 33.

19. Ibid., p. 39.

20. For a critical analysis of the evidence that cholesterol reduction will improve health, see P. J. Palumbo, "National Cholesterol Education Program: Does the Emperor Have Any Clothes?" *Mayo Clinic Proceedings,* vol. 63 (1988), pp. 88–90. See also J. McCormick and P. Skrabanek, "Coronary Heart Disease Is Not Preventable by Population Interventions," *Lancet,* vol. 2, no. 8615 (1988), pp. 839–41. Eight of ten people with three major heart attack risk factors will not have a heart attack in the next ten years, and most people who do have a heart attack will have few if any of the risk factors. Number of years of education is a better predictor of low risk of heart attack than absence of all the major heart attack risks. See S. L. Syme, "Social Support and Risk Reduction," *Mobius,* vol. 4 (1984), pp. 44–54.

21. L. A. Peplau, "What Homosexuals Want," *Psychology Today,* Mar. 1981, pp. 28–38.

22. J. Goldstein, *The Experience of Insight* (Santa Cruz, Calif.: Unity Press, 1977). See also J. Shapiro and D. Shapiro, "Perceived Reward of Intimacy: An Investigation of Males and Females," manuscript. University of California Irvine Medical Center, 1983. p. 209.

23. Shapiro and Shapiro, "Perceived Reward of Intimacy."

24. E. Fromm, *The Art of Loving* (New York: Harper and Row, 1962).
25. J. Bardwick, *In Transition* (New York: Holt, Rinehart and Winston, 1979).
26. H. S. Sullivan, *The Interpersonal Theory of Psychiatry* (New York: W. W. Norton, 1953).
27. G. E. Vaillant, "Natural History of Male Psychological Health: Correlates of Successful Marriage and Fatherhood," *American Journal of Psychiatry,* vol. 135 (1978), pp. 653–59. See also his *Adaptation to Life* (Boston: Little, Brown, 1977).
28. Students at Harvard University watched a film of Nobel Peace Prize winner Mother Teresa working with the poor in Calcutta, and their immune systems (levels of the immunity substance salivary IgA, which helps fight off colds and infections) strengthened. When the same students watched a film of Attila the Hun, they suffered weakened immunity (their IgA levels fell). See D. C. Mc-Clelland, "Motivation and Immune Function in Health and Disease," paper presented at the meeting of the Society of Behavioral Medicine, New Orleans, Mar. 1985.
29. For an easy-to-read summary of this research, see J. Lynch, *The Broken Heart: The Medical Consequence of Loneliness* (New York: Basic, 1979).
30. Shapiro and Shapiro, "Perceived Reward of Intimacy," p. 211.

CHAPTER 7

1. For an excellent description of the rise of selfishness in America, a movement urged on by the sex syndicate, see J. L. Collier, *The Rise of Selfishness in America.* New York: Oxford University Press, 1991.
2. The journal of the American Psychological Association, *The American Psychologist,* has dealt with this growing problem dozens of times. Both the American Psychological Association and the American Psychiatric Association have passed recent resolutions to strengthen their codes of ethics against such abuse, but most sex therapists are not regulated by or accountable to either of these groups or state laws.
3. For elaboration on this point, see S. Persons, *The Decline of American Gentility* (New York: Columbia University Press, 1973).

CHAPTER 8

1. As quoted in S. McCammon, D. Knox, and C. Schacht, *Choices in Sexuality* (Minneapolis–St. Paul: West Publishing, 1993), p. 378.
2. Kumu hula or Hawaiian cultural specialist and teacher Frank Kawaikapuokalani Hewett teaches the perpetuation of the dynamic Hawaiian culture and celebrates that culture in his instructive music and dance. See his *E Ho Omau Ka Ha O ka Hawaii.* Honolulu: Tropical Music, 1993. For a description of the cultural tradition of passing on the last breath, see M. K. Pukui, E. W. Haertig, and C. A. Lee, *Nana I Ke Kumu (Look to the Source)* (Honolulu: Hui Hanai, 1983).
3. D. Ackerman, *A Natural History of the Senses* (New York: Random House, 1990), p. 126.

4. As quoted in ibid., p. 378.

5. For a full discussion of the instrumental male and the expressional female, see C. Tavris, *The Mismeasurement of Woman* (New York: Simon and Schuster, 1993).

6. J. M. Rosenzweig and D. M. Dailey, "Dyadic Adjustment/Sexual Satisfaction in Women and Men as Affected by Psychological Sex Role Self-perception," *Journal of Sex and Marital Therapy,* vol. 15 (1989), pp. 42–50.

7. For a clear review of this new research area, see G. Cowley, "The Future of AIDS," *Newsweek,* Mar. 29, 1993, pp. 46–53.

CHAPTER 9

1. W. Masters and V. Johnson, *Human Sexual Response* (Boston: Little, Brown, 1966).

2. For a complete discussion of the inaccuracy of the four-stage model of human sexual response, see L. Tiefer, "Historical, Scientific, Cultural, and Feminist Criticism of the Human Sexual Response Cycle," *Annual Review of Sex Research,* vol. 2 (1991), pp. 1–23.

3. See S. Wilson and T. Barber, "The Fantasy-Prone Personality," in A. Sheikh, ed., *Imagery* (New York: John Wiley, 1983), pp. 340–87.

4. See E. Vance and N. Wagner, "Written Descriptions of Orgasm," *Archives of Sexual Behavior,* vol. 5 (1976), pp. 87–98. In this study, male and female descriptions of orgasm were so similar that a panel of psychologists and physicians could not distinguish them by gender.

5. Ibid., p. 86.

6. For one of the best descriptions of the discoveries that led to the "mind revolution," see K. Pelletier, *Mind as Healer, Mind as Slayer* (New York: Delacorte, Seymour Lawrence, 1977).

7. See R. Flaster, ed., *The New York Times Book of Science Literacy* (New York: Times Books, 1991), pp. 115–16.

8. Larry Ephron, as quoted in L. Dossey, *Meaning and Medicine* (New York: Bantam, 1991), p. 139.

9. The ancient Hawaiians and their healers and priests, the kahuna, practiced a form of medicine based on the collective health of their community, harmony with nature, and love. See L. R. McBride, *The Kahuna: Versatile Mystics of Old Hawaii* (Hilo, Hawaii: Petroglyph Press, 1972).

10. B. Lown, "Basis for Recurring Ventricular Fibrillation in the Absence of Coronary Artery Disease and Its Management," *New England Journal of Medicine,* vol. 294, no. 12 (1976), pp. 623–29.

11. S. Ohno and M. Ohno, "The All Pervasive Principle of Repetitious Recurrence Governs Not Only Coding Sequence Construction but Also Human Endeavor in Musical Composition," *Immunogenetics,* vol. 24 (1986), pp. 71–78.

12. Quoted in F. Wilczek and B. Devine, *Longing for the Harmonies* (New York: W. W. Norton, 1989).

13. See E. T. Hall, *Beyond Culture* (New York: Doubleday, Anchor Press, 1976).

14. Reported in Dossey, *Meaning and Medicine,* p. 145.

15. J. Grinberg-Zylberbaum and J. Ramos, "Patterns of Inter-hemispheric Correlation During Human Communication," *International Journal of Neuro-*

science, vol. 36 (1987), pp. 41–55. See also "Silent Communication Increases EEG Synchrony," *Brain/Mind Bulletin,* vol. 13, no. 10 (1988), pp. 1 ff.
16. Ibid.
17. J. Achterberg, *Imagery in Healing* (Boston: Shambhala, 1985).
18. W. Brand and M. Schlitz, "A Method for the Objective Study of Transpersonal Imagery," *Journal of Scientific Exploration,* vol. 3, no. 1 (1989), pp. 43–63.
19. See C. Douglas, "The Beat Goes On," *Psychology Today,* Nov. 1987, pp. 37–42.
20. M. S. Gizzi and B. Gitler, "Coronary Risk Factors: The Contemplation of Bigamy," *Journal of the American Medical Association,* vol. 256, no. 9 (1986), p. 1138.
21. M. Ueno, "The So-called Coition Death," *Japan Journal of Legal Medicine,* vol. 17 (1963), p. 330. See also T. P. Hackett and J. F. Rosenbaum, "Emotion, Psychiatric Disorders, and the Heart," in E. Braunwald, ed., *Heart Disease* (Philadelphia: W. B. Saunders, 1980), pp. 1923 ff.
22. D. Aldridge, "The Music of the Body: Music Therapy in Medical Settings," *Advances,* vol. 9, no. 1 (1993), pp. 17–36.
23. As quoted in ibid., p. 17.

CHAPTER 10

1. J. Krishnamurti, *The First and Last Freedom* (San Francisco: Harper and Row, 1954), p. 228.
2. Ibid., p. 177.
3. Ibid., p. 177.
4. Ibid., p. 231.
5. Quoted in A. Luks, "Helper's High," *Psychology Today,* Oct. 1988, pp. 39–42.
6. H. E. Fisher, *Anatomy of Love* (New York: W. W. Norton, 1992), p. 56.
7. J. L. Collier, *The Rise of Selfishness in America.* (New York: Oxford University Press, 1991), p. 200.
8. As quoted in *Playboy,* Jan. 1974, p. 65.
9. Reported by the Sex Information and Education Council of the United States by Peter Scales, a research analyst studying sex education programs for the federal government.
10. J. Krishnamurti, *First and Last Freedom,* p. 228.
11. N. H. Clark, *Deliver Us from Evil* (New York: Vintage, 1963), p. 82.
12. The source for the data supporting these conclusions is in H. B. Biller and R. S. Solomon, *Child Maltreatment and Paternal Deprivation: A Manifesto for Research, Prevention, and Treatment* (Lexington, Mass.: Lexington Books, 1986).
13. See the work of M. Seligman, *Learned Optimism* (New York: Random House, 1991).
14. H. B. Biller, and R. S. Solomon, *Child Maltreatment and Paternal Deprivation: A Manifesto for Research, Prevention, and Treatment* (Lexington, Mass.: Lexington Books, 1986).
15. Ibid., p. 153.
16. D. A. Smith and G. R. Jarjoura, "Social Structure and Criminal Victimiza-

tion," *Journal of Research in Crime and Delinquency,* vol. 25 (Feb. 1988), pp. 27–52.

17. Quoted in *New York Times,* July 12, 1990, p. C14.

18. I. Reiss, *The Social Context of Premarital Sexual Permissiveness* (New York: Holt, Rinehart, and Winston, 1967), p. 173.

19. B. F. More et al., "Effects of Variant Types of Child Care Experience on the Adaptive Behavior of Kindergarten Children," *American Journal of Orthopsychiatry,* vol. 58 (Apr. 1988), p. 297.

20. Collier, *Rise of Selfishness,* p. 251.

21. M. Blum, *The Day Care Dilemma* (Lexington, Mass.: D.C. Heath, 1983), p. 84.

22. For a clear and well-documented presentation of the data on the effects of the neglect of our parenting responsibilities, see Collier, *Rise of Selfishness.*

23. *Statistical Abstract of the United States,* 1989, United States Printing Office, Washington, D.C., pp. 688–89.

24. Ibid., p. 424.

25. W. Harris, *Inside America,* p. 355.

CHAPTER 11

1. Anthropologist Helen Fisher writes about the "four year itch" or the fact that divorce most often occurs around four years of marriage. H. E. Fisher, *Anatomy of Love* (New York: W. W. Norton, 1992), p. 109.

2. See M. R. Liebowitz, *The Chemistry of Love* (Boston: Little, Brown, 1983).

3. P. Bohannan, *All the Happy Families: Exploring the Varieties of Family Life* (New York: McGraw-Hill, 1985), p. 147.

4. See M. Beattie, *Co-Dependent No More* (New York: Harper and Row, 1989); J. Bradshaw, *Bradshaw On: The Family* (Deerfield Beach, Fla.: Health Communications, 1988); A. W. Schaef, *When Society Becomes an Addict* (New York: Harper and Row, 1988).

5. See M. Lievine and R. Troiden, "The Myth of Sexual Compulsivity," *Journal of Sex Research,* vol. 16 (1988), pp. 347–63.

6. E. Coleman and B. Edwards, "Sexual Compulsion vs. Sexual Addiction," *Sex Information and Education Council of the United States Report,* July 1986, pp. 7–10.

7. D. McClelland, "Inhibited Power Motivation and Blood Pressure in Men," *Journal of Abnormal Psychology,* vol. 88 (1979), pp. 182–90.

8. For example, R. J. Sternberg proposes three types of intelligence—academic, practical, and creative. See R. J. Sternberg and R. K. Wagner, eds., *Practical Intelligence: Origins of Competence in the Everyday World* (New York: Cambridge University Press, 1986). See also R. J. Sternberg, *Beyond IQ: A Triangular Theory of Intelligence* (New York: Cambridge University Press, 1985). Sternberg has extended his approach to loving style. See his "A Triangular Theory of Love," *Psychological Review,* vol. 93 (1986).

CHAPTER 12

1. J. Kellerman et al., "Looking and Loving: The Effects of Mutual Gaze on Feelings of Romantic Love," *Journal of Research in Personality,* vol. 23 (1989), pp. 145–61.
2. G. B. Shaw, *Man and Superman,* 1903.
3. E. Hoffman, *Huna* (West Chester, Pa.: Whitford Press, 1981).
4. See L. Wheeler, H. T. Treis, and M. H. Bond, "Collectivism-Individualism in Everyday Social Life: The Middle Kingdom and the Melting Pot," *Journal of Personality and Social Psychology,* vol. 57 (1989), pp. 79–86.
5. See H. D. Triandis, "The Self and Social Behavior of Differing Cultural Contexts," *Psychological Review,* vol. 98 (1991), pp. 224–53.
6. D. G. Myers, *The Pursuit of Happiness: Who Is Happy and Why?* (New York: William Morrow, 1992), pp. 147–48.
7. See M. Stroebe, M. Gergen, K. Gergen, and W. Stroebe, "Broken Hearts or Broken Bonds: Love and Death in Historical Perspective," *American Psychologist,* vol. 47, no. 10 (Oct. 1992), pp. 1205–12.
8. G. D. Gorer, *Death, Grief, and Mourning in Contemporary Britain* (New York: Doubleday, 1965).
9. M. M. Gergen, "Social Ghosts: Opening Inquiry on Imaginal Relationships," paper presented at the ninety-fifty annual convention of the American Psychological Association, New York, Aug. 1987.
10. M. Seligman, "Why Is There So Much Depression Today?" in *G. Stanley Hall Lectures,* I. S. Cohen, ed., vol. 9. Washington, D.C.: American Psychological Association, 1989.
11. A. J. Cherlin, *Marriage, Divorce, Remarriage* (Cambridge: Harvard University Press, 1981).
12. P. E. Lampe, ed., *Adultery in the United States: Close Encounters of the Sixth (or Seventh) Kind* (Buffalo: Prometheus Books, 1987).
13. As quoted in P. Bohannan, *All the Happy Families: Exploring the Varieties of Family Life* (New York: McGraw-Hill, 1985).
14. H. E. Fisher, *Anatomy of Love* (New York: W. W. Norton, 1992), p. 72.
15. See T. Stoehr, ed., *Free Love in America: A Documented History* (New York: AMS Press, 1979).
16. P. L. ven den Berghe, *Human Family Systems: An Evolutionary View* (Westport, Conn.: Greenwood Press, 1979).
17. As quoted in D. G. Myers, *Psychology* (New York: Worth, 1992), p. 581.
18. See E. Friedl, *Women and Men: An Anthropologist's View* (New York: Holt, Rinehart and Winston, 1975).
19. Ibid.

CHAPTER 13

1. As unbelievable as the reports about the skills of the Hawaiian kahuna may seem, they are well documented in several sources. At a time when European doctors were bleeding patients with dirty hands, the kahuna were performing medical procedures we are only learning about today. See L. R. McBride, *The Kahuna: Versatile Mystics of Old Hawaii* (Hilo, Hawaii: Petroglyph Press, 1972).

2. For an interesting discussion of the relationship between connection and healing in ancient Hawaii, see E. Hoffman, *Huna: A Beginner's Guide* (West Chester, Pa.: Whitford Press, 1976).

3. It used to be believed that we lose about 100,000 nerve cells per day after age thirty. New research indicates that "use it and you won't lose it" is the rule of brain function with age. See H. Brody, "Organization of the Cerebral Cortex II: A Study of Aging in the Human Cerebral Cortex," *Journal of Comparative Neurology,* vol. 102 (1955), pp. 511–56.

4. For a complete description of the relationship between fitness and aging, see W. Evans and E. H. Rosenberg, *Biomarkers: The Ten Determinants of Aging You Can Control* (New York: Simon and Schuster, 1991).

5. See Harvard Medical School psychiatrist G. Vaillant's study of hardy persons in *Adaptation to Life* (Boston: Little, Brown, 1977).

6. W. F. Fry and W. A. Salameh, eds., *Handbook of Humor and Psychotherapy: Advances in the Clinical Use of Humor* (Sarasota, Fla.: Pro Resource, 1987).

7. See J. Goodman, ed., *Laughing Matters* (A Quarterly Magazine on Humor). The Humor Project, 110 Spring Street, Saratoga Springs, N.Y. 12866.

8. For an excellent and easy-to-read book about laughter, humor, and health, see C. W. Metcalf and R. Felible, *Lighten Up: Survival Skills for People Under Pressure* (New York: Addison-Wesley, 1992).

9. R. Rosen, "Alcohol and Drug Effects on Sexual Response: Human Experiments and Clinical Studies," *Annual Review of Sex Research,* vol. 2 (1991), pp. 119–79.

10. J. Susset et al., "Effects of Yohimbine Hydrochloride on Erectile Impotence: A Double-Blind Study," *Journal of Urology,* vol. 141 (1989), pp. 1360–63.

11. W. H. Frey et al., "Effect of Stimulus on the Chemical Composition of Tears," *American Journal of Ophthalmology,* vol. 92, no. 4 (1981), pp. 559–67.

12. For example, the Fourth International Conference on the Psychology of Health, Immunity, and Disease lists dozens of the most current presentations and most prestigious and respected researchers in mind-body healing, but there are no programs dealing with sexuality. The National Institute for the Clinical Application of Behavioral Medicine, Hilton Head, S.C., Dec. 9–12, 1992.

13. See Evans and Rosenberg, *Biomarkers.*

14. Ibid., p. 23.

15. For a complete description of the sex muscles, see K. L. Jones, L. W. Shainberg, and Curtis O. Byer, *Sex and People* (New York: Harper and Row, 1977), pp. 126–28.

CHAPTER 14

1. A report on ABC Television's *20/20* reviewed several recent findings about the centenarians in Georgia that point to optimism, engagement, regular activity, lack of depression, and ability to cope with loss as key variables associated with living long and well. Other studies on long life confirm the findings outlined in this chapter. See K. Pelletier, *Longevity: Fulfilling Our Biological Potential* (New York: Delacorte, 1984).

2. As reported by ABC News, *20/20,* Transcript 1249, Nov. 20, 1992.

3. M. Seligman, *Learned Optimism* (New York: Random House, 1991).

4. See A. Storr, *Churchill's Black Dog, Kafka's Mice, and Other Phenomena of the Human Mind* (New York: Ballantine, 1988). In this book, Storr discusses the role of chronic depression in the lives of some of the great minds of our time.

5. See C. G. Jung, *Psychological Types,* vol. 6 of Collected Works, trans. R. F. C. Hull (London: Routledge and Kegan Paul, 1953–1979), paragraph 613.

6. See G. Bachmann, "Sexual Dysfunction in the Older Woman," *Medical Aspects of Human Sexuality,* Feb. 1991 vol. II, 42–45.

7. F. Beach, ed., *Human Sexuality in Four Perspectives* (Baltimore: Johns Hopkins University Press, 1978), p. 118.

8. A. Merriam, "Aspects of Sexual Behavior Among the Bala," in *Human Sexual Behavior: Variations in the Ethnographic Spectrum,* eds., D. Marshall and R. Suggs (Englewood Cliffs, N.J.: Prentice-Hall, 1971).

9. J. Bretschneider and N. McCoy, "Sexual Interest and Behavior in Healthy 80- to 102-Year-Olds," *Archives of Sexual Behavior,* vol. 15, no. 109 (1988).

10. R. Greene and S. Field, "Social Support Coverage and the Well-being of Elderly Widows and Married Women," *Journal of Family Issues,* vol. 10 (1989), pp. 33–51.

11. R. Weizman and J. Hart, "Sexual Behavior in Healthy Married Elderly Men," *Archives of Sexual Behavior,* vol. 16 (1987), pp. 39–44.

12. K. J. Gergen, *The Saturated Self: Dilemma of Identity in Contemporary Life* (New York: Basic Books, 1991).

13. J. W. Cullon, B. H. Fox, and R. N. Isom, eds., *Cancer: The Behavioral Dimension* (New York: Raven Press, 1976).

14. As quoted in D. Gradey, "Think Right, Stay Well?" *American Health,* Nov. 1992, p. 54.

15. As quoted in S. McCammon, D. Knox, and C. Schacht, *Choices in Sexuality* (Minneapolis–St. Paul: West Publishing, 1993), p. 513.

16. See R. S. Eliot and D. L. Breo, *Is It Worth Dying For?* (New York: Bantam, 1984).

17. This same finding is reported by D. Ornish in his *Dr. Dean Ornish's Program for Reversing Heart Disease* (New York: Random House, 1991).

18. L. Temoshok, *The Type C Connection* (New York: Random House, 1992).

19. T. J. Litman, "The Family as the Basic Unit in Health and Medical Care: A Social Behavioral Overview," *Social Science and Medicine,* vol. 8 (1974), pp. 495–519.

BIBLIOGRAPHY

Achterberg, J. *Imagery in Healing.* Boston: Shambhala, 1985.

Achterberg, J., and G. F. Lewis. *Imagery and Disease.* Champaign, Ill.: IPCA, 1984.

Ader, R. *Psychoneuroimmunology.* New York: Academic Press, 1981.

Ader, R., and N. Cohen. "CNS–Immune System Interactions: Conditional Phenomena." In *Behavior and Brain Sciences,* vol. 8, 1981.

Alves, R. *Tomorrow's Child: Imagination, Creativity, and the Rebirth of Culture.* New York: Harper and Row, 1972.

Angell, M. "Disease as a Reflection of the Psyche." *New England Journal of Medicine,* vol. 312, no. 24 (1985).

Bardwick, J. *In Transition.* New York: Holt, Rinehart, and Winston, 1979.

Baskin, Y. "The Way We Act." *Science,* vol. 85 (Nov. 1985).

Barthrop, R. W., et al. "Depressed Lymphocyte Function After Bereavement." *Lancet,* vol. 1 (1978).

Berkman, L. F., and S. L. Syme. "Social Networks, Host Resistance, and Mortality: A Nine-Year Follow-up Study of Alameda County Residents." *American Journal of Epidemiology,* vol. 109, no. 2 (1979).

Bernstein, R. L., and A. C. Gane. "Koro: Proposed Classification for DSM III." *American Journal of Psychiatry,* vol. 147 (1990).

Besedovsky, H. "Hypothalamic Changes During the Immune Response." *European Journal of Immunology,* vol. 7 (1977).

Biller, H. B., and R. S. Solomon. *Child Maltreatment and Paternal Deprivation: A Manifesto for Research, Prevention, and Treatment.* Lexington, Mass.: Lexington Books, 1986.

Blalock, J. E. "The Immune System as a Sensory Organ." *Journal of Immunology,* vol. 132 (1984).

Blazer, D. G. "Social Support of Mortality in an Elderly Community Population." *American Journal of Epidemiology,* vol. 115, no. 5 (1982).

Blum, M. *The Day Care Dilemma.* Lexington, Mass.: D. C. Heath, 1983.

Borysenko, J. *Guilt Is the Teacher, Love Is the Lesson.* New York: Warner, 1990.

Borysenko, J., and M. Borysenko. "On Psychoneuroimmunology: How the Mind Influences Health and Disease . . . and How to Make the Influence Beneficial." *Executive Health,* vol. 19, no. 10 (1983).

Borysenko, M., and J. Borysenko. "Stress, Behavior, and Immunity: Animal Models and Mediating Mechanisms." *General Hospital Psychiatry,* vol. 4 (1982).

Brand, W., and M. Schlitz. "A Method for the Objective Study of Transpersonal Imagery." *Journal of Scientific Exploration,* vol. 3, no. 1 (1989).

Brigman, D. D., and P. O. Toal. "Designing Imagery for Specific Conditions." Mansfield Center, Conn.: National Institute for the Clinical Application of Behavioral Medicine, 1991.

Brown, C. C., ed. *The Many Facets of Touch.* Skillman, N.J.: Johnson and Johnson, 1984.

Bruhn, J. G. "An Epidemiological Study of Myocardial Infarction in an Italian-American Community." *Journal of Chronic Diseases,* vol. 18 (1965).

Bruhn, J. G., et al. "Social Aspects of Coronary Heart Disease in Two Adjacent Ethnically Different Communities." *American Journal of Public Health,* vol. 56, no. 9 (1966).

Bullough, V. "Technology for the Prevention of 'Les Maladies Produites par las Masturbation.' " *Technology and Culture,* vol. 28, no. 4 (1976).

Byrd, R. C. "Positive Therapeutic Effects of Intercessory Prayer in a Coronary Care Unit Population." *Southern Medical Journal,* vol. 81, no. 7 (1988).

Caddileth, B. R., et al. "Contemporary Unorthodox Treatments in Cancer Medicine: A Study of Patients, Treatments, and Practitioners." *Annals of Internal Medicine,* vol. 10 (1984).

Campbell, E. R. "Patricia Sun." In Sy Safransky, ed., *A Bell Ringing in the Empty Sky: The Best of the Sun.* San Diego: Mho and Mho Works, 1985.

Cannon, W. B. *The Wisdom of the Body.* New York: W. W. Norton, 1942.

Chesney, A. P., and W. D. Gentry. "Psychosocial Factors Mediation Health Risk: A Balanced Perspective." *Preventive Medicine,* vol. 11 (1982).

Chopra, D. *Unconditional Life: Mastering the Forces That Shape Personal Reality.* New York: Bantam, 1991.

Clark, N. H. *Deliver Us from Evil.* New York: Vintage, 1963.

Coe, C. L., et al. "Effect of Maternal Separation on Humoral Immunity in Infant Primates." In N. H. Spector, ed. *International Workshop on Neuroimmunomodulation.* Bethesda, Md., 1985.

Cohen, S., and G. M. Williamson. "Stress and Infectious Diseases in Humans." *Psychological Bulletin,* vol. 109 (1991).

Collier, J. L. *The Rise of Selfishness in America.* New York: Oxford University Press, 1991.

Corballis, M. C. *The Lopsided Ape.* New York: Oxford University Press, 1992.

Counch, J. "Relief of Migraine Headache with Sexual Orgasm." *Headache,* vol. 27, no. 5 (May 1987).

Cousins, N. *Head First: The Biology of Hope.* New York: E. P. Dutton, 1989.

Covey, S. *The Seven Habits of Highly Effective People.* New York: Simon and Schuster, Fireside Books, 1990.

Cowley, G. "The Future of AIDS." *Newsweek,* March 23, 1993, pp. 46–52.

Dass, R. *Journey of Awakening: A Meditator's Guidebook.* New York: Bantam, 1978.

Davies, R. *The Lyre of Orpheus.* Harmondsworth, England: Penguin, 1989.

Dienstfrey, H. "What Makes the Heart Healthy? A Talk with Dean Ornish." *Advances: The Journal of Mind-Body Health,* vol. 8, no. 2 (1992).

Dixon, B. "Dangerous Thoughts: How We Think and Feel Can Make Us Sick." *Science,* vol. 86 (Apr. 1986).

Dossey, L. *Meaning and Medicine.* New York: Bantam, 1991.

————. "The Role of Consciousness in Health: Emerging Models of the Mind." In *Depth Perspective on Psychoneuroimmunology and the Mind/Body Connection.* Mansfield Center, Conn.: National Institute for the Clinical Application of Behavioral Medicine, 1991.

Douglas, C. "The Beat Goes On." *Psychology Today,* Nov. 1987.

Dreher, H. "Behavioral Medicine's New Marketplace of Clinical Applications: A Report on a Conference." *Advances,* vol. 8, no. 2 (1992).

Dreschler, V. M., et al. "Physiological and Subjective Reactions to Being Touched." *Psychophysiology,* vol. 22 (1985).

Eccles, J. C. "How Mental Events Could Cause Neural Events Analogously to the Probability Fields of Quantum Mechanics." Paper presented at the annual meeting of the Society for Neuroscience, Dallas, 1985.

Eibl-Eibesfeldt, I. *Ethology: The Biology of Behavior.* New York: Holt, Rinehart, and Winston, 1985.

————. *Human Ethology.* New York: Aldine de Gruyter, 1989.

Ferrucci, P. *What We May Be: Techniques for Psychological and Spiritual Growth.* Los Angeles: J. P. Tarcher, 1982.

Fillion, T. J., and E. M. Blass. "Infantile Experience with Suckling Odors Determine Adult Sexual Behaviors in Male Rats." *Science,* vol. 213 (1986).

Fisher, H. E. *Anatomy of Love.* New York: W. W. Norton, 1992.

Flaster, R., ed. *The New York Times Book of Science Literacy.* New York: Times Books, 1991.

Frankl, V. E. *Man's Search for Meaning.* Boston: Beacon Press, 1962.

Franks, J. D. "Nature and Functions of Belief Systems: Humanism and Transcendental Religion." *American Psychologist,* vol. 32, no. 7 (1977).

Freud, S. *Civilization and Its Discontents.* New York: W. W. Norton, 1961.

Fromm, E. *The Art of Loving.* New York: Harper and Row, 1962.

Gerber, R. *Vibrational Medicine.* Santa Fe: Bear and Company, 1988.

Givens, D. B. *Love Signals: How to Attract a Mate.* New York: Crown Publishers, 1983.

Gizzi, M. S., and B. Gitler. "Coronary Risk Factors: The Contemplation of Bigamy." *Journal of the American Medical Association,* vol. 256, no. 9 (1986).

Glaser, R., et al. "Stress, Loneliness, and Herpes Virus Latency." Paper presented at the meeting of the Society of Behavioral Medicine, Philadelphia, May 1984.

Goldstein, J. *The Experience of Insight.* Santa Cruz, Calif.: Unity Press, 1977.

Greely, A. M. *Faithful Attraction.* New York: Tor, 1991.

Green, A. W. "Sexual Activity and the Postmyocardial Infarction Patient." *American Heart Journal,* vol. 89 (1975).

Green, R., ed. *Human Sexuality: A Health Practitioner's Text.* Baltimore: Williams and Wilkins, 1975.

Grinberg-Zylberbaum, J., and J. Ramos. "Patterns of Inter-hemispheric Correlation During Human Communication." *International Journal of Neuroscience,* vol. 36 (1987).

Gupta, U., and P. Singh. "Exploratory Study of Love and Liking and Type of Marriages." *Indian Journal of Applied Psychology,* vol. 19 (1982).

Hackett, T. P., and J. R. Rosenbaum. "Emotion, Psychiatric Disorders, and the

Heart." In E. Braunwald, ed. *Heart Disease.* Philadelphia: W. B. Saunders, 1980.

Hales, D., and R. Hales. "The Bonding Hormone." *American Health,* Nov.–Dec. 1982.

Hall, E. T. *Beyond Culture.* New York: Doubleday, Anchor Press, 1976.

————. *The Silent Language.* New York: Doubleday, 1959.

Hall, J. G. "Emotions and Immunity: Letter to the Editor." *Lancet,* Aug. 10, 1985.

Hayden, G. G. "What's in a Name? 'Mechanical' Diagnosis in Clinical Medicine." *Postgraduate Medicine,* vol. 75, no. 1 (1984).

Henson, R. A. "Neurological Aspects of Musical Experience." In M. Critchley and R. A. Henson, eds. *Music and the Brain: Studies in the Neurology of Music.* London: William Heinemann Medical Books, 1977.

Hess, E. H. *The Tell-tale Eye.* New York: Van Nostrand Reinhold, 1975.

Hooper, J., and D. Teresi. *The Three Pound Universe.* New York: Dell, 1986.

Howard, J. W., and R. M. Dawes. "Linear Prediction of Marital Happiness." *Personality and Social Psychology Bulletin,* vol. 2 (1978).

Huxley, A. *Tomorrow and Tomorrow and Tomorrow.* New York: New American Library, 1964.

Institute of Medicine. *Behavioral Influences on the Endocrine and Immune Systems.* Washington, D.C.: National Academy Press, 1989.

Investigations [The Research Bulletin of the Institute of Noetic Sciences], vol. 1, 1990.

Irwin, M., M. Daniels, T. L. Smith, E. Bloom, and H. Weiner. "Impaired Natural Killer Cell Activity Following Bereavement." *Brain, Behavior, and Immunity,* vol. 1 (1987).

Jaret. "Our Immune System: The Wars Within." *National Geographic,* vol. 169 (June 1986).

Jemmott, J. B., and S. E. Locke. "Psychosocial Factors, Immunologic Mediation, and Human Susceptibility to Infectious Diseases: How Much Do We Know?" *Psychological Bulletin,* vol. 95 (1984).

Jemmott, J. B., and K. Magloire. "Academic Stress, Social Support, and Secretory Immunoglobulin A." *Journal of Personality and Social Psychology,* vol. 55, no. 3 (1988).

Jung, C. G. *Memories, Dreams, Reflections.* Edited by Aniela Jaffé. Translated by Richard Winston and Clara Winston. New York: Vintage, 1965.

Justice, A. "Review of the Effects of Stress on Cancer in Laboratory Animals: Importance of Time of Stress Application and Type of Tumor." *Psychological Bulletin,* vol. 98 (1985).

Kabat-Zinn, J. *Full Catastrophe Living: Using the Wisdom of Your Body and Mind to Face Stress, Pain, and Illness.* New York: Delta, 1990.

Kaminer, W. *I'm Dysfunctional, You're Dysfunctional.* Reading, Mass.: Addison-Wesley, 1992.

Kaplan, E. A. "Hypnosis and Pain." *American Medical Association Archives of General Psychiatry,* vol. 2 (1960).

Kaplan, G. A., et al. "Depression Amplifies the Association Between Carotid Atherosclerosis and LDL, Fibrinogen, and Smoking." *Mental Medicine Update,* vol. 1, no. 2 (1992).

Kaps, R. *Timelock.* New York: Ballantine Books, 1991.

Kellerman, J., et al. "Looking and Loving: The Effects of Mutual Gaze on Feelings of Romantic Love." *Journal of Research in Personality*, vol. 23 (1989).

Kenrick, D. T., and S. Gutieeres. "Contrast Effects and Judgments of Physical Attractiveness When Beauty Becomes a Social Problem." *Journal of Personality and Social Psychology*, vol. 25 (1989).

Kiecolt-Glaser, J. "Clinical Psychoneuroimmunology in Health and Disease: Effects of Marital Quality and Disruption." Paper presented at the annual meeting of the Society of Behavioral Medicine, San Francisco, Mar. 1986.

Kiecolt-Glaser, J., and R. Blaser. "Major Life Changes, Chronic Stress, and Immunity." *Advances in Biochemical Pharmacology*, vol. 44 (1988).

Kiecolt-Glaser, J., et al. "The Enhancement of Immune Competence by Relaxation and Social Contact." Paper presented at the annual meeting of the Society of Behavioral Medicine, Philadelphia, May 1984.

———. "Psychosocial Modifiers of Immunocompetence in Medical Students." *Psychosomatic Medicine*, vol. 46, no. 2 (1984).

Kimzey, S. L. "The Effects of Extended Spaceflight on Hematologic and Immunologic Systems." *Journal of the American Medical Women's Association*, vol. 30, no. 5 (1982).

Kimzey, S. L., et al. "Hematology and Immunology Studies: The Second Manned Skylab Mission." *Aviation, Space, and Environmental Medicine*, Apr. 1976.

Kinsey, A., et al. *Sexual Behavior in the Human Female*. Philadelphia: W. B. Saunders, 1953.

———. *Sexual Behavior in the Human Male*. Philadelphia: W. B. Saunders, 1948.

Kline, D. "The Power of the Placebo." *Hippocrates*, May–June 1988.

Kobasa, S. C. "Stressful Life Events, Personality, and Health: An Inquiry into Hardiness." *Journal of Personality and Social Psychology*, vol. 37 (1979).

———. "Test for Hardiness: How Much Stress Can You Survive?" *American Health*, Sept. 1984.

Kolodny, R. "Sexual Dysfunction in Diabetic Females." *Diabetes*, vol. 20 (1971).

———. "Sexual Dysfunction in Diabetic Men." *Diabetes*, vol. 23 (1974).

Kolodny, R., W. Masters, and V. E. Johnson. *Textbook of Sexual Medicine*. Boston: Little, Brown, 1979.

Kornfield, J. "Intensive Insight Meditation: A Phenomenological Study." *Journal of Transpersonal Psychology*, vol. 11 (1979).

Krishnamurti, J. *The First and Last Freedom*. San Francisco: Harper and Row, 1954.

Kreiger, D. *Foundations of Holistic Health: Nursing Practice*. Philadelphia: J. B. Lippincott, 1981.

———. *The Therapeutic Touch*. Englewood Cliffs, N.J.: Prentice-Hall, 1979.

Ladis, A., B. Whipple, and J. Perry. *The G-Spot and Other Recent Discoveries About Human Sexuality*. New York: Holt, Rinehart and Winston, 1982.

Larson, B. *There's More to Health Than Not Being Sick*. Waco, Tex.: World Books, 1984.

LeShan, L. *How to Meditate*. Boston: Little, Brown, 1974.

Leskowitz, E. "Life Energy and Western Medicine: A Reappraisal." *Advances*, vol. 8, no. 1 (1992).

Lieblum, S. "Vaginal Atrophy of the Postmenopausal Woman." *Journal of the American Medical Association,* vol. 249, no. 16 (1983).

Liebowitz, M. R. *The Chemistry of Love.* Boston: Little, Brown, 1983.

Lief, H. *Sexual Problems in Medical Practice.* Monroe, Wis.: American Medical Association, 1981.

Locke, S., and D. Colligan. *The Healer Within: The New Medicine of Mind and Body.* New York: E. P. Dutton, 1986.

Lovejoy, O. C. "The Origins of Man." *Science,* vol. 221 (1981).

Lown, B. "Basis for Recurring Ventricular Fibrillation in the Absence of Coronary Artery Disease and Its Management." *New England Journal of Medicine,* vol. 294, no. 12 (1976).

Luks, A. "Helper's High." *Psychology Today,* Oct. 1988.

Luks, A., and P. Payne. *The Healing Power of Doing Good.* New York: Fawcett Columbine, 1992.

Lynch, J. *The Broken Heart: The Medical Consequences of Loneliness.* New York: Basic, 1979.

Mace, D., and V. Mace. *Marriage East and West.* New York: Doubleday, 1960.

Mack R. "Occasional Notes: Lessons from Living with Cancer." *New England Journal of Medicine,* vol. 311, no. 25 (1984).

MacLean, P. "On the Evolution of Three Mentalities." In S. Arieti and G. Chrzanowski, eds. *New Dimensions in Psychiatry: A World View.* Vol. 2. New York: John Wiley, 1977.

Maddi, S. R., and S. C. Kobasa. *The Hardy Executive: Health Under Stress.* Homewood, Ill.: Dow Jones–Irwin, 1984.

Masters, W., and V. Johnson. *Human Sexual Inadequacy.* Boston: Little, Brown, 1970.

———. *Human Sexual Response.* Boston: Little, Brown, 1966.

McBride, L. R. *The Kahuna: Versatile Mystics of Old Hawaii.* Hilo, Hawaii: Petroglyph Press, 1972.

McClelland, D. C. "Motivation and Immune Function in Health and Disease." Paper presented at the meeting of the Society of Behavioral Medicine, New Orleans, Mar. 1985.

Meaneuy, M. J., et al. "Effects of Neonatal Handling on Age-related Impairments Associated with the Hippocampus." *Science,* vol. 239 (1988).

Melenchuck, T. "Why Has Psychoneuroimmunology Been Controversial?" *Advances,* vol. 2, no. 2 (1986).

Minkler, M. *Social Networks and Health: People Need People.* Series on the Healing Brain. Cassette no. T 57. Los Altos, Calif.: Institute for the Study of Human Knowledge, 1988.

Money, J. *The Destroying Angel: Sex, Fitness, and Food in the Legacy of Degeneracy Theory, Graham Crackers, Kellogg's Corn Flakes, and American Health History.* New York: Prometheus Press, 1985.

———. *Love and Love Sickness: The Science of Sex, Gender Difference, and Pair-bonding.* Baltimore: Johns Hopkins University Press, 1980.

More, B. F., et al. "Effects of Variant Types of Child Care Experience on the Adaptive Behavior of Kindergarten Children." *American Journal of Orthopsychiatry,* vol. 58 (Apr., 1988).

"Mounties Tried Crude Test in Gay Purge During the 1960s." *Detroit News* and *Detroit Free Press,* Apr. 25, 1992.

Myers, D. G. *The Pursuit of Happiness: Who Is Happy and Why?* New York: William Morrow, 1991.

National Academy of Sciences. *Bereavement: Reactions, Consequences, and Cure.* Washington, D.C.: National Academy Press, 1984.

Nerem, R. M., M. J. Levesque, and J. F. Cornhill. "Social Environment as a Factor in Diet-induced Atherosclerosis." *Science,* vol. 208, 1452 (1980); *Newsletter of the Institute of Noetic Sciences,* vol. 13, no. 3 (1985–86).

"New Technologies Detect Effects of Healing Hands." *Brain/Mind Bulletin,* vol. 10, no. 8 (1987).

Nilsson, L. *The Body Victorious.* New York: Delacorte, 1987.

Norris, P. A. "Clinical Psychoneuroimmunology." In J. V. Basmajian, ed. *Biofeedback: Principles and Practice for Clinicians.* Baltimore: William and Wilkins, 1988.

Offray de la Mettire, J. *Man: A Machine.* London: G. Smith, 1750.

Ohno, S., and M. Ohno. "The All Pervasive Principle of Repetitious Recurrence Governs Not Only Coding Sequence Construction but Also Human Endeavor in Musical Composition." *Immunogenetics,* vol. 24 (1986).

Ornish, D. *Dr. Dean Ornish's Program for Reversing Heart Disease.* New York: Random House, 1991.

Ornish, D., et al. "Can Lifestyle Changes Reverse Coronary Atherosclerosis? The Lifestyle Heart Trial." *Lancet,* vol. 33, no. 6 (1990).

Ornstein, R., and D. Sobel. *Healthy Pleasures.* New York: Addison-Wesley, 1989.

Pearsall, P. *SuperImmunity: Master Your Emotions and Improve Your Health.* New York: McGraw-Hill, 1987.

———. *SuperMarital Sex: Loving for Life.* New York: Doubleday, Ivy Books, 1987.

Peck, S. *The Road Less Traveled.* New York: Simon and Schuster, 1978.

Pelletier, K. *Longevity: Fulfilling Our Biological Potential.* New York: Delacorte, 1984.

———. *Mind as Healer, Mind as Slayer.* New York: Delacorte, Seymour Lawrence, 1977.

Peplau, L. A. "What Homosexuals Want." *Psychology Today,* Mar. 1981.

Perper, T. *Sex Signals: The Biology of Love.* Philadelphia: ISI Press, 1985.

Persons, S. *The Decline of American Gentility.* New York: Columbia University Press, 1973.

Pert, C. B. "The Wisdom of the Receptors: Neuropeptides, the Emotions, and Bodymind." *Advances,* vol. 3, no. 3 (1986).

Petterson, K. "Crisis Can Help Couples Rebuild Stronger Marriages." *USA Today,* Apr. 22, 1992.

Platonov, K. *The Word as Psychological and Therapeutic Factor.* Moscow: Foreign Language Publishing House, 1959.

Pooling Project Research Group. "Relationship of Blood Pressure, Serum Cholesterol, Smoking Habit, Relative Weight, and ECG Abnormalities to Incidence of Major Coronary Events: Final Report on the Pooling Project." *Journal of Chronic Disease,* vol. 31 (Special issue, 1978).

Pratt, G. K. *Your Mind and You.* New York: Funk and Wagnalls, 1924.

Quinn, J. *An Investigation of the Effects of Therapeutic Touch Done Without Physical Contact on State Anxiety of Hospitalized Cardiovascular Pa-*

tients. Ph.D. diss. New York University, 1982. University Microfilm no. DA8226788.

———. "Therapeutic Touch as Energy Exchange: Testing the Theory." *Advances in Nursing Science,* vol. 6 (1984).

Reiss, I. *The Social Context of Premarital Sexual Permissiveness.* New York: Holt, Rinehart, and Winston, 1967.

Reite, M. "Touch, Attachment, and Health: Is There a Relationship?" In C. C. Brown, ed. *The Many Facets of Touch.* Skillman, N.J.: Johnson and Johnson, 1984.

Rogers, M. "The Influence of the Psyche and the Brain on Immunity and Disease and Susceptibility: A Critical Review." *Psychosomatic Medicine,* vol. 14, no. 1 (1979).

Root-Bernstein, R. S. "Sensual Education." *The Sciences,* vol. 30, no. 5 (1990).

Rubin, L. *Erotic Wars.* New York: Farrar, Straus and Giroux, 1990.

Sadoff, D. A. "Value of the Human Body: Letter to the Editor." *New England Journal of Medicine,* vol. 308, no. 25 (1983).

Safire, W., and Safir, L. *Words of Wisdom.* New York: Simon and Schuster, 1989.

Scherwitz, L. Paper presented at the Clinical Application of Behavioral Medicine Third Annual Conference, Orlando, Florida, Dec. 4, 1992.

———. "The Psychology of Health, Immunity, and Disease." Paper presented at the Clinical Application of Behavioral Medicine Third Annual Conference, Orlando, Fla., Dec. 4, 1992.

Scherwitz, L., et al. "Self-involvement and Coronary Heart Disease Incidence in the Multiple-Risk-Factor Intervention Trial." *Psychosomatic Medicine,* vol. 48, nos. 3 and 4 (1989).

———. et al. "Type A Behavior, Self-involvement, and Coronary Atherosclerosis." *Psychosomatic Medicine,* vol. 45, no. 1 (1983).

Schlieger, S. J., S. E. Keller, and M. Stein. "The Influence of Stress and Other Psychosocial Factors on Human Immunity." Paper presented at the thirty-sixth annual meeting of the American Psychosomatic Society, 1979.

Schrödinger, E. *What Is Life? and Mind and Matter.* London: Cambridge University Press, 1969.

Schultz, W., et al. "Vaginal Sensitivity to Electric Stimuli." *Archives of Sexual Behavior,* vol. 18 (1989).

Seligman, M. E. P. "Helplessness and Explanatory Style: Risk Factors for Depression and Disease." Paper presented at the annual meeting of the Society of Behavioral Medicine, San Francisco, 1986.

Selye, H. *The Physiology and Pathology of Exposure to Stress.* Montreal: Acta, 1950.

———. *Stress Without Distress.* Philadelphia and New York: Lippincott, 1974.

Sexuality and Health Forum [Benjamin Cummings], issue 8 (Fall 1992).

Shapiro, J., and D. Shapiro. "Perceived Reward of Intimacy: An Investigation of Males and Females." Manuscript. University of California Irvine Medical Center, 1983.

Shealy, C. N., and C. M. Myss. *The Creation of Health: Merging Traditional Medicine and Intuitive Diagnosis.* Walpole, N.H.: Stillpoint, 1988.

Sheldrake, R. *New Science of Life.* Los Angeles: J. P. Tarcher, 1981.

———. *Newsletter of the Institute of Noetic Sciences,* Oct. 1992.

Siegel, B. *Love, Medicine, and Miracles.* New York: Harper and Row, 1986.
————. "Response to Dr. Spiegel." *Advances,* vol. 8, no. 1 (1992).
Silbner, J. "Metaphors in Immunology." *Science News,* vol. 130 (Oct. 18, 1986). "Silent Communication Increases EEG Synchrony." *Brain/Mind Bulletin,* vol. 13, no. 10 (1988).
Sklar, L. S., and H. Anisman. "Stress and Cancer." *Psychological Bulletin,* vol. 89 (1981).
Smith, D. A., and G. R. Jarjoura. "Social Structure and Criminal Victimization." *Journal of Research in Crime and Delinquency,* vol. 25 (Feb. 1988).
Smith, E. M., and J. E. Blalock. "Human Lymphocyte Production of Corticotropin and Endorphin-like Substances: Association with Leukocyte Interferon." *Proceedings of the National Academy of Sciences,* vol. 78, no. 12 (1981).
Sobel, D. S. *Social Networks and Health.* Series on the Healing Brain. Cassette no. T5-7. Los Altos, Calif.: Institute for the Study of Human Knowledge, 1984.
Solomon, G. F., S. Levine, and J. K. Kraft. "Early Experiences and Immunity." *Nature,* vol. 220 (1968).
Solomon, R. L. "The Opponent-Process Theory of Acquired Motivation: The Costs of Pleasure and the Benefits of Pain." *American Psychologist,* vol. 35 (1980).
Sontag, S. *Illness as Metaphor.* New York: Farrar, Straus and Giroux, 1978.
Sostek, A. J., and R. J. Wyatt. "The Chemistry of Crankiness." *Psychology Today,* Oct. 1981.
Spiegel, D. "A Psychosocial Intervention and Survival Time of Patients with Metastatic Breast Cancer." *Advances,* vol. 7 no. 3 (1991).
————. "Reply to Dr. Siegel." *Advances,* vol. 8, no. 1 (1992).
Spiegel, D., et al. "Effects of Psychosocial Treatment on Survival of Patients with Metastatic Breast Cancer." *Lancet,* vol. 2, no. 1 (1987).
Sternberg, R. J. *Beyond IQ: A Triangular Theory of Intelligence.* New York: Cambridge University Press, 1985.
————. "A Triangular Theory of Love." *Psychological Review,* vol. 93 (1986).
Sternberg, R. J., and R. K. Wagner, eds. *Practical Intelligence: Origins of Competence in the Everyday World.* New York: Cambridge University Press, 1986.
Sullivan, H. S. *The Interpersonal Theory of Psychiatry.* New York: W. W. Norton, 1953.
Syme, S. L. "Social Support and Risk Reduction." *Mobius,* vol. 4 (1984).
Thomas, C. "Stamina: The Thread of Human Life." *Journal of Chronic Diseases,* vol. 34 (1981).
Thomas, P. D., J. M. Goodwin, and J. S. Goodwin. "Effect of Social Support on Stress-related Changes in Cholesterol Level, Uric Acid Level, and Immune Function in an Elderly Sample." *American Journal of Psychiatry,* vol. 142, no. 6 (1985).
Tiefer, L. "Historical, Scientific, Cultural, and Feminist Criticism of the Human Sexual Response Cycle." *Annual Review of Sex Research,* vol. 2 (1991).
Udelman, D. L., and H. D. Udelman. "A Preliminary Report on Anti-depressant Therapy and Its Effects on Hope and Immunity." *Social Science and Medicine,* vol. 20, no. 10 (1985).

U.S. News and World Report, July 6, 1992.

Ueno, M. "The So-called Coition Death." *Japan Journal of Legal Medicine,* vol. 17 (1963).

Vaillant, G. E. *Adaptation to Life.* Boston: Little, Brown, 1977.

————. "Natural History of Male Psychological Health: Correlates of Successful Marriage and Fatherhood." *American Journal of Psychiatry,* vol. 135 (1978).

Vance, E., and N. Wagner. "Written Descriptions of Orgasm." *Archives of Sexual Behavior,* vol. 5 (1976).

Weiss, S. J. "Psychophysiological Effects of Caregiver Touch on Incidence of Cardiac Dysrhythmias." *Heart and Lung,* vol. 15 (1986).

Whitcher, S. J., and J. D. Fisher. "Multidimensional Reactions to Therapeutic Touch in a Hospital Setting." *Journal of Personality and Social Psychology,* vol. 37, no. 1 (1979).

White, J. *The Meeting of Science and Spirit.* New York: Paragon House, 1990.

Wilbur, K. *No Boundary: Eastern and Western Approaches to Personal Growth.* Boston: Shambhala, 1985.

————. "Where It Was, There I Shall Become: Human Potential and the Boundaries of the Soul." In R. W. Walsh and D. Shapiro, eds. *Beyond Health and Normality.* New York: Van Nostrand Reinhold, 1983.

Wilczek, F., and B. Devine. *Longing for the Harmonies.* New York: W. W. Norton, 1989.

Williams, R. *The Trusting Heart.* New York: Times Books, 1989.

Willis, C. "Back Off, Buddy: A New Hite Report Stirs Up a Furor over Sex and Love in the Eighties." *Time,* Oct. 12, 1987.

Wilson, S., and T. Barber. "The Fantasy-Prone Personality." In A. Sheikh, ed. *Imagery.* New York: John Wiley, 1983.

Wirth, D. P. "Unorthodox Healing: The Effect of Noncontact Therapeutic Touch on the Healing Rate of Full Thickness Dermal Wounds." Unpublished study. Healing Sciences International, 29 Orinda Way, Box 1888, Orinda, Calif. 94563.

Wood, C. "The Body Electric in England." *Advances,* vol. 3, no. 2 (1986).

World Health Organization. "Report on Reproductive Health." June 1992.

Wortman, C. B., and R. C. Silver. "Coping with Irrevocable Loss." In G. R. VandenBos and Brenda K. Bryant, eds. *Cataclysms, Crises, and Catastrophes: Psychology in Action.* Washington, D.C.: American Psychological Association, 1987.

Zilbergeld, B. *The New Male Sexuality.* New York: Bantam, 1992.

————. "Married Women Can Have the Best Sex Lives." *Redbook,* Apr. 1988.

Zillman, D. "Effects of Prolonged Consumption of Pornography." In D. Zillman, et al., eds. *Pornography: Research Advances and Policy Considerations.* Hillsdale, N.J.: Erlbaum, 1989.

Zimmerman, J. T. "Laying-on-of-Hands and Therapeutic Touch: A Testable Theory." In M. L. Albertson, D. S. Ward, and K. P. Freeman, eds. *Paranormal Research.* Proceedings of the First International Conference on Paranormal Research, Fort Collins, Colo., July 7–10, 1988.

Zuckerman, M. "Dimensions of Sensation Seeking." *Journal of Consulting and Clinical Psychology,* vol. 36 (1971).

ACKNOWLEDGMENTS

Ua ola loko i ke aloha.
(Love gives life within.)

This book, my life, my love, and all of my work come from the *aloha* I share with *'ohana*—my family. My mother Carol's and my deceased father Frank's *aloha* for each other and their *kamali'i* (children)—my brother Dennis and me—continues to nourish, inspire, and protect us. My wife, Celest Kalālani, is one with me forever in *aloha,* and our *kamali'i,* Roger and Scott, have overcome tremendous obstacles and will always be the pride and joy of my life. To my *'ohana* and all of my *'aumākua* (ancestors) I pray *maoli ola kākou*—may we live forever!

Authors find it difficult to thank all of those who made their work possible. In my case, I express my appreciation and debt to an entire culture whose people are the greatest healers in the world. Like my own *'ohana,* the Hawaiian people have endured and continue to suffer great challenges to their survival, yet their *mana* (energy), their spirit of *lōkahi* (unity), and their infinite *aloha* (loving kindness) are growing stronger than ever. My most sincere *aloha* to my friend kumu (teacher), Frank Kawaikapuokalani Hewett, with whom I pledge to work with all persons of Hawai'i *e ho'omau ka ha o ka Hawai'i*—to perpetuate the breath—the sacred and divine spirit—of the Hawaiian culture to which I owe so much.

Me ke aloha pumehana (my warmest love and appreciation) to *kupuna* Aunty Betty Jenkins, *tūtū* mama, and all of the *kūpuna* (loving elders) of Hawai'i who shared their *'ile kumu* (wisdom) with my wife and me and gave us our Hawaiian names. *Mahalo nui loa* (thank you very much) to Fred Cachola and everyone at Kamehameha Schools and to Vivian Ing and all of the *'ohana* at the Parent Community Networking Centers of Hawai'i for making us feel welcome in paradise.

A special *mahalo* to my editor, Erica Marcus, for her tireless work and patience and to her assistant, Renana Meyers. I hope we can work together again.

Finally, for my own healing and new beginnings, I say *mahalo nui loa* to my home and healing place—Maui, Hawai'i. *A he nani no'oe, e Maui*—Maui is so beautiful, the very best!

Ho'omaka Hou—To Begin Again,

Paul Ka'ikena Pearsall
Kihei, Maui
December 18, 1993

INDEX

Sickness:
   as enemy, myth of, 28–29
   necessity of, 24
   responsibility for, 44–46
Sickness Shame Syndrome, 46–48
   survey on, 48–51
Siegel, Bernie, 44–46
Sinai Hospital (Detroit), 4, 107
Single parents, 159–61
Smiling, 16
Solomon, Richard, 47
Somatosensory affective deprivation (SAD)
   syndrome, 199
Sound, sexual, 141–46
Spiegel, David, 45–46
Spitz, Rene, 11
Squeeze technique, 112
Stages of sexual response, 136
Stamina, sexual, 209–10
Storge love, 73
Stress, 66
   of love, 75
Stress Without Distress (Selye), 178
Sublimation, 205
Substance P, 122–23
Suffering, dividends of, 51–52
Surrogacy, 110, 162
Surrogate touch, 62–63
Swencionis, Charles, 8
Sympathetic nervous system, 55, 56
Sympathy, 46
Synchronicity, 144–46
   cerebral, 147–48

T cells, 36
Tears, 215–16
Tenderness, template for, 204
Thomas, Carolina, 90
Thoreau, Henry David, 21

Thought patterns, sexual healing, 95–97
Thrill seekers, 69–70, 75–77, 152–53
Thymus gland, 82
Tindall, Brett, 132
Tomlin, Lily, 120
Tool, body as, 202
Touch, immune system and, 61–65
Trust, 17
Turn-ons, myth of, 81–82

Unethical practices of sex therapists, 116–17
Urethral sphincter muscle, 219
"Us" factor, 15

Vaginismus, 111, 117
Value-free orientation, false claims of,
   115–16
Values, impulses versus, 126
Variety, need for, 126, 149–50
Violation of privacy, 116
Virginity, 110
Visualization, 42–43
Voluntary nervous system, 55
Vulnerability, 17

Wade, Carole, 126
Walsh, Roger, 43
Walster, Ellen, 70
Weeping, 16
Welsh, Anthony, 1
West, Mae, 220
White, George, 70
Withdrawal phase of relationship, 174
Workout, sexual, 210–11
World War I, 132
Worthiness, windows of, 197–98, 206

X-rated videos, 111–12, 143

Yoga, 42